A LONG WAY FROM MISERY

Jack Turner
and
Jacqui Halpin

Published by Crown Mountain Press 2016

Copyright © 2016 Jack Turner and Jacqui Halpin

All rights reserved. No part of this publication may be reproduced, stored in a retrieval system, or transmitted in any form or by any means, electronic, mechanical, photocopying, recording or otherwise, without the prior written permission from the publisher.

A catalogue record for this book is available from the National Library of Australia.

Creator: Turner, Jack, 1926- author.

Title: A long way from Misery / by Jack Turner and Jacqui Halpin.

ISBN: 9780994496300 (paperback) / 978-0-9944963-1-7 (e-book)

Subjects: Turner, Jack, 1926-
Sheep shearers (Persons)--Australia--Biography.
Country life--Australia--20th century--Biography.
Australia--Rural conditions--20th century.
Australia--Social life and customs--20th century.

Other Creators/Contributors:
Halpin, Jacqui, author.

Dewey Number: 636.0092

Book cover design and formatting services by BookCoverCafe.com

Disclaimer
Some names, places and identifying details have been changed to protect for privacy and maintain their anonymity. I may have changed some identifying characteristics and details such as physical properties, occupations and places of residence. This book contains cultural and indigenous references and language for the purpose of telling the story and is not meant to offend or have any ill intent towards real life culture or indigenous people. Every effort has been made to ensure that this book is free from error or omissions. However, the author, publisher, editor or their agents or representatives shall not accept responsibility for any loss or inconvenience caused to a person or organisation relying on this information.

www.blackjackturner.weebly.com
www.jacquihalpin.com
www.facebook.com/jacquihalpinwriter

For Mum and Dad, and Misery.
For the mates who lived these stories with me.
For my wife, Betty, for putting up with me for over fifty years.
For my great family that I love.
And for the brothers I've lost; wish you could have read it.
— Jack Turner

For my dad for trusting me with his story.
For my mother for her love and support, and for answering thousands of questions.
For my wonderful family for their love and laughter, and for sharing me with this book all these years.
For my friends, who have patiently listened to me and will be as relieved as I am that this book is now in print.
For the Ridge Writers who helped me start this journey, and for my Write Links friends who helped me finish it.
— Jacqui Halpin

Preface

I grew up with my father's stories. I heard them at every family gathering. My favourites always began with, 'Down on Misery...' Misery was the farm my dad grew up on, but the stories he told weren't manufactured myths. They were accounts of his life, verified by his many siblings. These anecdotes were always entertaining and I never tired of hearing them. It wasn't until I was grown up with children of my own, that I realised the importance of these stories as part of Australia's social history. They weren't just extraordinary tales of an ordinary bloke, they provided a fascinating glimpse into our nation's past. My father's family was fairly typical of the era, and yet unique. The jobs Dad did and the life he led were characteristic of the time, and yet he was exceptional. This book narrates the exploits of his youth. It is an account of his incredible stories, his distinctive family, and his remarkable life.

Jacqui Halpin

Introduction

Jack Turner's my name. I was born in Rylstone, New South Wales, on the twenty-third of December, 1926. The eldest of ten children, I never had an education—at least not one from a classroom. I got me education in the bush. I don't think I missed out on much. I've always got by. And if there's one thing growing up in the bush taught me, it was how to depend on meself and make do. This book tells the story of what my life was like, when and where I grew up, and the antics, adventures and mishaps I managed to survive. I lived in a very different time, a time that has now gone. That's why there have to be books like this one, because when all us old buggers are gone, who'll remember what it was like? Who'll tell our stories?

Chapter One

Mudgee

My dad was a twin born to Harry and Hannah Turner in the back of a dray at the foot of Mt Marsden. They were on their way from their farm at Glen Alice to the midwife in Rylstone. They never made it. Me father, Stanley, and his twin brother, Arthur, were delivered by their mother.

After she had them, Grandad said, 'We may as well go home now, Hannah.' So he turned the bullocks and dray around and they went back to the farm.

My mum had it a bit easier than that. I was born in the house of friends that she and Dad were staying with in Rylstone, so at least the midwife was close by.

When I was about two we went to live with Mum's mother and sister in Church Street, Mudgee. Mudgee's about thirty-five mile north-west of Rylstone and that's where Mum's family lived.

Grandma Fitler's house was an old brick place. It must have been built in stages, I think. There were two bedrooms, a dining room and kitchen in the front half, and out the back were two bedrooms and another room Mum used as a kitchen.

We lived in the back half of the house. Aunty Lu and Grandma lived in the front half. There was a laneway that run down the side of the house. Across the laneway lived Mum's brother, Fred. He was a plumber and he owned Grandma's house and the one he lived in. Further down the laneway was his plumbing shed, and a stable with a couple of trotters in the yard.

There was another old shed in this yard and that's where Herbie, another of Mum's brothers, used to live. He was a plumber too, but he was a drunkard bugger and didn't do a lot of work. He was a pretty smart codger just the same. He used to ride his pushbike around and when he saw someone he knew, he'd stop his bike and without taking his feet off the pedals, he'd balance there while he rolled a smoke and had a yarn.

After me sister, Marie, was born, we moved into another old house up behind Grandma's. Me next sister, Carmel, and me brother, Bryan, were born in Mudgee. Dad worked on the sewerage line there, pick'n'shovelling. There wasn't a lot of work around because of the Depression, so he did one week on and one week off. Relief work they called it. They rotated people each week to give more people work. Married men got preference when they were putting people on. Dad wasn't real big but he was pretty fit and could work hard. They used to put him in as leader for the other workers to follow. He said he felt sorry for the men who weren't used to shovelling. He'd show them what to do and try to look after them a bit. There were city blokes there who'd never had a shovel in their hands before but they had to do whatever work they could get. Times were tough.

On his weeks off, Dad would go away rabbit-trapping, shearing or droving around Rylstone. Sometimes he'd do fencing. Money was pretty scarce during the Depression but we always had a bit of flour for a scone or a rabbit to eat.

I remember we used to have porridge, or burgoo as we called it, every morning for breakfast. We never lived flash, but we never went hungry either.

We all had a pair of hand-me-down shoes, but we only ever wore them to go into town, no matter how cold it was. We wore hand-me-down clothes too. I remember wearing Dad's old clothes. They were miles too big but they did the job. I never had a belt. I used one of Dad's old ties. Anything would do as long as it held your trousers up.

The sewerage work didn't last long, so after that Dad was away droving, trapping or shearing most of the time. He'd only come home of a weekend, now and again, from wherever he was. I remember he always had a good, smart dog with him. At that time he had an old cattle dog called Booby. Us kids used to take Booby with us when we were walking down the street in Mudgee. If we said, 'Up a tree, Booby', he'd try and run up the nearest telephone pole. One day, me sister and I were walking down the street and this other kid come up and give me a whack in the ear. Well, Booby run up, grabbed him by the arse of his pants and shook him. It frightened buggery out of him.

On the night Bryan was born, old Booby was outside—Dad never had a dog in the house—but he kept scratching and howling at the door and putting on a dreadful row. Finally, Dad went out to see him. He flew in past Dad, into the bedroom where Mum was, looked her over and back outside he went. When the baby was born a few hours later, he carried on the same way until Dad let him in. He tore in, had a look at the baby in the cot, give a bit of a yodel and then out he went again, happy.

I remember Mum was bathing Bryan one day, he couldn't have been more than a couple of weeks old, when Uncle Herbie come home drunk, picked Bryan up, balanced him on one hand and was waltzing around the room with him.

Mum was chasing him and yelling, trying to get Bryan back off him. After that she used to lock the door when she seen him coming. 'Here comes the cat,' she used to say. Everyone used to say that when they seen him coming, 'Here comes the cat.'

I can't remember exactly how old I was when we left Mudgee, but I was around six or seven. At some time—I don't know when—Dad had bought two hundred and fifty acres, thirteen miles outside of Rylstone, on the Cox's Creek road. It was between two mountains, the Dairy and the Crown. He called it Misery Farm. Before we moved in, I used to go with Dad to help clean up and get the old hut ready for us to move out to.

While Dad was cleaning up the farm, we rented a house in Rylstone. One day, I was playing around on the roof of this house and when I went to get down, I slid down the ladder instead of climbing down, and got a splinter about four inches long in me rump. I went in to Mum, bellowing and howling. Dad was home at the time. They tried to get it out but they couldn't. It was in too deep for them to get a hold of.

So Dad said, 'I'd better give him some harnessthetic.' That's what Dad always called anaesthetic. The next thing, he give me a clip under the lug and knocked me clean out. When I woke up, he'd cut the splinter out with his old, cut-throat razor.

That anaesthetic was a favourite of Dad's. There were a lot of bloody things got anaesthetic —dogs, cats, kids. He knew just how hard to hit them to put them out for a few minutes or however long he wanted.

We stayed in that rented house for four or five weeks and then we shifted out to the farm. Dad carted everything out there with a horse and an old spring cart. It only took a couple of trips. We never had much in them days.

Mudgee

*Me, aged 9 months, with **Booby** and **Auntie Lu** in the laneway between Grandma's house and Uncle Fred's house, Church Street, Mudgee. 1927*

*Me, aged about 2 years, driving "Bunny", with me cousin **Nita**, Uncle Fred's daughter. Bunny was the name of Uncle Fred's trotter. 1929*

Chapter Two

Misery

Misery Farm had an old stone hut on it. I reckon it might have been built by convicts. It was covered on the outside with hand-cut timber slabs and had a tin roof. There were only three rooms—a bedroom, a dining room and a kitchen. The partition walls were made of wattle and daub. That's wattle sticks covered with clay. We used to whitewash the inside now and again to keep it clean. We'd patch up any gaps or holes with clay, or with a paste made of flour and water that we'd stick a bit of paper over. Sometimes the cracks in the exterior walls were so big you could look through and see old Jim Howe, our neighbour, driving past in his horse and sulky.

The front and back doors were timber. There were no locks or anything. I don't remember if they even had a handle. We just used a stone or an old flat iron to keep them closed.

The floor of the old house was made of bare unpolished boards. There was a casement window in the wall of each of the two front rooms. The dining room had a big open fireplace. The fire was going all day and night in the winter.

At the back of the house was the kitchen. It wasn't real big, about nine foot by six foot. It had a little storage room at one end where Mum used to keep bags of flour and sugar and jars of stuff. There were no shelves. She just used to store things on the floor or on the old bit of a bed that was in there for anyone who came to stay. Up the other end of the kitchen was an old wood-burning Crown stove. There was a small dresser in the kitchen too, that Mum kept stuff in. The kitchen window was a bush window—boards nailed together on a hinge that you propped open with a stick.

In the kitchen Mum had a big stew pan. It was about two foot six across and six inches deep. It was made of cast iron and glass blown on the inside. If we had a glut of tomatoes, she'd make tomato relish or when the blackberries were in season, she'd make blackberry jam in it. I think Mum used to lift the pan up onto the stove on her own but she had to get a couple of us kids to help her lift it down when it was full, it was so heavy. Gee, it was a bloody big pan. It took up the whole stove.

Uncle Fred made up a bit of wire for Mum to use for cutting the necks off bottles. She used to make all her jars that way. When she made relish, she'd fill up the jars, melt some fat and pour it over the top to seal it. For a lid, she'd stick a bit of brown paper over the top of the jar with a paste made from flour and water. Relish would keep for ages like that but it never lasted too long in our house.

I remember her making biscuits. She used to call them hard-timers. If she knew someone was coming, she'd say, 'I'd better bake some hard-timers.' They'd have been made with the cheapest ingredients and would have been the quickest to make, too, but they went down all right. Quite often our meal of an evening would be puftaloons. They were like fried scones that we had with treacle or cocky's joy. We had our main meal at lunch time, or dinner time we called it. It was always breakfast, dinner and tea when I was young.

Mum used to cook a lot more on the open fire in the dining room than on the old stove. It was quicker and she had more room. All us kids would sit around the fire in the dining room at breakfast time, cooking our toast. Even the little fellas that could only just wobble about, they'd be sitting down with a toasting fork and a bit of dodger, cooking it. We all had to cook our own toast and give Mum a bit of a hand.

We ate in the kitchen when there were only a few of us. There was a small table in there that Mum used as a workbench. As the family got bigger we ate in the dining room. It had a big, old wooden table about nine foot long and four foot wide. You could easy fit a dozen or more people round it. It took up nearly the whole room. There was only the table and chairs, a bit of a sideboard and an old lounge chair in the dining room. We'd sit around the table at meal times, all together, yapping away, telling what happened and what didn't. When Dad was home he'd be there, too. We'd all sit around together and have our meals.

None of the chairs around the table matched. They were just whatever Mum or Dad could scrounge up. Mum would go to the auction in Rylstone every now and then and buy a chair or two if one broke or another kid come along. Us kids were buggers to rock around on them and break them. They often had loose legs. Some of the chairs were made out of the wooden crates they used to cart kerosene or benzene tins in.

I remember we always had a hot dinner of a Sunday. Mum would rake up something, baked veggies and a roast of some sort. Even if it was only a couple of rabbits, she'd have a roast. When we had a roast chook, we never ate young chooks— they were for laying. We'd get an old hen, get a teaspoon of vinegar, hold its mouth open and pour the vinegar down its neck an hour before we cut its head off. That softened the meat and made it tender. After dinner we'd always have some jelly or junket for dessert. I used to think that was great.

When we first moved out to Misery us kids slept on the floor of the dining room. When more kids come along Dad built a verandah out the front. The floor was made of concrete that he mixed up on a sheet of tin with a shovel. The ends were enclosed with corrugated iron. The front was open. We sewed flour bags together with twine to make blinds. In the winter, we'd hang the bags down with a stick in the bottom to hold them there and in summer when it was hot, we'd just roll them up.

We had an old billy goat and sometimes he'd break his chain and come in and start chewing the blankets. The little kids used to get a fright and start screaming. One night he got in even when the blinds were down. There were kids running everywhere, screaming in the pitch black.

Back then bakers used to buy their flour in 160-pound bags. They were like corn bags. We used to buy them from the baker's shop in Rylstone. You could buy a dozen flour bags for a shilling. We made the waggas for our beds—that was the main blanket—out of flour bags—three or four flour bags sewn together side by side. Dad made a double bed one once, for his and Mum's bed, and covered it with rabbit skins. He sewed different coloured rabbit skins in a pattern all over this wagga. Geez, it was pretty, and worth a lot of money. All the rugs for our horses and cows were made out of flour bags, too.

We used to always kiss Mum good night when we went to bed. We'd say, 'Good night, Mum. Hope you have a good sleep. Don't you hope I have a good sleep?'

That used to be a real saying with us. Even when I grew up, if I was late home from a dance—it could be three o'clock in the morning before I got home—I always went in and kissed Mum good night before I went to bed. 'Hope you have a good sleep. Don't you hope I have a good sleep?' We'd always say that to one another.

The old hut only had a 100-gallon water tank, so we had to cart water from the swamp, which was about two hundred yards from the back of the house and had a creek running through it. It had running water all the time and was beautiful drinking water. There was a doctor who used to come out every weekend from Kandos to get water from our creek. We used to cart it up to the house in kerosene tin buckets, billycans and milking buckets. Mum would have a yoke across her shoulders with a bucket or kerosene tin on each end. Us kids would carry buckets, too. The buckets would get smaller with the size of the kids, right down to the littlest carrying a jam tin full. Mum used to cart water right up until a week or two before she was due to have the next baby. We had to cart all the water for drinking, washing and bathing.

On washday Mum would get out the little round washtub and do the washing out in the open. One of me brothers, Peter—he was the next one born after Bryan— when he was little he used to call red things blue. Anyhow, one day, he was sitting out in the yard while Mum was doing the washing. Suddenly, he said to Mum, 'Gee, this is a pretty little blue spider I got here.' Mum thought, blue ... that means red! She jumped up and got it off him. He'd been sitting there playing with a red-back spider. How he didn't get bit we'll never know. Peter was called Peter after Peter Pan, the horse that won the Melbourne Cup a couple of weeks before he was born.

Once a week we'd take the washtub inside, cart up the water, heat it up and all have a bath. The baby and youngest would go first, followed by the older ones, then Mum and Dad. We'd add a bit more water after each few. It wasn't a very big tub, looking back. I don't know how Mum and Dad even fit in it. I'm sure they were dirtier after they'd had the bath than before they got in. Sometimes in the summer we'd just leave the washtub out in the yard and bath out there.

Mum and Dad had the only bedroom. There was a cot in their room for the baby and the older kids slept on the verandah. There were two double beds on the verandah with a couple or three kids in each. As more kids come along I think we got a couple of single beds and put them on the verandah as well. If any of us were sick and Dad was away, we'd sleep in with Mum. In the summer, sometimes we'd drag our beds out from under the verandah and just lie out under the stars to cool off.

There was an outhouse down the yard on Misery, between the house and the swamp. It was made out of tin with a bit of a door and a dirt floor. Dad cut the top out of a kerosene tin and put it under a wooden bench he made up with a hole cut in it for a seat. We used newspaper for toilet paper. Every week Dad would take out the tin and dig a hole somewhere round the yard and empty it. Burying the dead he called it. Every week he had to bury the dead.

Mum had another five kids after we moved out to Misery. Whenever the newest baby come along, if any of us older kids was nursing it, Dad would yell out, 'Don't break him!' Didn't matter if it was a girl or a boy, he'd say 'him'. They used to get tipped out of the pram often enough despite what he said. Us kids took it in turns wheeling the baby around when it cried.

Mum used to go into town the week before she was due and stay at Mrs Wyldes's house in Rylstone. She was the midwife. Peter, Maureen, Tony, Pat and Larry were all born when we lived on Misery.

One time when Mum went into town to have a baby, she left Dad at home to look after us. He'd help us cook and take care of the place. Me sister, Marie, was a bugger for putting her feet up on me legs whenever we were sitting at the table. This particular morning we were all sitting around the table having breakfast, burgoo and a cup of tea, when Marie put her feet up on me legs. I thought, I'll fix you. I put me spoon in me hot cup of tea and left it there for a while. We were all sitting there nice and quiet when I dabbed the hot spoon on her foot. She let out a bellow, kicked the table up in the air and spilt Dad's tea. Well, he went bloody berserk! He threw his tea out the window as well as his plate of burgoo, and the pot, and out the door he went, roaring. Holy, bloody hell, he was wild. He left us alone for the rest of the day and didn't come home till dark.

When we were young, Dad would say, 'I'll give ya a penny if ya go without sugar or milk in ya tea for a week.' When the week was up, if we'd gone without, he'd say, 'It ain't payday this week.' Payday never come. I don't think he ever paid up. In the finish, Mum and Dad were the only two who took milk and sugar in their tea. When we were out in the bush, Dad would have to pick the ants out of his tin of sugar before he could use it. I used to think it was great I didn't need it. He'd always take a tin of powdered milk with him, too.

One day, Mum got something in her eye and no one could see what it was or get it out, so it got worse. After a couple of days it got so bad that she couldn't stand the daylight, so we had to go into town at night to the doctor.

First, I had to go and find old Maudy—our carthorse—harness her up and put her in the buggy. We put the kids in the back, Mum and Dad on the front seat, and headed off for town in the dark. Old Maudy had stringhalt and it used to take us an hour or more to go the thirteen mile into town. On the way in I used to have to get out and open the gates. There were about six gates on the way in. Dad used to keep going—he wouldn't stop when he got through the gate. I had to chase after him and get in the buggy. I was scared as buggery I'd get left behind in the dark.

Dad's mother lived in Rylstone, up on the hill near the hospital. She lived there with Dad's sister, Em. Aunty Em was blind. Grandad had died by this time. I was only about seven when he died. All I can remember about him now was that he had a big, white beard. We got to town about midnight and woke Grandma up. She had to find a place for us all to camp. The house only had about three rooms and an open verandah. The next day Mum went down to the doctor to get her eye fixed. Her eye was all right after she'd been to the doctor so we went back out to Misery that day.

Mum got a lot of migraines, 'bilious attacks' she called them. She used to get them fairly often and she'd be sick in bed. Dad was away a lot of the time so me and the older girls had to look after the kids as best we could and do what she'd tell us while she was lying there, poor bugger. I remember once she had a stew pan of jam cooking when she got a bilious attack. She was lying in bed and when she sang out to us to come in, she was that sick she couldn't tell us what to do. She just kept winding her hand around and around, mumbling, till one of us woke up that something on the stove had to be stirred.

Chapter Three

More Misery

One year, the parson up on the hill in Rylstone died. He had a heap of clothes and someone asked Mum if she wanted them and she said she did, so we got all his old clothes. Dad got the parson's big, black hat and he used to wear that around. Gee, he looked wild wearing that. He'd wear it while he was digging up the paddock. Before we got a plough horse, Dad dug up a fair bit of ground with a shovel. He used to dig at night for hours with just the light from a lantern that he'd hang on a forked stick. He'd be talking away to himself while he was digging. Three or four acres he dug up with a shovel. He'd dig all day and half the night to get the ground ready to sow. Corn, oats, potatoes and turnips, that's mainly what he grew.

The first year he grew oats, he cut it with a reaping hook. Us kids used to have to tie it up in bundles or sheaves, which we then arranged in a stack of ten or so and left for a couple of days to dry. Then we'd cart it into the old tin hay shed where we'd cut it up for chaff to feed the horses and cows. Dad had an old, hand-operated chaff cutter. One of me sisters would feed the hay into the cutter and I'd have to turn the handle. Marie was feeding it this day while I was turning the handle. Just as the handle got to the top and I was straining hard to push it down, she knocked it out of gear somehow. The handle flew down and so did I. I bashed me head on the concrete floor and knocked meself out.

Later on, Dad got a scythe from somewhere. He thought he was made then, with a scythe. That's all we ever had to harvest with. We grew oats and corn for the cattle and horses. We made our own porridge out of the corn. We used to put it in a sugar bag and belt it with a hammer or a rock. Gee, she was pretty rough burgoo. We grew stuff mainly to feed ourselves and the animals. Dad would go away to work during the week and come home of a weekend to work the farm, but she wasn't good enough to make a living off. Our income was mostly from Dad shearing, and rabbiting, and working other places. The farm only just fed us. We used to live on blackberries sometimes. They grew wild on Misery. Mum used to make blackberry jam and stew them for sweets.

When we were little, before we got big enough to start and do much work around the place, we used to play cowboys and Indians. We'd go up in the scrub and cut sticks and make horses out of them to ride. We'd gallop around the house and the yard chasing each other. We had great fun. When I got a bit bigger, I'd dig one of the suckers up out of the ground. They had a knob on the bottom of them about as big as a tennis ball. The black fellas call them nulla nullas. I'd get one of them and I'd go and knock bunnies over with it. You can throw them a fair way and pretty straight, too, when you get used to them.

As we got a bit older and the family got bigger, we had to do a lot more work around the place. Marie, the eldest girl, made the bread and helped

Mum look after the little ones, and Whopper and I did the ploughing. We called Carmel, Whopper, or Wop for short. She was so little that Dad used to joke and say, 'Isn't she a whopper?' and the name stuck. She and I were both too little to get onto the horse. I used to throw a rope around his neck and lead him up to a stump or fence so I could stand on that to reach to put the winkers and collar on him. I'd have to climb up onto him from there. When Wop had to get on him, she'd do the same, or if I were there I'd leg her up. When I got big enough to reach up and grab onto his mane, I'd hang onto his mane and climb up his front leg to get on. I'd have no boots on so I could dig me toes into his leg. Whopper was too little to steer the horse with the long reins walking beside the plough. If he shook his head he'd pull her off her feet, so she had to ride him bareback and steer him with short reins. I'd be behind steering the plough. That's how little we were when we had to do the ploughing. We had to plough twenty-two yard wide of land whenever Dad told us to.

Dad would say, 'I'll measure out a land and you plough it tomorra.' He'd take twenty-two big steps and that's how wide we'd have to plough it. We'd plough that, whatever length he wanted it. When we'd finished ploughing the paddock, we had to scarify it. We'd get the scarifier and go across the paddock the opposite way to what we ploughed. Then we'd harrow it to break up the clods, then Dad would sow it and then we'd have to harrow it again to cover the seed. That was our day's work. But we used to have great fun ploughing.

One day, Wop was riding the horse and Dad was ploughing, but Wop didn't keep the horse in the furrow, so Dad picked up a clod of dirt and threw it at her. It hit her in the head and knocked her clean off the horse.

Gee, we thought that was funny. We still talk about it now, how much fun we had ploughing.

Wop and I used to get up to mischief sometimes. We'd get around the back of the house near the chimney and roll up stringybark in newspaper and sit there smoking it. Soon as we'd hear someone coming, we'd stomp on it and put it out. How the hell it never harmed us I'll never know.

Sometimes we'd steal a watermelon from our neighbour, Jim Howe. He had a property just up the track from Misery. He always had fruit trees growing and a few watermelon vines in the summer. Wop and I would sneak up to his place, pinch a watermelon, run back into the bush, break it open and we'd into it. Till one day he fired a shot at us. I don't reckon he was trying to shoot us, just frighten us. We heard the shot and took off. We got the message after that and didn't go back. We'd have got a bloody hammering off Mum or Dad if they'd found out we'd been pinching stuff so he probably did us a favour.

When we first moved out to Misery, we only had one horse, old Maudy. Later on, we got a couple of draught horses. Dad made up an old slide—a forked stick with some boards nailed across the top of it and a bit of wire and a chain to hook it onto the swingle bar. The horse would pull it around the paddock and we'd pick up wood on it and drag it back down to the house to cut up. Then Dad got a little tank. We used to go down and half fill it up with water and the horse would pull it up to the house to save us carting it. We couldn't fill it all the way up or the horse wouldn't have been able to pull it.

One draught horse was a real good horse we called Socks. We'd been working him hard this day, so Dad said, 'Give Socks an extra bucket of corn tonight. He's been workin' real hard.' Dad thought he was doing him good.

When Dad come to put a rug on him, Socks bucked and farted and took off up the road. 'Gee, he's a good horse,' said Dad. 'But I don't know what's up with him.'

Next morning, we got up, and Socks was dead right in the middle of the bloody track. Too much corn will kill them. They get all fevered up. Dad didn't know that. He thought he was giving him good tucker. Socks was too big for us to move, so we had to burn him where he was and make a track around him.

I had other work to do as well as ploughing. I had to go and get the cows from up the paddock and bring them home to milk. This particular day I was feeling lazy, so when this old cow stopped, I sat down on the ground and grabbed a hold of her tail. 'Get-up!' I said. 'You can drag me home.' As she was walking down the track pulling me behind her, I got even lazier and lay down on me belly. After a while, she stopped. 'Get-up!' I yelled and grabbed her by the leg.

Well, she let drive and kicked me straight in the forehead and split it clean open. Up I got, staggering all over the road, and down I went to Mum. The blood was pouring out and there was a flap of skin hanging down over me eye. Mum got a bit of a fright when she saw me, she thought I'd lost me eye. I've still got the scar. It wasn't stitched of course. If we'd gone into town to the doctor every time someone got hurt, we'd have hardly ever been home. Mum fixed it up with Rawleigh's ointment and some sticking plaster.

Everything got fixed up with Rawleigh's ointment. A salesman used to come around selling all the Rawleigh's products. Medicines and ointment and stuff like that. We always had a tin of it in the cupboard. I think Mum must have bought the stuff in bulk—she used that much of it.

More Misery

We had a couple of cows for milking. One would be drying up just as the other one was in calf and coming up ready to milk. I was milking this old cow this day and she kept swishing her tail and hitting me in the face. So I tied her tail up with a bit of wire that was on the rail and started milking again. Next thing, she's whacking me again with her tail. I thought, I'll fix you, and I got her tail and plaited it around the rail so she couldn't flick me with it. Anyhow, I finished milking her and took off the leg rope and let her out of the bale but I forgot to undo her tail and she pulled six or eight inches of her tail off. After that us kids used to put it on and pretend it was a beard.

Another time I was milking the cow and instead of putting the leg rope on her I just sit down to milk her. I had half a bucket of milk when she lifted her foot up and put it straight in the bloody bucket. I wasn't game to tell Mum, so I just scraped the rubbish off the top of the milk and took it up to the house.

There was a big storm on one day, so Dad told us kids to stay inside and he'd milk and feed the cow. He got the bin of chaff and the milking bucket and down he went to the bale with his big overcoat on. On his way down the old cow was trying to get at the feed and Dad tripped somehow and fell on the ground. The bin of chaff went out in front of him and the cow stepped over him to get at the chaff and put her front feet on the sleeve of each arm of his coat, pinning him to the ground. He was bellowing his head off but we couldn't hear him over the storm, with the tin roof rattling. One of us looked out after a while and here's Dad pinned to the ground under this cow, out in the middle of the storm, while she's eating away out of the bin. I had to get me corn bag on—that's what we used for a raincoat—and run out and get the bin of chaff so the cow would follow me and get off him.

Then I ended up having to milk her cos he was covered in mud and wet as buggery. It was lucky for her he was wet and cold and had to go inside cos he was that mad, he'd have killed her if he'd stayed there any longer.

One time on Misery, me sister Marie and I had a pet lamb each that we used to bottle-feed. We fed them cow's milk but before we fed them we'd heat up a poker in the fire and stick it in the bucket of milk to stop the lambs getting scour, that's diarrhoea. We put a red-hot poker in the milk before we fed any baby animal. The little lamb that Marie had was the wildest bloody thing you've ever seen and a frightened little bugger, too. She called it Peggy and mine was Percy. One of me brothers had got a little, pull-along horse and cart for Christmas. Not long after Christmas, Marie and I were out the back feeding the lambs while Mum and Dad were standing out the front looking up at the weather and talking. When we'd finished feeding the lambs, I tied this horse and cart onto the end of Peggy's long tail and let her go. She took off baaing, and around the house she flew, right past Mum and Dad. But she went one side of Dad and the horse and cart went the other and pulled his legs right out from under him. Down he went. Gee, I got a bloody hammering from Dad out of that.

We always had a cattle dog on the farm and a few rabbit dogs and roo dogs. They were usually greyhound or staghound crosses, anything with a bit of pace. One day, a bloke in town give Dad an old, ex-racing dog, which Dad brought home—he thought he might catch a rabbit or two. We called him Dick after the joker that give him to Dad. Anyhow, one day, Mum and I went to town and Mum decided to buy a new milking bucket. We usually used kerosene tins to do the milking and get water. But she bought this milking bucket and that night I milked the cows and then I had to feed the poddy calves. They were way up the paddock near some blackberry bushes and an old well.

More Misery

I was trudging along when I heard rattling and here's this greyhound behind me. He must have broken his chain.

When I'd finished feeding the poddys, I said to this dog, 'You can carry this bucket back instead of me, mate.' I hooked the bucket to his chain and said, 'Get home!' Well, he took off with the bucket clanging behind him. The more noise it made, the faster he ran, and the faster he ran, the more noise the bucket made. He went straight up through the scrub, howling.

When I got home, Mum said, 'What's up with the dog?'

I'd have been in plenty of trouble if she'd known what happened to her new bucket so I said, 'The billy goat chased me and the dog, and knocked the bucket down the well.' The bucket was torn off the chain and left all battered up in the scrub. Mum never saw it again. That old goat got the blame for a lot of things.

I remember when Dad bought that old billy goat. We'd gone into town in the buggy, Mum, Dad and however many kids there were at the time. While we were in town, Dad got this goat off somebody and he put him in the back of the buggy. The other kids were in the front with Mum but I had to stay in the back with this bloody goat and he used to bite like mad. Anyhow, we got to the first gate coming home and I got out to open it and Dad took off trotting in the buggy. I had to shut the gate, run after him, and jump up into the buggy from behind. I was bloody terrified of this goat biting me. I was yelling and screaming and carrying on but Dad just kept going. I had to get up into the buggy with this billy goat biting me.

On Misery there were a heap of blackberry bushes. They were growing everywhere. You'd dig them up and they'd grow again. They were all over the swamp.

When Dad brought this goat home, he put him on a long lead in amongst the blackberry bushes and left him there till he'd eaten them all and there was nothing else to eat. Then he shifted him from there far enough out so he could reach the next lot. Everywhere he tied that bloody goat, the blackberries never grew again. I had to hold him while Dad moved the crowbar he was chained to, and every time he used to bite buggery out of me shins. It's a wonder the hairs grew on me shins, cos he chewed off the blackberries and they never grew back.

Chapter Four

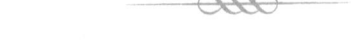

Plenty of Misery

When Dad was home and not working away, he'd sometimes cut mine props for the coalmines at Kandos and Charbon. He'd cut down trees between about six to ten inches across the base. He taught me to climb up the tree he was going to cut down and he'd tell me which way it was going to fall and which side to sit on. He used to say, 'Don't jump off till I tell ya and ya won't get hurt.'

So I used to sit in the tree and he'd cut it down and when it got about three or four feet off the ground, I'd jump off it. I got good at it and never hurt meself. I got that good at it that I'd climb a tree and wait, and when a cow or a steer or a horse would come poking past, I'd wait till it got just underneath me and I'd jump onto him. I used to get some lively bloody rides.

Talking of lively rides, I give one of me little sisters a lively ride once. I got on this little poddy calf we had and rode him around the paddock. He couldn't throw me, so I got me little sister, Maureen, and said, 'Here, get on this fella.' I put her on him and he threw her. I said to her, 'Get back on him again.

He won't throw ya this time.' And I tied her legs together underneath him and let him go. Well, he galloped around the paddock and he couldn't throw her, so he stopped bucking and started feeding. Then I got the old, blue cattle dog, Lassie, and skitched him onto the calf. Away it went straight through a heap of blackberry bushes with her tied on his back screaming her head off.

I could be a bit of a handful when I was young. I remember one time on Misery, when I was about eight, Mum was telling me to do something and I was buggering around not doing it, and then I started to give her cheek. She went to hit me so I run out the door and started poking me tongue out at her. She had a carving knife in her hand at the time and she let drive and threw it straight at me. As I turned to run, it stuck right in me hip. I've still got the bloody scar.

She got a bigger fright than me. She thought I'd duck out of the way but I wasn't quick enough that time. She had to patch me up. 'That's ya own bloody fault for givin' cheek,' she said. It was no good of running away from Mum if you'd done something wrong. She'd sit up all night waiting for you to come home to give you a hammering, so you might as well stay there and cop it. 'Ya gotta come home to sleep,' she'd say.

It was around the same time that I was down at Billy Mills's place. His family had a property next to Misery called The Dairy. It was across a little bit of a creek. They had a big, double-furrow disc plough sticking up out of the shed where Billy and I were playing. I come charging around the shed straight into the pole of the plough that was sticking up in the air. It split me head right open. They patched me up and took me home to Mum. Mum had me in the dining room, sitting in the lounge chair, when Dad come home.

That lounge chair was our hospital bed. Everyone went there when they were sick.

'Jack's been knocked out. He's crook,' she said.

After tea, Dad said to Mum, 'You go to bed, I'll watch him.'

Well, I got sillier and sillier with the concussion. I was trying to climb the fireplace and was playing up all night. Mum come out in the morning and said, 'How's Jack?'

'The bastard's mad,' Dad said. 'I don't know what we're gunna do with him.'

I got better but Mum had been really worried. She told me later, she'd said to Dad, 'What are we gunna do, Stan? What are we gunna do if he dies?'

Dad had said, 'If he lives, he lives, and if he dies, he dies.' One of Dad's favourite sayings was, 'What's to be, will be.'

After we'd been on Misery for a year or two, Dad built on a skillion roof out the back for a washhouse. I was knocked up chasing bloody hammers when he was building that. He had three hammers: a boot-maker's hammer, a claw hammer, and a shoeing hammer. They used to go through the air plenty of times. Every time he hit his finger, he'd throw the hammer down towards the swamp and I'd have to go and get it. As I was coming back, another one would be sailing over me head.

There was tin down one side and at the back of the washhouse. The other side closest to the kitchen door was open as far as I can remember. We used to keep the harnesses in there. It was built for a washhouse but it got used for dumping everything.

Not long after he built the washhouse, the crows were playing up, stealing eggs and causing trouble. Dad spotted one in a tree out the back this day and decided to shoot him. He had an old, single-barrelled shotgun that someone had given him.

I didn't know he was after the crow this day. I come running around the back of the house just as Dad was leaning out the window of the washhouse taking aim at the crow. The gun went off just as I went sailing past. It blew the hat I was wearing clean off me head! That was the end of that shotgun. Dad doubled it in half around the nearest post. It was a dangerous bloody thing. The hammer wouldn't stay cocked and it could go off at any time.

I reckon I was about eight or nine by now and I'd never been to school. None of us had. But Mum and Dad wanted us to have a schooling. So Dad borrowed money from the bank and got his brother-in-law, Bob Hobby, to build a schoolhouse for us on Misery. It was made out of corrugated iron. Mum and Dad had been told that if they could get enough kids to go to the school, the government would fund a teacher to teach us. But there weren't enough kids in the area so the schoolhouse was built but we had no teacher. Mum and Dad then decided that we'd better go into town to school. That didn't last long, though. Marie was sick a lot of the time with asthma and bronchitis, so she didn't go to school much. I don't think Wop had much schooling while we were out on Misery either. And I wasn't interested in going. There was too much to do on the farm.

But I do remember, one morning, taking Wop into town to go to school. We got in the horse and sulky and off we went. There was a big, heavy gate between our property and Mills's. The rails were at least six to eight inches across and fifteen foot long. Wop got down to open the gate for me. Off she ran backwards, carrying the rail, pulling the gate open. Then she tripped over an anthill. The rail hit her in the head and pinned her to the ground right on top of this huge meat ant nest. She was screaming like buggery, but the horse had taken fright, so I had to get him and quieten him down, then run back and see to Woppy.

By the time I got to her she was covered in meat ants and they were having a great feed. I dusted off the ants as best I could and got her into the sulky and back home to Mum. She was silly as buggery with the concussion by the time I got her home. She was pretty crook for quite a while there. She got over it but she used to get terrible headaches after that. We found out nearly fifty years later, when she had to have some neck x-rays, that her neck had been broken at some early stage in her life. She reckons it must have been when the rail hit her in the head. We never knew her neck was broken.

Soon after that Mum and Dad thought they should get us to school, so they rented a place at Woodlawn, about four or five miles out of Rylstone. It was an enormous bloody house but we only rented half of it. It had big stables and lots of paddocks. We left Misery and got a bloke to cart us to the new place in a ute. It was dark by the time we got to this joint and gee it was a spooky-looking place. We couldn't find anything and Mum was upset and worried. Us kids were all bloody frightened to be in these big rooms. You could hear the echoes when you were talking. It frightened buggery out of us. It was a lot different to our old hut on Misery. We were only there a week and I don't think any of us kids went to school. We were too bloody upset and we hadn't got things organised to do anything really. So we packed up and went back out to Misery again.

After we got back to Misery, Dad's twin brother, Arthur, come out to do a bit of work and stayed a while with us. One night he said he'd have to singe his hair because he needed a haircut. He got a couple of matches and sat down and started to burn the ends of his hair to singe it. Then he said to me and Whopper, 'Here, youse can singe it around the back.'

Whopper and I started to singe the back of his hair with the matches, but they kept going out. So we got a sheet of paper, rolled it up, lit it and put it on the back of his head. All of a sudden the paper set full alight and set his hair on fire. He jumped up waving his hands around and patted the fire out. We got a bit of a fright but not as much of a fright as he got.

We used to play cards of a night after tea. We'd all be sitting around the table in the dining room, near the big fire if it was winter, playing cards. We'd play a game called animal grab. You had to make a noise like an animal when you seen two of the same cards. Uncle Arthur reckoned he was going to be a rooster but instead of saying cock-a-doodle-do, he'd say 'wok who'.

He used to play tricks on us all the time. One night, he said to me, 'Here, you put that hat on and go outside the door and I'll whistle ya in, bareheaded.'

I thought, my bloody oath ya won't. This is easy. So outside I went. I put me hat on and pulled it down over me eyes. He whistled and I marched through the door. 'Here ya are,' I said, 'I got me bloody hat on.'

'Yeah,' he said, 'but I said *I'd* be bareheaded.' He was bareheaded. Well, that buggered me straight away.

When we got a bit older, Marie and I used to look after the younger kids during the day when Mum went into town to have a baby. Dad would be home of a night. But one time Mum got her sister's daughter, Moya, to come down from Mudgee and look after us. Dad must have been away at the time. She should have got a Victoria Cross for bravery. I was a holy bloody terror. One day, while she was looking after us, I come charging through the house with a carving knife stuck halfway down me throat. I'm buggered if I know how I got it there now. I only did it to give her a fright. It worked. It frightened buggery out of her. She thought I was going to die.

Mrs Wyldes, the midwife in Rylstone, had a couple or three rooms and Mum used to stay at her place. I'd take her in in the cart or the sulky, whatever we had at the time, about a week before she was due to have the baby. She'd stay there till the baby was born, then she'd come back to the farm. I remember going to town one time to see her. I had me horse tied up in Mrs Wyldes's yard. Mum must have been in labour cos she told me to get going. So out I went and got me horse. Mrs Wyldes come running out. 'Don't go yet,' she said to me, 'just stay outside for a while.'

I stayed outside for half an hour or so, then I was just going out the gate when she come running up and said, 'Tell them out at the farm, it's a girl.' It must have been Patty. I rode back out to Misery and told them all it was a girl.

When Larry was born a couple of years later, I was in town visiting Mum, and her sister, Aunty Cis, had come down for the day from Mudgee to see her. There was a diesel rail motor used to run between Mudgee and Lithgow every day. She'd get that down in the morning and go back on it in the evening. When it was time to get the train back, Aunty Cis went off down to the station.

I was getting me horse to go back out to Misery when Mrs Wyldes come running out and said, 'Ride down to the station and tell your aunty it's a boy.'

I rode down to the station and told Aunty Cis it was a boy. Then I rode back to Misery and yelled out as I was coming down the track to the house, 'It's a boy! It's a boy!'

Chapter Five

Misery at Christmas

Mum and I used to go to town once a fortnight, on pension day, to get groceries. Dad was on a war pension cos he'd had two fingers blown off in the first war. We'd take the sulky with old Roany—she was the sulky horse that replaced Maudy. We'd leave the other kids at home for Marie to look after. We had to go across Mills's, then through Rawdon Station. Rawdon was a large sheep station. There was a big hill on the Misery side of Rawdon. People called it The Gap. It was pretty steep on the side coming from Rylstone out. Coming home with the groceries, we'd have a full load on the sulky—50-pound bags of flour and about the same of sugar, plus all the other shopping. When we got to the foot of The Gap we'd give the old horse a spell for a while. Then we'd get out and push, Mum on one side of the sulky and me on the other. We'd help push the horse and sulky all the way up the hill. Mum sure earned her money. She'd be six months pregnant and still pushing the sulky.

It took about an hour to get into Rylstone and an hour to get home again. Mum would tell me lots of things on those trips. All about her life before she got married, and yarns about what happened in the early days. She told me that she and her brother, Fred, used to go to the races together all the time and have a bet. He kept trotters that he used to drive. One day, he and Mum picked out four horses to bet on. They put in five bob each and were going to have an all up bet on the four of them. That meant that if the first horse won his race, all the winnings went onto the second horse you bet on, and all the winnings from that horse, if he won, got put onto the third and so on. So they picked these horses out but something happened and they couldn't get to the races. So they give the money to their brother, Herbie, and asked him to put the money on for them. They heard that the four horses won, and it was a bloody lot of money, too. They had a plan that if they could win a lot of money, they'd buy a property together and breed and train trotters. They were waiting, all excited, for Herbie to come home with their winnings. When he come home that night, he was drunk as buggery. He'd spent their money at the pub and hadn't put the bets on.

On one trip to town, Mum told me that years ago in Mudgee, long before she was married, a young woman disappeared from Mudgee. They thought she'd been murdered but they couldn't find any trace of the body. Sometime later, a man was driving his horse and sulky along the Lue road towards Mudgee one night, when he saw a figure dressed in white sitting on a fence post by the side of the road. When he got near it, it got off the post and walked down to a nearby dam and disappeared into the water. He raced off to Mudgee and told the police what he'd seen. The next day, the police dragged the dam and found the body of the missing woman.

Mum also told me that when she was a girl, there was a freak snowstorm in Mudgee. She and her sister, Lu, were throwing snowballs at people when they walked past their house in Church Street. One of the people that come past was Buckaroo Mary. They threw a snowball at her and knocked her hat off her head. Now Buckaroo Mary was a real strange lady. Everyone was wary of her. As she come walking back past the house she had a snowball in her basket. When Aunty Lu poked her head up over the railing on the front verandah, Buckaroo Mary let drive with the snowball. Aunty Lu ducked. The snowball hit the front door and a jagged piece of bottle stuck in the door. She'd covered a piece of broken bottle with snow and thrown it so hard at Aunty Lu that it stuck straight in the door. The marks from it were still there years later, cos Mum showed them to me.

On another trip to town, Mum was telling me about a bloke she used to knock around with before she got married. Jack was his name. He and his father owned the funeral parlour in Mudgee. He was a bugger to drink and his father didn't like him drinking. Anyhow, he was having a drink in the morgue this day when he heard his father coming with someone to view a body. He had nowhere to hide, so he jumped into an empty coffin and pulled the lid on. His father didn't know which coffin the body this person wanted to look at was in. He was going around lifting the lids off one at a time. He got to the coffin Jack was in and pulled the lid off. As he did, Jack sat up. His father and the person with him got such a fright they both fainted.

Every shopping trip, Mum would buy us a cowboy comic that she'd read to us at night. Us kids used to get up on the side of the mountain and play cowboys and Indians. We used to be Cowboy Charlie and his off-sider—I think his name was Curly. We had an old cave at the foot of the Crown Mountain that we called our hideout. We cut a few saplings to lean up against the front of it to make a bit of a shelter.

Billy Mills, the young fella from the property next to us, was a couple of years older than me. He would buy a *Tarzan* comic every time he went to town. Billy was like me and he couldn't read, so he'd come up home and Mum would read the comics to him and us kids. Most nights after tea she'd read something to us. When Dad was home she'd read *Robbery Under Arms*. If there was nothing to read, we'd play cards.

We had no electricity out on Misery. No electric lights, just the old kerosene light with the glass top and a couple of hurricane lanterns to see us to bed or to go outside with. They would stay alight in the wind and rain. Sometimes, instead of reading or playing cards, we'd just sit there making animals with our hands, putting the shadows on the wall and seeing who could make the best. We used to come up with some great little ones. We'd play cards till late, then we'd have tea and toast, then off to bed, and up and at it early again the next day.

Sometimes we'd play cards till midnight. We'd play cards or Mum would read till the moon went down so it was dark enough to go spotlighting. Spotlighting was when we went out shooting hares and rabbits that were getting at the crops. We joined three two-cell torches together and made one big one. I think Billy Mills come up with the idea. It took us a while to find a bulb strong enough that wouldn't blow when we switched it on. It was a powerful light and would mesmerise the bunny while you shot him. We were only allowed to use it for spotlighting. We'd go spotlighting often. Sometimes it was every night for a while. It all depended on the moon and how many animals were getting at our crops. We'd all still get up at daylight, summer or winter. Dad used to be up before daylight every day. He'd have the fire lit and be smoking his pipe waiting for daylight so he could go out and get started on whatever he had to do.

One time, we went to town on a Saturday and there was a cowboy picture on at the picture show in the old town hall. Dad let me stay at Grandma's place overnight so I could go to the pictures. There was a bloke coming out to Misery from Rylstone the next day, to see Dad about something, so he brought me back out. I seen a cowboy picture with Roy Rogers or one of them. I thought I was bloody made to see that.

Around that time, Barney, the owner of the paper shop in Rylstone, was losing a lot of stock and money in the night. He went to the copper and said, 'There's someone breakin' into me shop of a night. So I'm goin' down there tonight with a gun, and I'm gunna wait in the shop and see who's pinchin' me stuff, and I'll catch him.'

'Righto,' said the copper.

So that night he went down to the shop. In them days the old electric light had a long cord hanging down from the ceiling that you had to pull to switch the light on or off. Barney hooked a lump of string onto that and took it behind the counter and hid there with his gun, and waited. There was a swaggie camped out on the racecourse in Rylstone, and it was him that was pinching the stuff. Well, he come in this night, jimmied the shop door open and started picking stuff off the shelves, and went to the till to get the money out. Just then Barney pulled the light on. 'Reach for the skies or I'll blow ya in halves,' he said, and held the bloody gun on this fella. He rung the copper and the copper come and pinched the bloke. Barney was getting around town the next day saying how he told this fella, 'Reach for the skies or I'll blow ya in halves.'

If we were running out of tucker and it wasn't pension week, or if the sulky had broken down, then I'd ride me horse into town to get supplies.

I rode Roany into town this day. She was only young at the time and a big sort of a mare. I tied her to the fence under the shade of a tree in the grocer's yard down the end of town. Away I went, shopping and yarning and everything I had to do. I was just walking back down the street with the sugar bags full of groceries, when I looked up and here's old Roany walking out of the yard and down towards the river. She'd rubbed the bridle off.

I raced down the road, grabbed the bridle off the fence and ran after her yelling out to her, but she just kept trotting on about three or four hundred yards in front of me. She walked down to the river and crossed. I got wet crossing the bloody river after her. Out onto the main road, the Lue road, she went, still a couple of hundred yards in front of me. She wouldn't stop and I couldn't catch her. She kept going and got to the turn off where we had to turn right. There was a gate there for horses and livestock to go through and next to it was a cattle grid for cars to drive over. We used to call them 'ramps' in them days. The gates were always closed, you had to get down and open them to lead your horse or whatever through. I thought, I'll get her here. She stopped at the ramp and I got within one hundred yards of her—and ya wouldn't believe it—she walked straight across the bloody ramp. She just put her foot on each bar and walked across it as easy as winking. She followed the road right through to the next gate and ramp keeping a couple of hundred yard in front of me. She got to it and done the same bloody thing. She followed the road to the third ramp, crossed that one, then the road turned. One road went up to Cox's Creek and the other went up to Cox's Crown, towards Misery. She turned towards Misery and up the bloody Gap she went. When she got to the other side of The Gap in the Rawdon paddock, where Mills's place started, there was a baton gate on hinges there and no ramp, so she had to stop. The bastard! I had to walk all the way home to there and carry all the tucker and the bridle. I was a bloody long time getting home. Mum said, 'What happened?'

'Bloody Roany got away on me and wouldn't let me catch her. She come right to the last gate here before I could get her.'

Mum used to buy presents all through the year, whenever she went into town, and hide them away for Christmas. Sometimes, she used to go to town with the Millses from next door if they had room in their car. She'd buy things at the shop, leave them there, and ask Mrs Mills to pick them up for her so we wouldn't see them. She used to hide them at Mills's place. Mills's place would be close on a mile to our place, across a little creek.

Mum and I would go down a day or two before Christmas to sort out all the presents. We'd put them in a big sack and hump them back from Mills's place. I used to feel like Santa Claus carrying a chaff bag full of toys back to Misery. Once we got near the house we'd hide the presents under logs and bushes and behind trees so they were close but where the kids couldn't find them. Sometimes, it was daytime when we went, other times it was at night and we'd take a hurricane lamp and walk across the paddock to Mills's.

Dad would be home at Christmas time. He had an old .38 calibre rifle. On Christmas Eve we'd all be sitting there at the table and he'd say, 'I'm gunna get the .38 and wait. I'll shoot that old bastard tonight.' It used to frighten buggery out of the kids. They thought he was going to shoot Santa Claus.

Mum and I would wait up till everyone had gone to bed. I'd be nodding off at the table and she'd nudge me and say, 'You can't go to sleep yet.' Once everyone was asleep, we'd go out by the light of the lantern and gather up all the presents we'd hidden. The kids would hang up an old pillowcase on the end of the bed and we'd sneak around putting presents in them. The girls would get dolls and stuff. We got socks or shirts or other clothes we needed. I remember one year I got a cap gun, another year a pull-along toy. Mum would put some boiled lollies in, too. When you paid your bill at the grocery shop, the shop keeper used to get a piece of brown paper, roll it up to make a cone shape, then he'd tip a heap of boiled lollies in and seal the top over. He'd give you something for paying your bill. We used to have an account at the shop that Mum paid monthly.

Sometimes, when we got older, we'd catch and skin a few bunnies and sell the skins and save the money up for Christmas. I can't remember what we used to buy Mum—it was a long time ago.

One year, Mum bought me a pair of long trousers. I thought that was great. They were me first pair of long pants. I'd only ever had shorts before that. I dressed up in them and went over to Mills's to show them. They'd just killed a calf and left the cow out in the paddock. She was pretty savage and as I come across the paddock she chased me. I ran and took a flying leap at a six-rung, barbed wire fence and caught me trousers on the top of it as I went over. It tore the bloody leg nearly off them. Me brand new trousers! Mum wasn't happy, and I wasn't happy about it either. I was screaming me head off about the wrecked trousers. I wasn't worried about me leg that I'd torn the hide off. We hardly ever got new clothes.

Another Christmas, Mum said Dad had to take us kids into town for shopping. She give us a couple of bob each to buy presents with. Dad was going to take us on Christmas Eve, but something went wrong with the sulky and Dad had to put another set of wheels on it. They had a left-hand thread on one side and a right-hand thread on the other. You had to put the axle in the right way round or the nuts would come undone and the wheels would come off. Anyhow, he put these wheels on the sulky, put Roany in the shafts to pull it and we all got in. We only went a hundred yards and one of the wheels fell off. He'd put the axle in the wrong way round. That was the end of the trip to town that Christmas, we never got in there.

Mum made a Christmas pudding and a Christmas cake every year. She'd make them a couple of months before Christmas and have the pudding hanging up somewhere in the house. I used to get sick of banging me head on the bloody thing. We'd have a roast and veggies, and Christmas pudding for Christmas dinner. I remember she always bought a bottle of port wine to make wine sauce for the pudding. She used to have a little drop of wine in a glass of lemonade at Christmas—that was all the alcohol she drank. I don't know what happened to the rest of the wine after that because she never drank it and Dad never drank either. The one bottle maybe lasted her a couple of years.

One year, Dad took our old, crippled mare, Maudy, over to Belmont Park Stud and got her in foal by Wee Donald. That was the little pony stallion over there. Anyone who had a Wee Donald pony had a really good pony. We didn't work her much after she come back cos we had Roany then and Maudy was getting a bit old and tottery. She had a little bay colt on Christmas Day. Dad christened him Rainbow.

I remember him coming in and saying to Mum, 'We've got a little bay colt with a star on his forehead … Rainbow.' He called him Rainbow because Captain Starlight's horse was called that in *Robbery Under Arms*.

When Rainbow got old enough, Dad broke him in. He used to ride him but he was a bit too flighty for us kids to ride, so Dad bought a little bay mare from a bloke in town for us to learn to ride on. She had a little filly foal at foot that he also bought. We called the filly, Peggy, and the mare, Dolly. She was our first pony. Dolly was a small, quiet pony perfect for me and the other kids to learn to ride on. She was pigeon-toed so Dad didn't want us galloping her or jumping anything. He thought she'd fall. I used to ride her around everywhere. After a while I got that good I thought I was bloody Lance Skewthorpe. I was galloping her everywhere and rounding everything up on her.

Unbeknown to Dad, I used to jump Dolly over logs, and I used to get Marie and Wop to lie under a blanket and I'd jump her over them. Then I told them to frighten her as she jumped over them. I used to yell out to them to move just as I got up to them, to frighten her. How one of them wasn't killed I don't know. What a bloody ratbag I was. Anyone would think we were trying our best to kill one another.

Chapter Six

Mountains of Misery

When I was about twelve Dad thought I was old enough to have a gun of me own, so he bought me a little bee-bee gun. I used to shoot snakes and birds with it. I thought it was great. One day, something jammed in it. So Dad had a look at it when he got home. He put it up to the side of his head and fired it. The pump-action handle that used to load the pellets snapped back clear across his knuckles and nearly smashed them. That was the end of that gun. It got wrapped around the bedpost. So then I just used to use Dad's .22 rifle.

Billy Mills and I used to go hunting together, chasing rabbits and climbing around the mountain. The mountain in front of Misery was called The Crown. There was an area on top of it about one hundred foot long, fifty foot wide and about twenty foot high, with not a foothold anywhere around it to climb up. We tried a few times till one day, Billy said, 'We'll make a ladder to get to the top.' He had a tomahawk with him. We cut down a sapling and laid it against the crown and climbed up it to the top. You could see for miles from up there.

We'd roll rocks down from the top. Gee, they used to clear some timber. There was one big rock we tried to push down but it was so big we couldn't move it. It would have been a good bit bigger than a 44-gallon drum. We dug around it and finally we started to get it moving. Billy said, 'You get under that side and I'll get under here. Put ya hand right under it and I'll lift from this side. You lift from that side.'

I put me hand right under and lifted, but a piece of rock on his end broke and down come the rock right on me finger. It was pinned under the rock and we had no hope of moving it. So Billy climbed down and cut down a sapling to use as a lever to lift the rock up enough for me to pull me hand out. Me third finger was split right down the middle. To this day there's still a scar on me finger. I'm looking at it now.

A cousin of mine, also called Billy, come to stay with us for a few days. Billy Mills and I decided to take him up the mountain. Away we went, climbing up the Crown till we got to the sapling we'd cut down in order to get to the top. Billy climbed up to the top first and kicked a rock off the side of it. Down come the rock and hit Billy Mac fair in the head, split his head open and knocked him out cold. We had to carry him down off the mountain, home to Mum, to patch him up. He was in pretty bad shape there for a while.

This Billy Mac and his family—there were seven or eight of them—sometimes come down in a car from Mudgee for the day. Billy's sister used to go out with a car salesman in Mudgee and he'd get a loan of a car for the day and bring the family down to see us. These cousins and I were all walking up to Crown Mountain this day. They were getting around acting all spooked, not being from the bush, when I saw this big line of cobweb between two trees. 'Look at the line,' I yelled. Well, I looked round and there was kids running every-bloody-where. They got such a fright. They thought there was a *lion*. I don't know what else they thought lived out in the bush.

Dad used to shear for an old bloke that had a Southdown sheep stud around the other side of the Crown Mountain to where Misery was. Anyhow, Dad come home one day and said they were looking for a young fella to do some work for them. So out I went. It was me first paid job. I was about twelve. The old man who owned the place had a stock and station agency in Rylstone, so one of his daughters run the farm. She wanted me to help around the farm and do hay making. When you're hay making you have to start early before the wind picks up, so I had to be there at four a.m. I had to get up pretty early cos I had to walk and it would have been a mile and a half through the scrub. I worked till breakfast—had to take me own tucker too—worked the rest of the day from seven-thirty till five-thirty, with an hour off for dinner. You had to boil your billy and everything in that time. I worked all week and Saturday till dinnertime, around twelve. Then she said to me, 'Here's ya pay, Turner.' And she give me five bob. 'I'll see ya Monday morning.' I could make more than that catching rabbits.

'I won't be back,' I said.

This woman's little brother lived on the property, too. Max was his name. All his sisters were grown up but he was younger than me. It was his birthday and he had no kids to share his birthday with. So he come over to our place. It would have been a good three-mile walk. He carted his cake, a candle and his present in a bucket. He come all the way over to our place to share his birthday with us. Marie spotted him coming down the track and went out. 'Here comes Max with his party in a bucket,' she yelled. Us kids thought it was great having a piece of cake and whatever he had with him. And he had plenty of kids to share his birthday with.

Dad and the bloke from a couple of farms up the gully were doing some contract work at that time, burning off for Rawdon Station. They used to camp out on the station and I had to cart their tucker out to them. One day, Mum made a bread and butter custard for Dad. She wrapped it up in a tea towel and said, 'Carry this over to ya dad while it's nice and fresh and hot.'

I put some other tucker in the saddlebag—well it was a corn bag made into a saddlebag—and carried the custard in me hand. I jumped onto Dolly and set off. Well, between opening gates and chasing roos, by the time I got over to where Dad was, it didn't look very fresh. I said, 'Here, Mum sent ya over this bread and butter custard.'

Dad opened it up and it was splattered everywhere. He said, 'It looks more like baby shit to me.'

Dad and the neighbour from across the swamp behind us, Tommy Gore, bought a couple a hundred sheep off one of Dad's mates. This mate and Dad grew up together in Glen Alice. Dad and I had to ride over and pick them up from his property on the Bylong road. It was a fair way. We had to ride across Rawdon Station to get there.

When we got there, they drafted the sheep out and then this bloke said, 'We'd better go and have some dinner now before ya take 'em home.' So in we went to have some dinner. They put some corned meat, potato and pumpkin in front of us. I went to eat mine when I spotted some maggots on me plate next to the meat. I was just about to say something, when Dad give me a rake up the shin with his riding boot and pointed down to his plate. He had maggots on his plate, too. He just scraped them to one side of his plate with his knife and made me do the same, and kept on eating. I had tougher guts back then than I've got now, I'll tell ya.

Horrie was an old bloke that had the property in behind the Dairy Mountain, up the other gully from us. His property backed onto the back of Rawdon. He was a pretty wild old codger. People reckoned he'd gone a bit strange. He'd been a schoolmate of Dad's down in Glen Alice. He used to come over for Dad to cut his hair now and again. Dad had given up smoking cigarettes by this time. He always smoked a pipe instead. He used to call his pipe his gun. 'Anybody seen me gun? Where'd I leave me gun?' he'd say, and us kids would run and find his pipe.

Well, Mum looked out the window this day and saw old Horrie coming across the paddock smoking a pipe. 'Here comes Horrie with his gun,' she said. Well, all us kids bolted in under the bed to hide from him. We thought he was coming to shoot us.

Talking of pipes reminds me of a trick we used to play on Dad. When cracker time come around, if we had any spare crackers and we could get at Dad's pipe, we used to shove a little Tom Thumb cracker in it. He'd pick it up and light it and it'd blow the bloody pipe out of his mouth. Geez, he used to bellow.

The mountain further up the gully behind Misery was called Wheelbarrow Mountain. Now Wheelbarrow Mountain got its name from a bloke that drew a block on the top of the mountain years before. He took all his belongings from Rylstone out to the mountain in a wheelbarrow. It's a fair bloody way, too. It'd be thirty mile, I reckon. Anyway, one day the dingoes were getting around up on Wheelbarrow Mountain. They'd been killing a few sheep. So Dad got an old draught horse from somewhere, took him up to the foot of the Wheelbarrow, shot him and poisoned him for dingo baits. He used to use strychnine. You could buy it at the chemist in them days.

A few days later, Dad said to Bryan and me, 'Ya'd better go and see if anything's been eatin' that horse.'

Away Bryan and I went on Dolly. As we got up through the scrub, we spotted a dingo and went after it on old Dolly, flat out. I sent her over a log but she tripped when she got over the top of it and fell arse over head. She knocked Bryan out and busted me up. I got him back on Dolly—she was all right—and got us home. He was crying and bellowing. He'd gone silly from the knock on his head.

When Dad got home, Mum said, 'Bryan's crook. He's been knocked out.'

'I'll look after him,' Dad said.

When any of us kids got sick, Dad used to say to Mum, 'Get a bed and put it on the floor and I'll sit and watch overnight.' He'd sit in the lounge chair in the dining room with an old mattress and a couple of blankets or a wagga next to it. He used to call it the sow's nest. 'Get into ya sow's nest,' he'd say. It stuck with us, and me brother, Peter, all his life, called his bed his sow's nest.

After he got Bryan settled, Dad asked me what happened, so I told him. Later that night, Dad was sitting in the dining room with Bryan wrapped up in a blanket, when Bryan started raving and yelling. He was still delirious. Dad asked him what happened. Bryan said, 'Jack hit me with a stick.'

Dad come out and give me a belting, then went back in to Bryan. After a while Bryan said, 'Jack threw me off Dolly.' So Dad come out again and give me another back-hander. Bryan was as silly as a wheel all night. He was all right the next day, once he got over his headache. I'm pretty sure he couldn't remember any of it, but I bloody could.

Another time, I was cutting firewood and Bryany—that's what I often called Bryan— come poking around picking it up. 'Get back,' I said, 'ya'll get in the way here. Ya'll get ya head cut off.' But he kept coming in and I kept chopping away, and I hit him in the bloody head with the axe and split it open. I had to take him in to Mum and she patched him up. He was all right after. Bloody lucky he wasn't killed I s'pose.

I'd learnt when I was little to call up a dingo for Dad to take a shot at. I'd got bloody good at it, too. I could howl the same as a dingo and he'd come to have a look. Back then I could tell a dingo's howl from a dog's. Now there are so many domesticated dogs that have interbred with them, it's hard to tell the difference. Dad would shoot as many dingoes as he could if they come close enough but they got pretty cunning after a while. They'd smell you if the wind was blowing that way. That's why we had to poison them if we could.

The dingoes were still bad even after we'd poisoned the horse for bait. So the farmers from Cox's Creek and the Bylong farmers got together in Rylstone and organised a dingo drive. The Cox's Creek blokes spread out across the Dairy, the Crown and the Wheelbarrow Mountains, shooting in the air and making a racket to drive the dingoes over to the Bylong side of the mountains, where the Bylong blokes were lined up waiting to shoot any dog that come along. Dad and I were with the Cox's Creek mob. When we got halfway there, all the Cox's Creek blokes met up for dinner. I suppose there was about a dozen or so of us. Dad and I had a lump of damper and a billy of tea for dinner. Two brothers that were there pulled out two great big pieces of steak and threw them on the coals to cook. They'd been in their bag half the day, out in the sun, no eskies or anything back then, and the bullock would most probably have been killed a week or so before, and no ice or fridges—they wasn't going to go hungry.

One year Dad and I trapped the Wheelbarrow Mountain for rabbits. I think it was the second winter before he went into the army. We had a hundred traps between us that we took up to the mountain. We'd set them, have dinner, then run a sundowner and come home. A sundowner is when you go round the traps just before dark and take out any caught rabbits and reset any traps that have gone off. Lots of things could set a trap off, the wind or a branch falling down, vibrations on the ground. A snap that's called, when a trap goes off without catching anything.

As well as the traps, all trappers carried trap papers. They were cut up bits of paper about four inches long and two inches wide that we put over the plate of the trap to stop dirt from getting under the plate and stopping the trap from going off. Dad used to get us kids to cut the papers up from old newspapers, magazines or bread paper. All groceries were wrapped up in paper in them days. We'd hook all the trap papers on a bit of wire and hang it on a button on our shirt or coat. Dad would spit on one corner of the paper and stick it on the plate so it wouldn't move off while he scratched the dirt over it.

The next morning we'd go up again around the traps. It'd be a good four or five mile up round the Wheelbarrow. We'd get up in the morning, go round the traps and reset them, skin the rabbits, bring the skins home and peg them out. By the time we'd pegged them out and had a feed, it was time to go back and run a sundowner. Then back home again that night, peg the skins out, then back up the mountain to the traps the next morning. It was bloody hard yakka.

Dad and I were up on the side of the Crown Mountain cutting horse yard rails one time. The Crown was thickly timbered right up to the foot of the mountain back then. The rails were about twenty foot long and six inches across.

As we were carrying one home, Dad on one end and me on the other, I tripped over a rock and crack went me neck. Pain shot through me neck, me shoulder dropped and me head flew round to the right. I was in awful bloody pain. Dad dropped the rail and dragged me home and put me to bed. The pain was terrible. I was yelling and couldn't do anything. Dad said, 'Ya'll be right tomorra.' But I wasn't. I had to keep me head on one side. Mum had to feed me soup.

After about a week, Dad said, 'Ya'd better ride into town and see a doctor about that neck. Ya been too bloody long layin' around doin' nothin'.' He saddled up a horse for me, a young one. I think he was breaking it in for someone. I got on him, and he threw me to buggery. Me neck went whoosh straight back round the other way and I was all right then. I never had to go to the doctor after all. But it was a bloody painful week, I'll tell ya.

Chapter Seven

Misery for Visitors

Sometimes people would call out to see us on Misery. We were in having dinner this day, when we heard a noise outside like someone was hitting a tin. 'What's that noise?' said Mum. She went and looked outside.

It was old Ali Box, the Indian hawker. He was standing on the fowl house with a stick, belting the roof and singing out, 'Anybody home, anybody home?'

Mum come in and said to Dad, 'Old Ali Box is out there.'

Dad went out and asked him in to have some dinner. Ali Box used to say grace before and after he had his dinner. He used to bless himself by throwing his open hands up past his head. Us kids used to reckon it looked like he said grace and then threw it away again.

Mum had a sore throat at the time. She could hardly talk. Old Ali Box asked her what was wrong and she told him she had quinsy. That's an abscess on your tonsils. Ali Box said, 'You get a teaspoon of black pepper and put him in some water and gargle your throat a couple of times and he's gone.

Fix him straightaway.' Mum did what he said and in a day or two she was as good as gold.

Dad had seen Ali Box in town a few days earlier and told him he had a carthorse for sale. Ali Box was after a horse to pull his goods cart around. After dinner, Dad went out and showed him the old horse we called Dick. Dad said, 'He'll pull all right. Go and yoke him up, Jack.' I put the collar and hames on him and took him up to the scrub where I hooked him onto a big log. Dad got me to pull the log around until it was between two trees. Then he give the horse a hit up the guts with a stick. The horse was digging a hole in the ground, heaving, trying to pull the log.

'Lull ill do, Stan, lull ill do,' old Ali Box yelled out, 'I'll buy him.'

He jumped on the horse bareback to ride him back to Rylstone. When he got to our first gate he yelled to the horse, 'Get up,' and pulled on the reins. Every time he wanted the horse to stop he'd say 'Get up' and every time he wanted him to go he'd yell 'Whoa'. The poor bloody horse didn't know whether he was coming or going.

Old Ali Box used to knock around Glen Alice when Dad was a kid. Dad told us that when Ali Box was younger, he was down on Rawdon Station one time and there was a bloke there that was saying what a good, strong carthorse he had. Well, Dad reckons they put a mark on the ground and Ali Box got hold of the axle of the cart and the driver flogged this horse to go forward but Ali Box pulled the horse and cart back over the line. He was a pretty strong man in his younger days. Dad also said that before he got a horse, Ali Box used to put all his goods in a tarpaulin, tie up the corners and carry it on his head. He reckoned it must have weighed quite a few hundredweight and he would walk for miles with it. Ali Box always wore a turban made out of about ten yards of blue material. I remember he used to say he was saving up to go back to India to die, and as far as I know he did.

As our family grew, we got too big to all fit in the sulky, so Dad got the coachbuilder in town to make us a new spring cart. The blacksmith and the coachbuilder in Rylstone were father and son. The father, who was the coachbuilder, had a real squeaky voice, so everybody called him Squeaky. His son, who was the blacksmith, was always nodding his head, so we all called him Noddy. So Squeaky made Dad this spring cart. It was painted a pretty green. It had one seat across it and had a lot more room than the sulky. We used to always go into town in that then.

Dad never had a car while we were kids. I remember Mum telling me one time that he bought the first Chev Four car that come to Rylstone. He was taking Mum to Kandos in it and going down a hill called Dog Trap—it was only five mile out of Rylstone. There was a horse and sulky driving along the road and he run straight up the back of it cos he didn't know where the brakes were. He pushed the horse and sulky off the road. That was the end of it. He come straight back to Rylstone and got rid of the car. He never drove again. He'd sooner have a horse and sulky. Every horse he got he broke into harness.

Before he broke Rainbow in, Dad decided to get him gelded—that's castrated. There was an old bloke in Rylstone who used to do it, old Thompson. Dad made arrangements for him to come out one Sunday and do Rainbow. This old fella never had a car or anything but there was a brother and sister in town who had a garage and they had a car hire service. The brother used to stutter like buggery. Old Thompson got him to bring him out to Misery. So out they come one Sunday. Mum got ready and cooked some scones and cakes for a big tea party for them.

Anyhow, they got Rainbow and took him down the yard away from the house and fixed him up. Old Thompson was there with blood all over him, and I was there with eyes and ears everywhere. They come up to the tank stand to wash their hands. Dad said to Thompson, 'What's the damage?'

I thought holy geez, he must have put a good cut in his hand, he's got blood everywhere. I thought Dad meant what's the damage to his hand but he meant how much money did he owe him. He said, 'Ten bob, Stan.' That was to do the horse and to pay for the hire car out and back. Geez, it must have been cheap, hey? Just shows you how cheap things were in them days.

Dad says, 'Come in and have a cup of tea.'

So in they come, old Thompson and this stuttering fella. Dad and all us kids were perched up at the table. Mum had the scones and cakes on the table and was handing the gear around and this stuttering bloke wanted the butter. Well, the bloody carry on he had to try and say butter. Us kids thought it was funny. We couldn't stop giggling, the poor bugger. After they went, every time we wanted the butter we'd say, 'Pass the but…but…but…butter.'

Mum or Dad would give us a backhander. 'Cut that caper out,' they'd say. They weren't gunna have us making fun of him.

Mum would only bring out the good crockery and linen when she knew visitors were coming. The best of it wasn't real flash but it was better than a poley cup with a chip out of it. (A poley cup, for people that don't know, is a crockery cup with the handle broken off.) One time me brother, Peter, nailed a poley cup to a piece of wood and never broke the cup. Years ago you could buy a handle for a cup if you broke the handle off. It was a piece of tin shaped like a handle that clipped under the cup and over the rim. You could buy a rubber spout for a teapot, too. You never threw anything out.

Uncle Herbie, Mum's brother from Mudgee, come out and did some work on Misery one time. He made a wooden gate about four foot high and about twelve foot long. It was the boundary gate between Misery and Mills's place. It replaced the gate that knocked Whopper over. The name of Cowboy Charlie's ranch in the comics Mum used to read us was 'New Hope' and Mum thought that would be a good name for Misery. She painted a sign on a piece of kerosene tin 'New Hope' and hung it on one side of the gate. There was still the sign that said 'Misery' on the front of the gate, though. So it said Misery as you were coming in to the property and New Hope as you were going out. Nobody called it New Hope. Every bugger in Rylstone only knew it as Misery. It was called that long before we went to live there. Dad had had the land for quite some time before we moved down. I think he'd bought it before he got married.

I remember Mum telling me that he was digging a well on Misery, sometime before we moved down from Mudgee, and he got appendicitis while he was down the well. He couldn't get out. Jim Howe, one of our neighbours on Misery, come past and found him and took him off to the doctor in Rylstone. They operated on him. Dad might have died down that well if Jim hadn't come along. Just bloody lucky, I guess.

Dad had left his coat and tobacco lying near the well and his old dog Booby was lying on it looking after it. Dad asked Jim to go and get it for him. But old Booby wouldn't let Jim anywhere near Dad's coat. I think he had to leave it till Dad went and got it himself. There were plenty of bunnies about so old Booby didn't starve.

Talking of wells, I remember one time there was a bit of a drought on. It hadn't rained for a long time and the creek we used to get our water out of was drying up and hardly running. Dad said, 'We'll have to dig a well.'

So he got Bob Hobby, his brother-in-law—the one who built the schoolhouse—to come out. He was a carpenter and a water diviner, too. He would hold a chip of wood behind his back and as soon as he got to where water was under the ground, his hands would start to shake. When they were young, Dad and his brothers used to dig holes of a night and bury tins of water for him to find. They used treacle or syrup tins, something with a lid on. They'd bury them two or three foot deep and cover over the ground so it didn't look like it had been dug up. Then Bob would come along of a night with a chip of wood or a stick and he'd find them every time. So anyhow, Dad got him to come out and divine for a well.

When he found a spot, Dad and I dug the well. After we got down a bit, Dad couldn't be digging because I wasn't strong enough to pull the bucket of dirt up. It was a four-gallon kerosene tin we used. So I had to get down and dig it and Dad would pull the bucket up. We dug down about eighteen or twenty foot before we got water. It took us a while. But when the water started to come in I had a job to get out of there in time. It come in real quick and come within two or three foot of the top of the well. We used to dip a bucket in and carry the water to the trough for the horses and cows, or cart it up to the house.

After we'd been on Misery a few years, Dad decided to put up a clothesline for Mum. Before that we used to hang the washing out on the fences and the sulky shafts. I didn't know Dad had put a clothesline up this day, and I come riding home from somewhere on Dolly, galloping along, yahooing, and around the house I went. I didn't see the clothesline. It hooked me straight under the chin and knocked me off the horse.

That was the fastest I'd ever been off a horse, except for the time Dad got a bloke out to do some sucker bashing for us. He was working up the paddock when I come riding past on Roany. She had a big lump of a foal at the time. I got talking to this bloke and he said to me, 'Can ya ride, Jack?'

I said, 'Yeah, I can ride any bloody thing. I'm a pretty smart joker.'

'Can ya ride that foal?' he said.

'Yeah. No trouble.'

The foal come up to take a drink from Roany and, as he did, I flew straight over onto his back. Well, he took off and let up with a heave and shot me straight up in the air. Down I come with me back right across a stump. It buggered me back. I've had a crook back ever since. Many years later, I went to a chiropractor and he took x-rays of me back. He looked at the x-rays and said he couldn't understand why I wasn't in a wheelchair. He said, 'The way I look at those x-rays, there's no possible way you could be walking.' And I shore for fifteen or sixteen years after that accident, so I've done a pretty good job. But it's a bloody crook back all right.

I went to the chiropractor just the other day and he said, 'It amazes me. I can't understand how you can still be walking about.' He said that it looked like my back had been broken at one time. I reckon I must have broken it with that fall. Of course, we never went to the doctor with things like that. It had to be serious before we went to the doctor. I just hobbled around for a while till it come good.

Not long after that, Dad was up around Lue and he bought me a little pinto pony, a pinto blue. Gee, he was a pretty little pony. He was a good horse too, he could go, and he was hardy. I didn't have a lot of imagination with animal names. I called him Pinto. I used to ride him everywhere.

Dad didn't have any work on at the time, so he decided to go over and visit his oldest brother, Bob, and have a yarn to him for a day or two.

Uncle Bob had a property of three or four hundred acres, down on the Capertee-Glen Davis road. He used to call it the Goanna Farm. It was covered in scrub. About the only thing that would grow on it was goannas. So Dad and I went over to see him.

I rode Pinto and Dad rode Rainbow. We had to ride across the mountain and through different properties—it'd be seventy or eighty odd mile. We come through the property of a bloke that Dad used to shear for. Jim he was called. We rode up to the house and Jim come out and met Dad at the fence. 'Ya can't stop Stan, cos Jimmy's dyin' and I gotta go back in to him.'

His son had cancer and was just on his last legs. He was only a young bloke too, about twenty-one. He had a lot of tragedy in his family, poor Jim. His wife only had one leg and one daughter died of pyorrhoea, that's an infection of the gums. She hadn't long got married and had a little baby.

We moved on and got to Uncle Bob's place. He had an old tin shack that was his house, with old iron frame beds up on kerosene tins. I remember one night, we were lying there in bed, and Uncle Bob was lying there with his hands folded across his chest. He said, 'Ya know Stan, one of these nights I'm gunna die, and by gee I hope it's tonight.'

Well, I never slept all night. Every time he made a sound I looked around at him to make sure he was still alive. It frightened buggery out of me.

Uncle Bob could tell some great yarns. He had two fruit shops in Sydney, as well as his property. His wife and kids lived in the house at the back of one of them. He'd go down there sometimes to keep an eye on them, and the shops. His eldest son, Norm, used to run the shops when he was away. Everybody in Rylstone would gather around Uncle Bob in the pub to hear his latest yarns when he come back from Sydney. He used to pretend to have some invisible friends. One he called Santy Claus, the other he called Pigeon's Milk—that was Santy Claus's son, and another he called Grasshopper. The kids used to think it was great fun listening to his yarns.

One time, he said he met Santy Claus, and Santy Claus was telling him that he had some roo skins that needed tanning. In them days we used wattle bark to tan the skins. Uncle Bob said that Santy Claus told his son, Pigeon's Milk, and Grasshopper, to go out into the bush and get him some wattle bark so he could tan the skins. He said Santy Claus told him that Pigeon's Milk and Grasshopper were away for hours and he was getting very worried about them. Then all of a sudden, back they come with two dogs. 'This is all we can find what'll bark,' they said. Uncle Bob was full of stories like that. We used to laugh our heads off. Everyone had fun when Uncle Bob was around.

Everyone had fun on Show Day, too. Rylstone had a show every year. We'd always go. There were merry-go-rounds and knock-em-downs. They had a cooking competition in the pavilion to see who made the best scones, and cakes, and jams. Mum never went in for any of it. She never had bloody time. The show would be half over by the time she got all the kids ready and got there herself.

There was always a riding competition, best lady rider, best gent rider and best kid rider. They always had a boxing tent, too. Me younger brother, Tony, went in the boxing competition sometimes, when he was old enough. We all had great fun at the show—it was a big day for Rylstone.

At the show they always had a pillow fight. They had a big, round rail about six or eight foot off the ground. Two blokes would get up on it with a bag of straw each and they'd belt one another with the bags till someone got knocked off. One year before the war, they had this pillow fight and everyone had been knocked off. I'd had a go, too. The two Abbott boys, Coogy and Jack, were the only two left to fight it out to the finish. They knocked one another off the rail, but they were still hanging on with their legs, upside down, flogging one another till the blood was flying out of them. I think they ended up having to call it a draw.

    I think it was the same year that they had catch-a-greasy-pig. They used to get a little sucking pig and grease his tail, then let him go in the showground and everyone would run after him and try and catch him. The two Abbott girls, Princie and Denny, caught the pig. They got it between them that year.

Chapter Eight

Dawson Street

When the war started in 1939, we didn't know for a while cos we never had a wireless. Dad had been away shearing. When he come home he told us the war had started.

During the war years, I can remember Mum saying to me when I was going out shooting, 'Leave me some of them bullets. Ya can't go using them all cos if the Japs come, I'm gunna shoot you all and then shoot meself. The Japs aren't takin' us.'

Dad enlisted for service about a year after the war started. He'd fought in the First World War and had the two middle fingers of his left hand shot off. He'd been injured by gunshots twice before that, but they sent him home after he lost his fingers. That was towards the end of the war.

We didn't know he'd joined up till he got his calling up papers at the start of 1941. His brothers, Bob and Cliff, also joined up. I remember looking at a photo of them all in uniform with their slouch hats on. Gee, they were a wild looking trio. They were sent to Orange because they were too old for combat. They had the job of guarding the internees.

When Dad got his call up he said to me, 'When I go into the army ya can have me saddle.' I'd never ridden in a saddle before. Us kids used to use a corn bag for a saddle so we didn't hurt the horse's back. We used to tie the bag on with a surcingle—that's like a girth.

The morning Dad left, he walked over to a neighbour's property and got a lift to town. We all stood outside and watched him go. As he was walking up the hill, I yelled out, 'Thanks for the saddle, Dad.'

When he left, I don't think we knew where he was going to be posted or even if he was staying in Australia. We only found out when he come home on leave that he'd been sent to Orange. I can't remember Mum being upset when he left. She was used to him being away. And nothing seemed to worry me. I had no more worries than a frog's got feathers. I was happy to get a saddle. That was the first day I rode in a proper saddle.

The year before Dad got called up, he decided to put a fence up and divide our front paddock into two. He and I split the posts and stood them. We put up one strand of barbed wire through the middle of the fence and then went in for dinner. While we were inside, something frightened the horses and Peggy run slap bang into the barbed-wire fence and tore a hole in her chest big enough to fit a football in.

'We'll hafta shoot her,' Dad said. I kicked up a fuss about shooting her, so Mum and I took her down the yard and got her in the crush. We sewed her up with ordinary cotton and filled the wound with Stockholm Tar. Mum stuck a patch of rag over it with sticking plaster to keep the flies away.

Dad said, 'Take her up to Wheelbarrow Mountain and leave her up there, her and her mother, and let her die. She'll do for dingo bait.' So I took Dolly and Peggy and turned them out on Wheelbarrow Mountain.

Just after Dad left to go to the war, I said to Mum, 'I'm goin' up to the Wheelbarrow to get old Dolly and see what happened to Peggy.' So away I went and found Dolly. She had a beautiful little filly with her that had a scar on its chest that looked just like a monkey's face. Peggy had survived. I brought them both home. Dad used to break in horses and he'd been teaching me how to do it ever since I'd learnt to ride. When I got Peggy home, I broke her into saddle. I used to ride her everywhere. Then I broke her into the sulky just before we went into Rylstone to live.

Before Dad went away to war, we'd planted a big paddock of corn on Misery. When he come home on his first leave he said to Mum, 'Ya'll hafta get Jack and try and get somebody else to give ya a hand pick that corn. It'll be ready in a couple a weeks.'

Our next-door-neighbour, Gordon Mills, went into town and organised a working bee and most of Rylstone come out to help. They got a council truck and all come out one Sunday. There were heaps of people. They picked the whole paddock of corn in one day—a tip-truck full. We used the schoolhouse Dad had got built as a storeroom. We took the corn there and filled the room with it. It was so full that we had to shut the door and throw the last bits of corn in through the windows.

Soon after that, Mum decided to move into town. She bought an old house in Dawson Street, Rylstone that we shifted into. Lenny Price, who was a cousin of ours, had a mail run. He'd cut the back off a car and made a little semi-trailer for it. He shifted us into town.

Mum was better off when Dad was in the army because of the allowance for all the kids. There were nine kids by then. She got a big war pension. She was better off than before or after the war. She borrowed the money from the bank and paid for the house. I think she paid a hundred pounds for it. We kept the farm as well. We had crops still growing on it and other folks used to keep their cattle on it.

The house in Dawson Street actually fronted onto a lane. It was the back of the house that faced Dawson Street. It was made of vertical split slabs of timber and inside they were papered with newspaper and painted over. The floor was bare boards. There was no electricity or running water. Out the back was a kind of laundry room and bathroom. Next to that was the dining room with a big open fire at one end. The kitchen was opposite, with a little wood stove. Like on Misery, Mum did most of her cooking on the open fire in the dining room. There was a space of a few feet between this back part of the house and the front part, with a covered walkway in the middle. The front part had a short hallway with a bedroom off on either side, then it opened up into a lounge room and Mum and Dad's bedroom run off the lounge room. There was an open verandah on the front.

When we first moved in, the little kids had the back bedrooms and Mum and Dad had the front one. Us bigger kids slept on the verandah. Later on, the girls had the back bedrooms and the boys had the verandah. Years after, Dad made bricks out of ash and cement and put a wall up about three foot high along the front of the verandah. We used to hang flour bags down to cover the gap if it was windy or wet.

In the front room—that's what we always called the lounge—we did all our entertaining. We had a gramophone and all the hillbilly records under the sun. When Dad was home he wouldn't put up with the noise. We had to stick a towel in the speaker to keep the noise down. He liked the cowboy records but he didn't like it too loud. He didn't go much on old

Bing Crosby either. 'Get that howlin' bastard off,' he'd say if we put one of his records on.

Blokes would come up home to watch Dad and us boys put the gloves on and go a few rounds. There was a big open fireplace that was going day and night in the winter. We'd sit in there and have tea and toast, and play cards till all hours.

I didn't go to school when we moved into town. The other kids that were old enough did. They went to the public school in Rylstone. It finished at grade six. All the older ones finished then, but the three youngest went out to the convent school in Kandos. They'd catch the bus out, up on the Kandos road. There used to be buses running every day that took all the workers out to the coalmines and the cement works at Kandos and Charbon.

Once we were in town, I used to go poking around the streets and I got to meet up with some mates. I reckon I'd have been about fourteen. Now and then, some of them would come out with me to Misery to shell corn. They thought it was great fun coming out to the bush. We'd go out in a horse and cart.

We were all happy to move into town but I'd go back out to the farm every few days to get things. Us kids used to pick blackberries to sell in town. That got us our picture money. That, and rabbiting— rabbit skins fetched a good price.

The pictures were in the dance hall. They projected the film onto a screen on the stage. Every Saturday night the pictures were on. We didn't go every Saturday. We'd usually only go if it was a cowboy picture or a comedy, Laurel and Hardy or the like. I can't remember how much it cost but it wasn't very much, maybe sixpence. The bloke that run the pictures did the picture show in Kandos as well. At interval, he'd bring the picture he showed at Kandos out to Rylstone and take the Rylstone one back to Kandos. It'd be five mile and he'd do that in the interval time. He must have been fairly flying.

As well as shelling corn, I had to go out to Misery and cut chaff. We fed chaff to our cattle and horses. We still had a haystack out there. One day, me and another young fella from town, who'd come out to give me a hand, were cutting chaff. When we got down to the bottom of the haystack we found a big heap of mice. We got a four-gallon kerosene tin that was made into a bucket and filled it up with mice and bits of hay. We put a bird wire lid over the top of it to keep them in. There would have been a couple of hundred mice in there. We took them back to town with us. Then we went up to the rubbish dump on the side of the hill near the common and found two big square biscuit tins. We punched some holes in the lids for air holes.

It was a Saturday. So that night we put the mice in the biscuit tins and went to the pictures. We had the biscuit tins under our overcoats. When we got into the picture show we went one on each side of the aisle. We'd made arrangements beforehand that at the right moment one bloke would cough twice—that was the signal. Then we'd put the tins down on the floor, take the lids off and go and get a pass to go to the toilets. You had to get a pass from the usherette to get back in if you left. The usherette, and often the copper too, would be up the back. So about half way through the picture, I coughed. We took the lids off the tins, got up straight away and got a pass. We went outside and waited around the side of the hall. After a couple of minutes the screaming started. The lights went on, and people come running out of the hall in droves. What a bloody racket! Then we took off.

We'd taken all our animals with us from Misery. We used to run them on the common. The common was a council run area of about a hundred acres. There were three commons in Rylstone. One was three mile out of town and the other two were in town, one either side of the Cudgegong road. The Cudgegong River run through the bottom common. It had a deep swimming hole in it that we called the Rocky Waterhole. That's where we used to swim. The other common was on the hill just above our house. We called that one the top common. You paid a shilling or something a month to graze your animals on it. We had a couple of horses and a couple of cows that we kept there. Our chooks we kept in a fowl house up the back of our yard. We kept our milking cow on the common, too. We used to go and bring her up to the house to milk her. After a few years, we built a round yard up behind the house for breaking in horses.

Dad would catch a train from Sydney when he come home on leave. We never knew when he was coming. He'd just turn up some mornings. The Mudgee mail train used to leave Sydney every night about seven or eight o'clock and get to Rylstone between five and six the next morning. Then it would go on to Mudgee and out to Coolah. It would turn round at Coolah and come back and get to Rylstone about nine o'clock at night on its way back to Sydney. When Dad was going back, I used to carry his kit bag for him down to the train. We all walked him back to the train. All us kids, trudging along behind him like a mob of ducks.

Dad come home on leave one time and he leased Misery out to a fella who put cattle on it. We still had a lot of our harnesses and our sulky out there in the schoolroom. I was still going out there to shell corn, and one day, two fellas come out with me. We'd shelled a couple of bags when a big, roan steer come wondering around the paddock near us. I lassoed him, pulled him up to our old house and tied him to a verandah post. I said to one of me mates, 'I'm gunna get on this fella and then you let him go.'

'Righto!' he said.

So on I got and he let him go. Well, ya wouldn't believe it, he went straight through the bloody house, bellowing and roaring and bucking. He got into the dining room and slipped on the floor and threw me. He got up, got me in the corner, and he come at me. I've still got a scar up me guts where he tried to rip it open. I was in trouble for a while there before I got away … and he wrecked the bloody house. The other fellas were as scared as buggery, but I thought it was the funniest thing I'd ever seen, this bullock wrecking the house.

I wasn't satisfied with that though, so we caught him again and I said, 'We'll have some fun with this fella.' We tied him up to a post and I got Dad's old breaking-in gig. A breaking-in gig is a sulky with long shafts. I made up a set of harnesses out of ropes and broken bits of leather and put the bullock in the shafts of the gig. I said to me mate, 'You get in the sulky and I'll get on the bullock and we'll have some fun.'

So I got on the bullock and me mate got in the sulky, then the other bloke let the bullock go. I tell ya, they're hard to ride at any time, but with the shafts of a sulky under me legs I had no chance. He bucked and bellowed and took off. I jumped off, but the poor fella in the sulky was too scared to move. He was screaming out, 'Help me! Help me!' as the bullock took off up through the scrub. We followed him and found bits of the sulky laying everywhere, and this fella lying in the scrub yelling. He had some hide off him but apart from that he wasn't hurt but it frightened buggery out of him.

Another time, we were out on Misery shelling corn, me and two mates from town. Billy Mills, me old neighbour, also had a couple of mates over from town. We all met up and were shooting bunnies up around the swamp. It was a warm sort of day so we'd all stripped off to our shorts. One of these fellas worked in a draper's shop in Rylstone. He was as white as a sheet and just had a pair of shorts on. He had a banana in his hand cos we were having dinner. He said to Billy, 'You're a bloody good shot with a rifle, aren't ya?'

'Yeah,' said Billy, 'I am.'

This kid peeled the banana and held it up in his hand. 'Can ya shoot this out of me hand?'

Well, Billy went bang with the .22 rifle he was carrying and this fella started to scream. 'You shot me! You shot me!' he was yelling. When the bullet hit the banana, the banana splattered all over this poor bastard, and it was red hot. He thought he was dying.

Billy wouldn't shoot a rabbit in a squat, he'd make it run and then shoot it. He never missed. He was a pretty good shot with a bow and arrow too. We'd make bows from little stringy bark suckers and a bit of string. The string you used to get around parcels back then was nearly as strong as rope. The arrows we made out of smaller bits of stringy bark. You could get some pretty straight ones. They had to be straight for making arrows.

One time, Billy got the cane stick off his sister's kewpie doll that she'd bought at the Rylstone show. He hammered a steel knitting needle into it and used that as an arrow. It'd go a long way.

One afternoon, I was down at his place and he was showing his brother-in-law how far he could fire this arrow straight up in the air. 'Look at this,' he said. He pulled the bow back hard and fired the arrow straight up in the air.

It went that high we lost sight of it. We were standing around wondering where it went, when down it come straight through the brim of Billy's hat and stuck in the ground at his feet. How's that for luck? A couple of inches further over and it would've gone straight into his bloody head.

Once when Dad come home on leave, he bought an old cart off someone. It had hard rubber tyres on it. One of the tyres kept coming off, so he tied it on with a bit of wire. He put a Bogan twitch in it. That's a piece of wire, doubled, and you twist it around with a pair of pliers and tighten it. He tied it on tight with this wire and when he cut the ends off, he curled them up a bit to stop them sticking straight out.

Anyhow, Mum told me this day to go out to Misery and get some more corn. I yoked old Roany up and put her in this rubber-tyred cart. Another young fella who was hanging around doing nothing come out with me. We went out, got the corn, picked a heap of blackberries, shot a bunny or two, and got in the cart to go home. As we were coming home, I got bored sitting in the cart doing nothing, so I stood up and jumped onto the wheel. As the cart was going along, I was running on top of the wheel thinking it was great fun.

This other kid was yelling at me, 'Ya silly bugger, ya'll hurt yaself.'

'Not me,' I said, and kept running along.

All of a sudden I slipped. Down I went and this Bogan twitch caught in me shin and tore a lump out of it about an inch long. I had to get it patched up by Mum when I got home. That's another scar I've still got.

Chapter Nine

On the Common

The old house in Dawson Street had a little 100-gallon water tank, with a tap poking through the kitchen wall. We had a big underground tank that used to catch the rest of the water from the roof. It was twelve foot square and about ten foot deep and had a pump on it. That's where our main water supply come from. We had to pump it up into a bucket and cart it into the house. When the pump buggered up, we just used to dip it up with a bucket.

There was a drought on this summer and a lot of people were out of water. The little 100-gallon tank was empty, so I got it and rigged it onto an old spring cart and started carting water for a living. I reckon I was about fifteen by then. I'd go down to the well on the bottom common, throw a bucket down with a rope on it, pull it back up full of water, then empty it into the tank till I filled it. Then I'd take it up to the house of whoever wanted it and empty it into their tank with a bucket. Two bob a load I got paid and I made enough money to keep meself and me horse. Gee, it was hard yakka, but between carting water and cutting firewood, I did all right around Rylstone for a while there.

Later on, I got two 44-gallon drums from somewhere and tied them onto a flat top that I'd made on top of the breaking-in gig. We were carting water this day, me and me brother, Bryan, and another fella. As we were going across the common, Bryan standing in one of the empty drums and this other kid standing in the other one, something frightened Rainbow and he took off. I got thrown off and the other kid jumped off, but Bryan couldn't get out of the drum. He got a rough ride all right. He was yelling, 'Stop him! Stop him!'

We caught Rainbow later but there was nothing left of the gig. As far as I know there's still parts of that gig laying around the common. Bryan survived but he wasn't real happy; he didn't go much on a rough ride. And it would have been a rough ride too because they're real long shafts on a breaking-in gig, to stop the new horse kicking the front out of it. With long shafts like that, when they get a go on, they whip like buggery.

Me youngest brother, Billy, was born after we moved to town in '42. That made ten kids. Mum was pretty busy all the time. She'd cook for us and nearly always a couple of mates would be there for a feed, too. People would ask her how she managed to feed so many and she'd say, 'I just add more water to the stew.' I'm buggered if I know how she did it—no electricity or running water, kids everywhere, and Dad away most of the time.

We had a couple of ferrets at one time that we used to take down to the bottom common, down on the flat, to catch rabbits. There were rabbits everywhere and plenty of warrens. We used to sell the skins and eat the meat. Mum would say, 'We got no tucker, ya better get a bunny or two.'

We used to catch them on the common. A lot of the kids in town would come with us. They thought it was great fun chasing rabbits out of the burrows with the ferrets. Gee, they come out in a bloody hurry. We had a heap of nets we used to put around the mouth of the burrows. One of the ferrets we had was a bludger of a ferret. If he could get hold of a bunny and suck the blood out of him, he'd stay in the burrow and go to sleep. We had to wait for hours for him to come out. We'd try and make a lot of noise to wake him up.

This day we were down on the common. It was getting late in the evening and this ferret hadn't come out and one of the kids said, 'Why don't we put a saucer of milk at the mouth of the burrow?'

Another kid said, 'We don't have any milk.'

So then he said, 'Why don't ya make a noise like a saucer of milk? Will he come out for that?'

One weekend, me and a couple of other young fellas I knew from around town went out shooting rabbits on the common. We got off the common a bit and onto a bloke's property. It had a set of cattle yards on it and a heap of cattle poking around. 'Come on,' I said, 'let's round some of these bullocks up and we can have a bit of a ride.'

'Like bloody hell,' they said. 'We're not gettin' on them.'

Anyhow, I coaxed these fellas into rounding them up and we put one in the yard and I got it in the crush. There were some pieces of rope tying the gates up, so I made a surcingle out of the ropes and put it on the bullock and told the other blokes to open the gates when I'd jumped on him. I got settled on him and they opened the gate, and he took off across the paddock, bucking. The bloke that owned the property must have had the phone on because there were two wires running across the paddock only about six foot off the ground. This bullock went straight through them with me on him and I got tangled up in them and pulled the wires down. I jumped off and we all took off back to town. The next week some bloke was going around town telling everyone that someone had pulled McQuiggin's telephone line down.

Once I got into town, I used to get into all the bloody trouble under the sun. The Mudgee to Sydney mail train used to come through every day. It got in about nine o'clock at night. There was a lady that was contracted to take the mail down to the train. The policeman usually went down with her. She'd take the bag of mail by car down to meet the train.

Well, one night, me and another fella got an empty kerosene tin, put about twenty little stones in it, screwed the lid back on it, got a lump of wire and tied it onto the diff of her car. She come out to take the mail down, got in her car and started to drive away, but it was making a terrible racket. So she stopped to have a look but she couldn't see anything. Away she went again. Again there was this terrible racket, so she stopped and had another look—couldn't see anything. We'd tied the tin where she couldn't see it. Away she drove again and when she got onto the bitumen road at the start of town the tin was dragging on the bitumen and sparks were flying everywhere. The copper saw her and yelled for her to stop. He thought her car was going to blow up. When he looked underneath and found the tin, he was bloody wild. I reckon he'd have shot us if he'd found out we did it. I think he had a pretty good idea who had done it but he never said anything to us. We were in the churchyard, watching from there. Gee, we laughed. We were crying we were laughing so much.

On another occasion, we got three or four gates from the blacksmith's shop. There was a row of trees growing down the centre of the main street. We tied one gate to a tree in the middle of the road and tied the rest of them together to make a fence, then run them across to the blacksmith's gate, blocking off the road. When she come down the street to the train, she couldn't get through. The copper was riding with her. He had to get out and undo them so they could get past. He wasn't real happy about it. It was a wonder he didn't come looking for me.

Me and another kid, called Alan, used to go buggering around down the street, getting up to all sorts of mischief. The council had just started putting up these rubbish bins. They were a four-gallon round tin that fitted into a wire frame fixed to a post. The bin just used to sit in the frame. 'Be tidy' bins they called them. Me and Alan would walk down the street wearing hobnail boots. I give this bloody tin a boot one night and up in the air it went, out of the frame it was in. Alan thought that was funny, so of a night we'd go down the street wearing hobnail boots and we'd give these bloody tins a boot and see who could kick them up the highest out of the frame.

One fella, who used to come to town of a weekend, called Ned, spotted us walking down the street one night and he seen us kick this bin. 'Geez,' he said, 'I'll have a go at that.'

When the next weekend come round, before he come into town, we half-filled one of these bins with sand. When we went down the street that Saturday night, Ned come with us. One of us had a go at the first bin. The second one, with the sand in it, was the one we let Ned have a kick at. When he was talking he never said, 'By the Christ', he said, 'byly cry'. So he says, 'Byly cry, I'll shift this one.'

He let drive with his foot and kicked the bottom of the bin and it never moved an inch. Poor bugger bloody near broke his ankle. He was yelling and hobbling around. That was the end of him coming with us kicking bins.

Around bonfire night, we used to get Tom Thumb crackers, little basket bombs and stuff like that. We'd let them off on bonfire night. It must have been just after bonfire night, when me and Alan were going down the street and we had a basket bomb left. We were walking along and we saw this old fella, Albert, who used to come into town from down along the other side of the river. He lived a couple of mile out of town with a joker he used to do a bit of work for. He'd help around the house and take this bloke's kids to school in his horse and sulky, and do their shopping. This day he was in town sitting in the sulky reading his list, when me and Alan spotted him. He wasn't far away from a rubbish bin. So I got this rubbish bin, Alan lit the basket bomb and put it under the horse's belly, and I put the bin over the top of it. We jumped back onto the footpath waiting for the basket bomb to go off. It went off with a bang. The bin flew up in the air and hit the horse in the guts. It jumped in the air and took off just as the copper come round the corner. The horse flew down the street with old Albert in the sulky, legs up in the air, wondering what the bloody hell happened.

The copper yelled out to us and we took off. Down the back of the shops I raced, down through the park and onto the bottom common. Rainbow was down that end of the common. No saddle or bridle, I just jumped on him and away I went out along the Cudgegong road. I buggered around all day out there. I never come home till late that afternoon.

That was the last bloody straw. The copper come up to Mum's and told her to tell me to go down to the police station. Down I went. He frightened buggery out of me. He told me if I kept playing up he'd send me to a kids' home in Orange for wayward boys. So that settled me down for a while.

Mum must have thought I needed something better to do with me time too, because she was looking in the AWU paper and saw a job for me. The AWU was a newspaper advertising for shearers, rouseabouts, station hands, all sorts of jobs on the land. It used to have one section for shearing sheds starting and cutting out. It would tell you what date a certain shed was going to start shearing and what sheds had just cut out, and when. Cut out is a shearer's term for when a shed finishes shearing all its sheep. Mum saw in the AWU paper that Cooba Station wanted shearers and rouseabouts. She wrote to Cooba and asked for a rouseabout job for me and they sent back word that they had a job for me and what day they were starting. I caught the train to Darlington Point. It was the first time I'd been that far away on me own and it was a bloody long way from home.

Cooba was five mile out of Darlington Point. They picked us up in a truck from the station. When I got there, it was the biggest bloody joint I'd ever seen. Someone told me that in the old days Cooba Station had one hundred and one stands in a straight line. A stand is where a shearer stands to shear the sheep. When I was there it had been mechanised. But in the early days they shore with a blade—a hundred and one shearers. There weren't that many shearers when I was there, though.

I was out at Cooba for seven weeks, picking up. There used to be one rouseabout for four shearers. A rouseabout's job was to pick up the fleeces and throw them onto the table for the wool roller to skirt and roll up and give to the wool classer. He also swept the board and was the tar boy, too. The tar boy dabbed tar on cuts or maggots on the sheep. The shearers would yell out, 'Tar boy! Dab it on and jump back.'

The rouseabout would grab the tar brush and dab it on the sheep where the cut was or the maggots were. Instead of tar, some sheds used KFM, which was a chemical. It stood for 'kills flies and maggots'. An aboriginal shearer told me that KFM was good stuff to toughen up your hands. So I used to rub it all over me hands and it toughened them up all right. Wool softened your hands see, all the lanolin in it, so you had to make them tough somehow.

Cooba was a big shed. They shore a hundred and seventy thousand sheep the year I was there, in that seven weeks. I can't remember exactly how many shearers they had that year but it was a bloody lot. It was the first time I'd been in a shearing shed and I decided then I wanted to be a shearer. When Cooba Station cut out, I went back home.

*Me on **Peggy**, trying to play the guitar. It's a wonder the bloody horse didn't throw me. That's me Tolty saddle I'm sitting in. I'd be around 15 in this photo.*

I took this photo of the family, around 1945, on me old box Brownie camera, and developed the film in the bathroom.

*Left to right, back row; **Wop**, **Marie**, **Bryan**.
Middle row; **Peter**, **Maureen**, **Tony**.
Front row; **Billy**, **Pat**, **Larry**.*

Chapter Ten

Bee Keeping, Boxing and Boundary Riding

After I come back from rouseabouting at Cooba, I done a bit of work for a carrier in Rylstone. Joe he was called. He used to cart all the goods from the train to the stores. It was me first proper job in town. I only worked a few hours a day with him, so he asked me if I wanted a job with his brother-in-law, Eric, who had a property and was a bee farmer.

'All right,' I said. I went home and told Mum I was going bee farming.

'Ya bloody fool!' she said. 'The bees will kill ya.'

She was worried because on Misery, a few years before, I'd got stung on the forehead by a bee and swelled up like a balloon. I couldn't even see—me eyes were swollen shut.

'I'll be right,' I said.

Anyhow, I rode me pony up to this bloke's place. His farm was about fifteen mile up Cox's Creek on a different sort of a track to where Misery was.

I got up there and said to him, 'I'm Jack Turner, the bloke Joe told ya about.'

'Oh, yes, Jack. How are ya?' he said. 'I'm not working the bees just yet, but I've got plenty of work here on the farm. I'm planting spuds and doing a bit of ploughing, ya can give me a hand. Thirty bob a week and ya keep.'

'That'll suit me bloody fine,' I said.

So I started working for him, ploughing, and sometimes in the evening we'd make up new frames for the bee boxes, and fix things up for when the bees started gathering nectar and pollen. He had eighteen or twenty hives in a paddock not far from his house. One day, after about a week, Eric said he'd better go up and check them, see if they had enough honey and were strong enough to shift. If they were, then we'd take them out to where the other hives were.

'Ya'd better put long trousers on and long sleeves, and here's a veil and a hat, put that on too,' he said. 'If ya get stung, don't pull the sting out, just scratch it off with ya fingernail. They're not real savage this mob, anyway.'

We went up to the boxes. The bees were buzzing around me and I got a few stings.

'They're not ready yet,' he said, 'we'll come back next week and shift them.' As we were going back me hands started swelling up. 'Don't worry about it,' he said, 'they'll swell like that for a while but then ya'll be right. They won't hurt after a while, ya'll get used to them.'

We worked around the farm for a week, then one evening we went up to the hives and put some cleats on the boxes and nailed a screen across the top to stop the bees from getting out. Then they were ready to shift.

He'd give the hives a puff or two of smoke to quieten down the bees while we were working with the hives. He said, 'We'll take the hives out to Tong Bong tomorrow.' We loaded them onto his little red Chev truck that night and set off before daylight for Tong Bong.

The grey gums were just starting to blossom. He reckoned he'd make a lot of money from the honey made from the grey gum blossom. We set the hives up where there were plenty of gum trees. He had over a hundred hives already there. Me hands swelled up as big as footballs from the stings, but after a few days they went down. They didn't swell again when I got stung.

We spent a few days there robbing the hives of honey. I got quite good at it. I thought it was a great job working among the bees. When the blossom was in full flower on the grey gums, the bees made that much honey we were busy every day from sun up till sun down. We were flat out for about six weeks. Collecting the honey, labelling the tins—they were sixty pound tins—and taking loads to town to put on the train to Sydney. Sixty to eighty tins at a time we'd be taking in. He sold most of it to W.D & H.O. Wills. It was a big British tobacco company. They used honey in the making of tobacco. They had a factory in Sydney.

When things quietened down, we went down to the Blue Mountains, to Katoomba, to get honey. The blossom was just starting to come out on the tea trees there. So Eric went and got permission to put hives in the grounds of the Queen Victoria Consumptive Home. It was a government-run joint. It was for the soldiers mainly. We transported the hives down by train. We went by truck and got there a day earlier and were waiting at the station when the train arrived. When the guard opened the van door, there were two or three hives that had tipped over and were open. Gee, there were some savage bloody bees around, I'll tell ya. Everybody bolted. None of the railway blokes would have anything to do with us. We unloaded them by ourselves. It took us a few loads to shift them.

We had two spots where we put the hives. One was down near the Western Highway and the other was off the beaten track a bit, up in the grounds of the Queen Victoria Consumptive Home. We camped in a tent there near the hives.

After a few days we started to extract the honey. We were robbing the hives near the Home this day, when a group of soldiers come down and asked if they could have some honeycomb. 'Yeah, ya can have some,' I said and give them some.

They were standing around near the hives eating honeycomb, when a bee come up and was buzzing around this baldy-headed fella. He started waving his arms around to shoo it away.

'Don't go wavin' ya arms around,' I said. 'Just stand still. It won't hurt ya.' There was only the odd one about. But this fella kept hitting at them and he got a bit closer to where Eric was robbing a hive. He was waving his hat and his arms around and all of a sudden the bees into him. He took off through the nearby bush like a kangaroo, belting himself with his hat to get them off him. We didn't see him again for honeycomb.

When we finished that lot of hives, we went back to the ones near the Western Highway. We camped there and started robbing those hives. One night a horse and cart pulled up with three or four young fellas in it. They were shifting up to Orange to live and they had all their gear in the cart. They had a cat with them, too. The next morning when they were packing up to get going they were singing out for this cat. It was all thick scrub around us. I was down in the scrub a bit and I started meowing.

'Here! He's over here,' they said and run over to where I was. I run around under a ridge to another spot and meowed. 'He's over here! He's over here!' they said and come running across. I ducked off again through the scrub and meowed again. 'Here, he's over here,' they said and run back.

'Come here Jack, ya lunatic,' Eric called out to me. 'Ya'll send those poor buggers mad.'

We were there for about six weeks. Then it was getting on for winter and the blossom was just about finished. Eric said, 'We might have to feed them if there's not enough blossom about anywhere.' To feed bees you just mix up sugar and water and that will keep them going for a while. We left the bees where they were and went back home. While we were there Eric went to Coonabarabran to look for blossom. When he come back he'd found a place in Coonabarabran.

So we went back down to Katoomba and shifted the hives up to Coonabarabran by train. We loaded the hives into a goods van for the goods train to pick up and drove the truck to Rylstone with all our gear on it. We got there a day earlier than the goods train and then caught the same train that the bees were on up to Coonabarabran. Eric had a pushbike he took with him. We unloaded the bees and got a carrier to take them out to the property where we were keeping them. Then we come back into Coonabarabran. Eric left his bike at some bloke's place and was going to ride out to the property in a couple of weeks' time to check on the hives.

We camped in town that night, in the fettler's hut right beside the railway line. We just laid our swags down on the ground. That night, while we were asleep, a goods train come along and stopped right outside the fettler's hut and let off steam. The hut filled with steam. Eric had to get out but I stayed asleep. The next day he told me about it but I hadn't heard a thing. After that we went home and he went back in a fortnight's time to check the hives. As he was riding out to the property where the bees were, he come across a big bull that had got out of a paddock and it was in the laneway. It took to Eric and he had to fight it off with the bike. It wrecked the bloody bike but he survived.

While I was working for Eric, he sold his little old Chev to another bee farmer up on Nullo Mountain and bought a bigger truck. This other farmer called North—I can't remember his first name—was keeping some bees down at Sofala. We had bees down there too, at the time. After a while, we brought our bees home and North was bringing his back later. I was in bed one night when Eric come and woke me. 'Come on, Jack,' he said. 'We gotta go down to Sofala. North's just turned his truck load of bees over on the Cudgegong Cuttings road.'

So away we went. What a bloody shemozzle we saw when we got there. Bees everywhere, and boxes smashed up all over the place, and the little Chev was wrecked. Just as well Eric had put fifteen or so empty bee boxes on his truck to take with us. We were all night and all the next day straightening them up and fixing boxes. We had to bring them all home on Eric's truck.

Eric's brother-in-law, Joe, had given away carrying by then and he was poking around doing nothing. He come up to the farm and was there for a couple of days. Then he asked me if I wanted to go rabbiting with him.

'I can get a paddock out at Bylong,' he said, 'down the bottom of Widden Mountain. One of me brothers-in-law works for the property owner and he'll let us go trapping there.'

I asked Eric if he'd be needing me for a while and he said he'd be right. So I packed me swag and got a heap of tucker and traps from home and down we went to the property in Bylong, in behind the Widden Mountain. We were trapping away there early one morning when I heard a dingo howling.

'There's a dingo up there in the mountain,' I said to Joe. 'Get the gun and I'll call him down here. We'll get a quid for this fella.' You got money for dingo scalps. I think it was about a quid a scalp.

He got the gun and sat down. I started howling and the dingo answered. I howled again and he answered. We went on like this for about an hour. Then there was a howl and I answered. 'He's comin'. He's movin', this fella,' I said to Joe. 'He's comin' around the side of the mountain.'

I kept howling, hiding behind trees, waiting for this dingo to come along. After another half an hour, along come a joker with a gun, sneaking through the scrub.

'G'day,' he said when he saw us. 'How are ya?'

'G'day,' we said.

'I thought that dingo was down this way,' he said, 'but he must be over on the other side of the mountain. I've been calling him,' he said. 'But he must have somethin' to eat over there because he won't come to me. I thought I'd better go to him.'

'He could have, too,' I said.

'Ya bloody fool, Jack,' Joe said. 'Tell him who it is.'

'What's up?' this bloke said.

'It's Jack,' said Joe. 'He's been calling ya.'

'Be buggered,' said this bloke. 'I've been chasin' dingoes all me life and he's the first bloody dog who's called me up yet.'

We were rabbiting about five weeks, then the rabbits were starting to get a bit scarce and Eric didn't need a hand, so I got a job boundary riding on Rawdon Station. Nine pound a month, and that was a calendar month. It was just after shearing and they'd started dipping the sheep. We used to get up at three o'clock in the morning and go out and dip the sheep, then we'd have breakfast. You'd take a bit of tucker with you for breakfast at seven. Then at half past seven you'd start your day's work and work till half past five.

It was a boundary rider's job to do just about everything. Check fences, burr cutting, marking sheep, patching up fences, shifting stock from one paddock to another. If there's a lot of grass called foxtails, the seeds from it can get in the sheep's eyes and they get infected. In your saddlebag you had a pair of shears, a pair of pliers and pair of tweezers. And another pouch with a bottle of sheep dip in it. If you saw a sheep with sore eyes caused by seeds, you'd catch him and pull the burrs out with your tweezers. If you saw sheep that were fly blown, you'd get the dog to round them up, then you'd go through them, cut the wool off that's blown, then put sheep dip on it. It was all sorts of work.

I was doing that for a few months, for nine pounds a month. You only got paid at the end of each month and by that time I owed nearly that much bloody money from borrowing it to keep me going.

While I was at Rawdon, Dad come home on leave and met up with a shearing contractor that was going to Monivae. It was a sheep station between Lue and Rylstone, a six-stand shed. Dad asked him if there was any chance of getting me a rouseabout job there. The bloke said he'd get me on and pick me up when he was ready to go.

Dad helped roll me swag before I left—he was still home on leave. The first thing he threw in it was a set of boxing gloves. He always had a set of boxing gloves and when we were kids, as soon as we were old enough, he'd kneel down on the floor so we could reach him, and teach us how to box. When he'd finished teaching us, he'd get up and Mum would put the gloves on and give him a bloody hammering. He used to think that was great fun.

'Put 'em on with any bugger who wants 'em on,' he said. 'It'll do ya good.'

I got to Monivae and unrolled me swag. I was in a room with another joker.

'Geez, kid, you must think you're bloody smart carryin' them around,' he said to me.

'Oh no,' I said. 'Dad just said to put 'em in and anyone who wants a glove, put 'em on with him.' So every shed after that I took me gloves with me and put them on with anyone who wanted to spar.

A few years later, I got a letter from Tom MacGuire. He was a Newcastle boxing trainer who trained Dave Sands and them. Dave Sands was the Australian and Empire Middle Weight Champion. The letter said, I'd like you to come and join my crew in Newcastle and I'll make you the fourth ace. He had the three Sand's brothers and they all had a title. They were the three aces. He was going to make me the fourth. I don't know how he found out I was handy with the gloves but bush telegraph has a habit of travelling long distances.

When Dad saw the letter he said, 'There ya go.'

'Not me,' I said. 'I'm not training. I know how to look after meself and that's all I want.' I didn't want to go over to Newcastle and tie meself down training. I was having too much fun hanging around the bush.

When I'd been at Monivae for a little while, I found out that this bloke that was in the room with me, Frank, it was his brother that bought Pinto off Dad.

I'd only had Pinto for a year or so when Dad sold him. I don't know why he sold him cos he was a bloody good pony. Anyhow, Frank's brother had broken Pinto into harness. He had a buggy with two in hand. That's what you call it if there are two horses pulling the buggy. He had Pinto and another blue the same as Pinto. He was coming home from the pub at Lue one night and a car run into him and killed him and both horses.

After Monivae finished, the contractor asked if I wanted to go out to Dabee. They were crutching out at Dabee Station and they wanted a rouseabout. So out I went sweeping up and cleaning up, me and another redheaded fella from town that was at Monivae with me. We went home first and got our horses and rode out to Dabee, me on Rainbow and him on his pony. It was only about six mile away. We left our ponies in the paddock while we worked.

One night, we decided to go into town, so we hopped on our horses and rode them into town and went up and saw Mum. Then we rode back out to Dabee. It was only about ten o'clock and the shearers and rouseabouts were in the mess hut playing cards. I rode to the door and jumped Rainbow up the steps and rode him up into the middle of the hut. Blokes went racing out of the hut in every direction while Rainbow was slipping and shying, and kicking stools all over the bloody place. By the time I got to the door at the other end of the hut there wasn't a bloke left in the place, they'd all cleared out.

When Dabee was finished I was back in town not doing much. There was a café in Rylstone, right opposite the police station. Mrs Bossley was the owner of the café. I used to get all me soft drinks and rubbish from there. One Saturday afternoon, I was riding Rainbow down the street and I rode him straight into the shop. I sung out, 'Hey, Mrs Bossley, is there any chance of me gettin' a pie?'

She come out from behind the curtain and here's me on me horse standing at the counter. Well, she let out a bellow and yelled, 'Get out of here you lunatic. The police are just over the road.'

I could do anything on Rainbow. He didn't like Dad though. He and Dad used to fight like buggery. He'd rear up any time Dad went near him. Mum reckoned he didn't go much on Peter either. She told me she was washing up one day and looked out the window onto the lane that run beside the house. She saw Rainbow feeding up one end of the lane and she noticed he was going backwards while he was feeding. Horses and cows usually go forwards as they're feeding. What's he up to, she thought? Peter was playing up the other end of the lane. She watched Rainbow back all the way up the lane and kick Peter behind the ear as he was sitting there playing. He had a horseshoe shaped mark behind his ear up until the day he died, and he was seventy-four when he died.

I was still in Rylstone, doing nothing in particular, when a joker come up to me and told me he had a contract for splitting four or five hundred posts for Dabee Station. Bird was his surname so we called him Feathers. He was a clever joker. He had a honey tin and he'd tap it and make a tune out of it and sing.

He said to me this day, 'I'm gunna get the posts from the mountain in front of Dabee. Do ya want a job with me?'

'Yeah, that'll do me,' I said.

'We'll climb up the mountain and cut the trees, bark 'em, then slide 'em down the mountain. We'll split 'em at the bottom,' he said.

So out we went and camped at the foot of the mountain in a tent. We'd climb up the side of the mountain, fell a tree with a cross cut saw, cut it off wherever we thought we'd get four or five lengths of post, bark it, then slide it down the mountain. When they're barked they're as slippery as buggery. They used to slide for a few hundred yards. By gee, they used to go.

There was a boundary rider that worked on Dabee. We used to call him Spike. He lived near the old slaughter yard, on the railway line in Rylstone, and had about fourteen or fifteen kids. He was a silly bugger, too. This particular day we were cutting down a tree and he come past—riding the boundary fence. Feathers yelled out to him. 'Spike, stay down there. We're comin' down in a minute. Don't come up.'

But Spike kept yelling back to us and coming up the mountain at the same time.

'Come on, Jack,' Feathers said to me. 'Let this log go.'

So we let the log go. Down the mountain it went, trees and rocks flying out beside it everywhere. Spike saw it coming and took off. He cleared the fence near his horse—never even touched the wire. Onto his horse he flew and off he went. We didn't see him again while we were splitting posts.

I was poking around town another time, and a bloke I knew come up to me. Motey we called him. He was the fella that Billy shot the banana out of his hand.

'What are ya doin', Jack?' he said.

'Nothin',' I told him.

'Do ya want to go rabbitin'?'

'Yeah, I'll go rabbitin',' I said. 'That'd be good. I can get us a paddock out at Tong Bong.'

'Ya got any traps?'

'Yeah, I got the traps all right.'

'Okay, we'll go. I'll get the tucker, you bring the traps.'

I took a horse and sulky and we loaded it up with all our stuff.

'Where are we goin' to camp?' he said.

'I'll just put a couple of sheets of bark up against the shafts of the sulky,' I said. 'That'll do us.'

'Bugger that! Me old man's got a tent.'

'Fair enough,' I said.

So he got the tent from his old man and away we went out to Tong Bong. We cut a few poles and pitched the tent and set our traps. We were trapping there for a day or two but weren't getting many rabbits. One evening we set the traps and I look up. 'We're gunna get a storm,' I said. 'We'd better do a sundowner early.'

We had tea, went out, did a sundowner and were back early enough before it got too dark. Anyway, we were sitting around the fire. 'I got a bottle of that keg rum,' Motey said. 'I got it when I was gettin' the groceries. Do ya want a snort of it?'

'I'm not old enough to drink,' I told him, 'but there's no bugger here to say anything, so I s'pose it won't hurt.'

I had one drink and then another. Gee, it'll set fire to ya this stuff, I thought. He had a few drinks, too. After a couple of drinks I climbed into me swag and fell sound asleep. In the morning I woke up and thought, what the hell happened here?

'What'd ya do to the bloody tent?' Motey said.

I looked up and there wasn't a sign of the tent. There were tree limbs blown down all around the camp, the wash bucket was gone and the cups and billy were blown to buggery. A storm had come through in the night and torn the tent to pieces. We found bits of it everywhere. We'd slept right through it. We never heard a thing.

'What'll Dad say?' Motey said.

'I don't know. But I'm bloody cold and wet.'

That was the end of him and his rabbiting. We packed up and went back to town. 'Bugger this bush,' he said. 'I don't like it out here.'

Chapter Eleven

Trapping with Dad

Dad was only away with the army for about eighteen months. Because they were short on shearers, all the farmers and the cockys in the area got together and sent a petition into the army to get Dad and another bloke back. Shearers were hard to get at the time cos a lot of them had gone away to the war. Dad was discharged and he got a shed up the Narango road, going up towards Nullo Mountain. It was the same place we visited on the way to see Uncle Bob—Jim's place, the bloke whose son was dying. Dad took me with him to teach me how to shear. It was only a little two-stand shed. I first learnt to shear there.

We were there for about three weeks. We drove out in a horse and sulky. When we went away shearing anytime, we'd always take a young horse to break into harness. A lot of times, you'd get a horse that's already broke into saddle and you think he's quieter than he is. You think he'll be easy to break into sulky, and nine times out of ten he'll kick the guts out of the sulky. It was always good experience for the horse to go on a long trip in a sulky.

At this shed, we used to eat in the house with Jim and his family and sleep in an old hut just opposite their house. The shearing shed was a good two hundred yards away from the house. Jim had another son just under joining-up age for the army. He was a big bugger, and strong.

One day, this young fella said to Dad, 'Turner, I'll race ya from here to the shed for a lottery ticket, and I'll pull the sulky. And I'll beat ya.'

'My bloody oath ya won't!' said Dad.

The next day, after dinner, Dad said, 'Come on, get the gig.' This young fella got the sulky and they lined up.

Old Jim said, 'Go!' And they took off.

Well, Dad had only just come out of the army so he was really fit, and he was always pretty fast, but this young bloke with the gig beat him by about twenty yards or more.

Dad had served with the Australian Infantry during World War One. He never spoke about it to us kids, but I remember if he was in a shearing shed or camping anywhere and another bloke come along, who'd also served in the war, I'd hear them have a bit of a yarn about it. I know he was wounded in action in France. He had the two middle fingers of his left hand shot off. That hand used to open up for years afterwards, at the start of the shearing season. It was so deep he had to pack it with cotton wool. Right up till the last year I shore with him, his hand would open up and he'd have to pack it. Trying to get a hold of big sheep with only the thumb and forefinger of his left hand and pull them out of the pen, that's what used to do it.

When we finished Jim's shed, we got another shed up in the same valley. It was another two-stand plant. They were the best places to learn how to shear and get in some practice. Dad was teaching me all the time and I was getting better and better. We were there about three weeks. When that shed cut out, we got another little shed on the way to Glen Alice. It was about a three-week shed, too. Then we went down to another place in Glen Alice, a four-stand shed called Warrengee. There were four of us shearing there and that's where I shore me first hundred. That's a hundred sheep in one day.

I shore me first hundred the day me mate got killed. Neville he was called. He used to come up home of a night with his guitar. He was a good little singer. He was working for a carrier in Rylstone. They had a load of wool on this day, coming down the Narango road. There were three of them in the truck. Neville was in the passenger seat, closest to the door. The truck turned over on the causeway just as they were going past a guidepost. The post went straight through the door, and Neville. Killed him stone bloody dead, poor bastard. He was only seventeen. Mum rung Warrengee that night and told the owner to tell me.

A few days later, I shore one hundred and four and was as pleased as punch. This job lasted about three weeks. I remember the old cook in that joint was deaf. The kitchen recess with the stove in it was pretty dark and it was hard to see and because he was deaf, he couldn't hear the kettle bubbling, either. So he used to take the lid off the kettle and dip his finger in to tell if the water was boiling or not.

After we finished at Warrengee, we went on to Umbiella. It was a six-stand shed but there was only me, Dad, and an old fella shore there this time. Then that was the end of the shearing for the year. I shore in five sheds and shore me first hundred so I was getting pretty good, or at least, I thought I was.

There was no more shearing work around, so Dad and I went down to Bogee Station in Glen Alice, poisoning rabbits. One day, just after dinnertime, we come back to the hut. We were camped in the shearers' huts there. At the end of the shearers' huts there was a tank stand and beside this was a big peach tree. It was summer time and the tree was loaded with peaches. We had a drink of water, then Dad told me to get up the tree and shake down some peaches for him. He always wore a suit coat, even in the summer out in the bush, he'd be dressed up with a suit coat on. I got up the tree and started to shake peaches down. Dad was underneath it, bending down picking them up, when I shook a bloody big, black snake out of the tree and it fell straight across Dad's back.

I yelled as it was going down, 'Look out! Snake!' But it hit Dad across the back.

He put his arms together to pull his coat around him and get out of the way of the snake, but as he did, he jammed the tail of the snake between his arm and his coat and pulled it towards his body. He was bucking and heaving trying to throw the snake off his back, but he didn't realise he had hold of the snake while he was doing it. Gee, it was funny watching him buck and leap till he woke up to what was happening, then he let his arm go and threw the snake to buggery. You could have rode Rocky Ned easier than Dad, the way he was bucking.

Later on, Dad and I were rabbiting down near Glen Alice on a station called Rose something. I can't think of the rest of the name. It was next to Goollooinboin Station. We camped in a shed and slept in an old spring cart. While we were rabbiting there, I went away for a couple of weeks to do some work for someone. When I got back, Dad told me that the people that owned Goollooinboin had had some friends come up from Sydney for a visit. It was a young couple with a little baby only a few weeks old. The mother had laid the baby outside on a rug to get some sun and gone back into the house. An eagle hawk had swooped down and picked it up. The baby was never seen again.

The bloke from the property on the other side to where we were camped was a share farmer on a pig farm. He had three little boys and a missus. In the middle of the night he come up to us singing out, 'Come and help me, Stan. Can ya come and look after me kids and me missus while I go to Glen Davis and get the ambulance?'

There were no telephones out where we were, so he had to ride his horse into Glen Davis to the closest ambulance. It'd be fifteen mile to Glen Davis. His wife was haemorrhaging. I don't know from where cos they never told me. I just remember there was blood everywhere. Dad went with Norm back to his place. I had to go out the other way a mile or so to get another lady to come and give us a hand to look after Norm's missus. In the pitch black, I had to walk over to a neighbouring property to get her. It's a real bushman's skill being able to find your way through the bush in the dark.

While she was getting ready and making arrangements with her kids for the older ones to look after the younger ones, I went and found her horse and harnessed up her sulky to take her over to Norm's place. Dad and her looked after Norm's missus till the ambulance got there and I looked after the kids. It was daylight before Norm got back with the ambulance to take her to Rylstone Hospital. The woman that come to help couldn't stay cos she had to get back to her family and look after her kids. Her husband was away somewhere. We had to stay with the kids for a week while Norm was away with his missus.

We had to milk the cows, and feed the pigs and the poddy calves. The kids would come with us. They had bare feet and the poddy calves were treading all over their feet. Tough little buggers they were. When we put them to bed of a night they used to get down on their knees and say their prayers.

'Please, God, bless Mummy and help her to get better. And bless Jack and Stan for looking after us.' Gee, they were great little fellas.

We didn't think Norm's wife would survive—the blood that she lost. But she did. She was away for a few weeks then she come back to the farm. It was a good week before Norm could leave her and come back to look after things. We had to forget about rabbiting. We were too busy looking after these kids, and the pigs, and milking cows. Years later, I taught the middle one of those kids to shear. When we were out at Warren, I got him a learner's pen there and I taught him how to shear.

Talking of kids, I remember that anytime Dad and I had a droving job on, or if we were going rabbiting, and it was school holidays, we'd take the kids with us. Me brothers and sisters I mean, not Norm's kids. One time, we had a droving job. We had to take some sheep up to Nullo Mountain, so the kids come with us. We got onto the travelling stock reserve the first night and camped there. We cut a heap of bush leaves and piled them up. We had a couple of big waggas with us. We put one down over the leaves and got the kids into bed, then put the other wagga over the top. Dad on one side and me on the other, and three or four, or probably five kids it would have been, in the middle.

He'd tell them a story, then he'd say, 'Fill ya pipe, Johnny, and we'll have a smoke before we go to sleep.' (Dad often called me Johnny cos I was christened John, but everyone else called me Jack.) Dad always smoked a pipe, so I smoked one, too. We'd have a puff of the pipe, then he'd say, 'Ya ready?'

We'd lift the wagga up with our feet and let it drop. It'd fall in under our feet and keep us warm through the night.

The next day we got up to Narango and camped on the reserve there with the sheep. Same procedure, we cut some bushes and put them down, spread the waggas out. The next day we got to the foot of the Nullo Mountain. We had to go up it. Dad had a lot of roo dogs, but he never had any good sheep dogs, so he got a loan of a couple or three dogs off different fellas. Well, geez, they were useless. We were going up the Nullo—it's narrow-gutted and hilly, a pretty steep mountain. In the cuttings it was all right putting the sheep through, but when we got to open ground with a slope on one side, the bloody dogs wouldn't do anything. Dad threw them over the side of the mountain and they took off for home. Me, Peter and Bryany had to do the bloody dog's work. Anyhow, we got the sheep up the mountain in the finish and camped there that night, and had another story. We packed up the next day and come home. The little kids had some great yarns to tell Mum when they got back.

Another school holidays, Dad and I were poisoning bunnies down near Glen Alice. To make the baits for poisoning rabbits, we'd dig up the roots of flat thistles. They had a big long root on them. We'd cut them into little pieces, wash them thoroughly, to get the smell of our hands off, put them in a dish with holes in the bottom to drain the water out, sprinkle them with sugar and put them in the sun to dry. They get sticky then, with the sugar on them. We'd sprinkle strychnine over them and shake them up well so the strychnine was mixed onto all the baits, then put them out to dry again.

We made a pair of wire tongs to pick the baits up, cos you can't touch them with your hands. We'd use the tongs to drop the baits in the holes we dug.

We'd still skin poisoned rabbits. But we had to be up well before daylight to get to the rabbits before the crows or the foxes got to them. It's slower to skin a poisoned rabbit cos he's been dead a couple of hours, so he's stiff.

Anyhow, we were working away, when Dad said to me, 'It's school holiday time, ain't it? Ya'd better go get the kids.'

So home I come in the sulky, got the kids, picked up their tucker and their swags and down to Glen Alice we went. We were camped in an old hut down there. It had a couple of spare bunks in it, a big double bed and plenty of room on the floor.

So we were all down there poisoning rabbits this day and Bryan was giving Dad a bit of cheek. Dad sung out to him and Bryany said something to Dad. He was fifty or sixty yards away, just climbing through a wire fence, when he give Dad cheek. Dad was using a setting hoe to dig the holes for me to drop the baits in. 'Don't cheek me,' he said, and let drive with this bloody setting hoe, straight at Bryany's head. It hit the wire and glanced off, otherwise it would have split his head clean open.

One other summer, we were down in Glen Alice poisoning rabbits for some fella. It was the school holidays and me younger brothers were down with us. One of me brothers, Peter, was a bit of a bugger for hunting around. He was stripped down to the waist this day, with only a pair of shorts on, and was poking his head in every log and hollow. Dad was digging the holes for the rabbit baits and I was dropping the baits in the holes. We were working our way through the bush, when Peter come flying out of the scrub screaming and throwing himself on the ground and rolling around.

Dad looked up and yelled to me, 'Johnny, Johnny, come here quick! Peter's had a bait.'

Dad thought he'd been poisoned but when we got up to him we could see he was covered in wasps. He'd stuck his head in a log straight into a wasps nest. They were all over him. Dad tore his suit coat off and wrapped it around Peter and threw him into a bush. They went after Dad then and we had to belt all the wasps off him. We spent a bloody hour chewing tobacco to put on Peter's wasp stings. He was in a bad way for a while there.

Peter was always hunting around. If he spotted a bunny, he'd pick up a stick or a stone, throw it at him and hit him every time. He had a bloody good eye.

Another day, on the same rabbiting trip, Peter was racing around in a pair of shorts with a knife in his belt. He used to reckon he was Tarzan. This day the dogs chased up an old roo. This old roo took off and straight down into the dam he went. The dogs were too bloody smart to go into a dam with a roo. We were following the roo, too, but Peter raced off ahead and flew into the dam. He was going to get this roo with his knife. The roo was out in deeper water than Peter could stand up in. He started splashing over to it.

Dad said to me, 'Quick, Johnny! Run down and get the roo before he gets Peter.'

I raced down to the dam, but before I got there, Peter had swum up to the roo and he couldn't stand up. The water was too deep. As soon as he got near the roo, the old roo grabbed him by the head and drove him down under the water. I had to go like mad to get to him before the roo drowned him. I had a long-handled setting hoe in me hand. I swam up behind the roo and give him a whack in the head and killed him. Then I had to dive down and grab Peter. The roo was treading on him by the time I got to him. He come up, spluttering. Another couple of minutes, he'd have been gone.

The same summer, Dad said he was going rabbiting on another property. He told me to come down the following week with some tucker. He asked me to take the brindle pup we had at home because he was about the right age to start working him as a kangaroo dog. He was about three months old and used to play around with the kids at home. I had a straight shaft sulky. It had a long tray underneath the seat with a wire basket that we'd fixed up under the axle to cart extra stuff in. I put the pup on the tray and all the tucker and the gear in there, too, and away we went.

Dad wanted me to meet him down at the Twenty-One Mile peg, to shift him up to another paddock that was better for rabbiting. On the way there, I had the pup under the seat and I was tormenting him all the time. It got so every time I put me foot under the seat he'd bite it. He was ropeable by the time I got to the Twenty-One Mile.

I met up with Dad and we threw all his stuff on the sulky. He hopped in the gig and away we went. When we got to the gate, I hopped out to open it and Dad drove through. As he did, he put his foot under the seat and this bloody pup grabbed him. Well, he let out a bellow, reached down and grabbed the pup by the scruff of the neck and hurled him out of the sulky. 'I'll give you bloody bite me, ya mongrel,' he said. The poor pup had to walk to the next paddock.

Dad always had half a dozen or so dogs for rabbiting and rooing. At one time I remember he had thirteen. He'd go out rabbiting or rooing with thirteen dogs but thirteen wouldn't necessarily come home. Some would get baits, and some would get too much harnessethic. He could have seven or eight dogs one week and be out looking for a new dog the next.

When Dad and I weren't rabbiting or shearing, we used to do any sort of work we could get. One time we were fencing out along the Cudgegong road and digging post holes two foot six deep. It must have been school holidays cos Tony was with us.

When we heard a car coming, Dad would say, 'Get Tony and put him down a post hole, Johnny.'

So I'd put Tony down a posthole. As the car was coming past, I'd grab Tony by the hair and lift him straight up out of it. People would nearly run off the road they'd be looking so hard. Gee, he was bloody little. No wonder he turned out to be a jockey. He was a tough little bugger, too. He reckoned that was why had no hair later on.

Then winter come and Dad and I went rabbiting again down near Mt Marsden. You'd poison the rabbits in the summer and trap them in the winter. The skins are better in the winter. Dad had a paddock down there that the owner said he could rabbit on. You couldn't just go rabbiting on anybody's property without their permission. We were camped in a hut down near the side of the mountain.

We were in the hut one night and we heard, 'Ahoy!'

Dad said, 'Go and see who that is.'

I went out. Not a bloody soul anywhere, so I went back in and said, 'There's no one there.'

Ten minutes later we hear, 'Ahoy! Ahoy!' again.

Dad said, 'Go and see who it is, there's some bugger there.' So out I went again and couldn't see anyone. Back in I went.

'There's nobody there. I can't see anyone.'

Five minutes later we heard it again. Dad said, 'I'll give this bugger something!'

So out Dad went and fired in the air with the rifle and an old mopoke took off from a tree nearby. He'd been having a great game with us.

Dad used to catch a lot of kangaroos as well as rabbits. He'd skin them and tan the skins. Every bed at home had a roo skin rug on it. He had skins stuffed in hollow logs everywhere. He'd tan the skins with alum and salt. Whenever we'd catch a roo, we'd skin it, salt the skin, put a bit of alum on it, and shove it in a hollow log. Then we'd come back in a few weeks' time, clean up the skin and salt it again. That's another real bushman's skill—remembering where you've put the skins.

One freezing winter afternoon while we were rabbiting on the side of Mt Marsden, Dad went off for a look around. A little while later he come back and said, 'Come with me. The dogs have bailed up a big roo and drowned him in the dam. Ya'd better come and get him out.' Down to the dam we went.

This big roo was right in the middle of the dam. 'It's too cold to get in there!' I said.

'You'll be right,' said Dad, 'I'll light a big fire.'

So I stripped off and went into the dam. By geez, it was cold. I'd nearly frozen to death before I got anywhere near the roo. Dad was pointing to it, showing me where to go. When I got to the roo, I had to dive down to get a hold of him, pull him as far as I could, then come up for air, and dive down and pull him again till I got him into shallow enough water so I could stand up. By the time I got him back to the bank I was screaming with the cold. I was blue. I've never been so bloody cold in all me life. Dad had lit a fire but I had nothing to dry meself with, and I couldn't get too close to the fire or it was painful, going from being so cold to the heat.

Another time, the dogs bailed up a big roo on the side of a mountain. We had a little Pomeranian-type dog with us this time that one of me sisters had got from somewhere. She wanted it as a pet but Dad said, 'I don't want any of these useless bloody things around the house. It can come with us rabbitin'.' I think he thought he could train it to get into a log after a bunny.

When the dogs had this roo bailed up, they were all standing around the roo not getting too close. This little dog called Stumpy Tail didn't know nothing about trapping. When she caught up to the other dogs she went charging straight in, yapping. The old roo just grabbed hold of her with his front paws and tried to rip her open with one of his back legs. But she was too small for him to reach with his back foot. He was biting her and she was yelping but he couldn't do too much damage to her.

'Quick, Johnny, get in and get him while he's busy,' said Dad.

I raced up behind the roo, hit him in the head with a setting hoe and killed him. Stumpy Tail had a bit of skin off her but she was all right. Lucky for her she wasn't any bigger or the roo would have ripped her open.

When it was cold, I used to wear Dad's old army overcoat rabbiting. In the mornings when we were going round the traps, we'd get the rabbit out and wring his neck straight away, but if I found a half-grown bunny that was good to eat, I'd put him in the pocket of me coat and tie it shut with a bit of wire. After we'd skinned the rabbits we'd caught and pegged out the skins, we'd have a feed. I'd get the bunny out of me pocket, kill him, skin him and cook him. Dad didn't go much on rabbit but I loved it. One time, we were out of tucker and he had to eat a rabbit. He put bloody near half a tin of curry powder in with it. It nearly burnt the arse out of the billy.

Whenever I was trapping with Dad, if we split up to trap on different properties, or if one of us went home for some reason, we'd send one another a smoke signal to let the other one know we'd got there all right. Dad would tell me to go over to such and such a place. 'Send me a smoke signal when ya get there,' he'd say. I'd light a fire and make it smoke well, so he'd see the smoke and know I'd got there okay.

If we'd arranged to go to a certain property or paddock from different areas, the first one to get there would put a stone on a certain post so the other bloke would know that he'd already gone past. Then the other fella would knock the stone off when he come past. There were no mobile phones back then and hardly any of the properties around the area had a telephone, but we had our ways of communicating.

*Me on **Rainbow** in the lane behind our house in Dawson Street around 1946.*

*Me and **Stumpy Tail**.*

Chapter Twelve

Black Jack Turner

When I wasn't shearing or rabbiting, I used to break in horses to earn a quid. I reckon I'd have been about sixteen. Dad had bought me a Tolty saddle when he come out of the army. They were made in West Australia. He paid thirteen quid for it. A big, kneepad saddle it was. Every bugger used to say, 'There's only starvation or a pretty girl will get you out of that saddle, Jack.' But I rode plenty of horses that found a way to get me out of it.

Anyhow, I met a bloke who was working on the railway in Rylstone. Arnold he was called. He was from Denman way, and he could ride a bit. We got to be mates. He could play the guitar and sing. He'd come up home of a night and we'd have some great old sing-a-longs.

Arnold said he'd give me a hand on the weekends, breaking in. I got a couple of horses to break in and worked on them during the week and got them ready to ride. Then we rode them about on the weekend. We were riding these two horses out on the common—we'd get them pretty quiet before we sent them back to the owner. Suddenly, I saw a black snake go into a log.

'Hold onto me horse,' I said, 'while I get this snake.'

Arnold was sitting on his horse and he put the reins of my horse over his elbow and was rolling a smoke. I was poking around trying to get a hold of the snake. Anyhow, I got him by the tail and heaved him out, but I couldn't think fast enough where to throw him, and I threw him straight over the neck of Arnold's horse. The horse got a bloody fright, give a snort, leapt in the air and took off. But it ran one way and my horse took off the other way and pulled poor Arnold clean out of the saddle. He was sitting on the ground wondering what the bloody hell happened.

One of Arnold's work mates knew a man that wanted a horse quietened down, so I said I'd be able to do it. He brought the horse up to our place and put him in the yard. I worked on him for a day or two, then the weekend come around. Arnold said we should take him out along the Pinnacle Swamp road and give him a try out to see how he'd go. I got my horse and he rode the one I was breaking in. We went out along the Pinnacle Swamp road. It was a bush track surrounded by scrub. After we got out a few miles from town, Arnold said, 'You wait here while I gallop this horse on its own for a bit to see how he goes.'

'Righto,' I said.

As soon as he got out of sight, I took me horse into the scrub and tied him up. I'll give this joker a fright, I thought. I climbed up into a tree and faced the way going back towards town and waited for him to come riding back. After a little while I heard a horse clopping along. Just as the horse cantered past the tree I jumped down onto its back behind the rider. But it wasn't Arnold. It was a bloody sheila riding back into town. She let out a scream and the horse took off. I had a bit of a job trying to quieten the horse and stop her from bashing me to get me off.

'Jack Turner!' she yelled, 'I'm telling the police on you.'

There were three Jack Turners in Rylstone when I lived there. There was one bloke who was deaf, so they called him Deaf Jack Turner. He was the oldest fella. He used to live on the common in an old tin hut. It was made from split-open kerosene tins. His son was crippled—he was Crippled Jack Turner. He had paralysis and was crippled from the hips down. He was a boot maker and lived down in the town. And then there was me. They used to call me Black Jack Turner because me hair was jet black. So there was Deaf Jack Turner, Crippled Jack Turner and Black Jack Turner, and people used to call us that so everyone knew who they were talking about.

While the war was still on, a couple of the cockys who were in the army come home on leave. There was a dance this night down at Bylong. One of the blokes borrowed his dad's big old Packard car. It was a six-seater. It had a bench seat in the front, a bench seat in the back and two extra seats in the middle that could fold down. He come into town with his brother and asked if I wanted to go with them. I told them I would. So they loaded up the car with whatever grog they could get, and a couple of other fellas.

I was about seventeen by then—old enough to have a drink if I didn't get caught. It was wintertime, so we were all dressed up in big army overcoats. As we were going down the hill to Bylong, we come sailing round a corner and there was a big, old wombat crossing the road. The car hit him and knocked him arse over head but didn't kill him. It just stunned him. The driver pulled up and I flew out of the car and grabbed him.

'What are ya gunna do with that?' he said.

'I'm gunna take him down to the dance and we'll have some fun with him,' I said.

I put him in a big bag and we left him scratching around in the back of the car while we went into the dance. We kept going out of the hall to get a drink of whiskey or schnapps. Then the barn dance come up. Everyone was going around in a circle doing the barn dance. I went out to the car, put me overcoat back on, got the wombat out and shoved him under the overcoat. I walked back right into the middle of the hall and dropped him. Well, this old wombat was running around, slipping and sliding, trying to get out of the place. You should have heard the ruckus. People were running and screaming, jumping up on one another's shoulders trying to get away from him. The MC was yelling out, 'Who did that? Who did that?' Me and the other blokes were outside, crying with laughter.

The MC of the dances at Bylong was a big, tall man, and a nice bloke he was, too. Harvey he was called. He had a little Chev ute. One Saturday night he had it backed up against the fence not far from the hall. Me and this other fella called Ross, went and got a lump of wire out of the fence next to the dance hall and tied it onto the fence post then onto the diff of Harvey's car. We went and sat in Ross's car and waited.

When the dance was finished, everyone started to leave. A bus used to take a lot of people down to the dance and home again. It took off with a load of people and everyone else was leaving, too. Harvey come out, locked up the hall and got in his car. We were on the other side of the road in our car. He started his ute up and drove away, but as soon as he got the full length of the wire, the car stalled. He got out and went around the back, couldn't see anything, so he got back in and started to go again. The same thing happened. He got out to have a look, then he saw us.

'You buggers! What are you up to? I'll kill you if I get hold of you,' he called out to us.

'It's not us,' we said. 'We're over here. It's not us doin' it.'

He started to go and the car stalled again. Well, he jumped out and run around the back of the car so fast, he tripped over the wire.

'I'll kill you bastards if I get hold of you,' he yelled at us. We got out of there pretty bloody quickly, laughing like mad.

When I wasn't working away with Dad, trapping or shearing, I sometimes did some work for Pat, one of the carriers in Rylstone. He was Ross's father. All his sons worked for him. He had an old white Whippet car. Ross used to drive this car and he asked me one day if I was going to the dance down at Ginghi. Ginghi was just before you got to Bylong, coming out from Rylstone. I said I was going so he said he'd take me. There was always a dance somewhere on a Saturday night.

It was during the war and we couldn't get any beer but he had a bottle of schnapps he said he'd take. That night we headed off to the dance at Ginghi. Because drink was in short supply, if anyone saw you had some grog they might pinch it and drink it themselves. So to hide it from everyone he put it under the bonnet on the engine of the car. We had a couple of dances and a yarn to a few people. 'Come on,' he said, 'we'll go and have a drink.'

Out we went, but we couldn't unscrew the lid off the bottle. He had a pair of multi-grips in his car so I used them to undo it. I put the bottle up to me mouth and had a swig. Gee, this is a bloody wild brew, I thought. It'd poison a brown dog. It was nearly boiling from being on the engine. Then he had some and sat it up underneath the bonnet again, and we went back into the dance hall.

I went to ask a girl for a dance. 'Have you and Ross been fighting?' she said.

'No, we haven't been fighting.'

'Yes you have,' she said. 'You've got blood all over your mouth.'

I looked over at Ross and his mouth was bleeding, too.

'Geez,' I said to him, 'we must have broken the top off that bottle.' I'd unscrewed it so hard, I screwed the neck of the bottle clean off. We were too bloody silly to realise that the bottle had cut our mouths. Lucky we didn't swallow any glass.

Another Saturday night, I was at a dance in Bylong. A bloke and his missus and kids come along in a horse and sulky to this dance. They tied the horse up at the fence near the dance hall and went inside. Me and another fella got this horse and took him out of the sulky. We had to go up a fair way to find a gate in the fence but we got him through the gate and brought him back. Then we put the sharves of the sulky through the fence and put the bloody horse back into the sharves again. Half way through the night Harvey, the MC, come out and saw what we'd done. He went back in and announced that some silly bugger had put a horse into the sulky with the sharves through the fence. The poor bloke that owned it had to come out and put it right. What a bloody ratbag I was.

One weekend there was a dance on at Lue. It was about fifteen miles from Rylstone. A bloke asked if I wanted to go to it.

'How'll we get there?' I asked him.

'We'll get a train.'

'That'll do us for goin' up, but there won't be a train comin' back.'

'There'll be a goods train sometime tonight. We'll jump on it.'

'That sounds all right,' I said.

So away we went to the dance up at Lue, dressed up in our Sunday best. The dance finished a bit after midnight. We went over to the railway line, which was only a couple of hundred yards away from the Lue Hall. We were sitting around the station smoking, waiting for a train. All of a sudden we saw the lights of a train coming. We hid off the track near the station. The train pulled up and the guard started hooking on a goods truck that was in the yard. While they were busy doing that we climbed up into an empty truck about halfway along the train. The train went on its way again and gee it got up a fair bit of speed.

'We'd better get off this before we get to Rylstone,' I said. 'Because they know us there. They'll know we're jumpin' the rattler, and we'll be in for it.'

'We'll be right,' he said. 'Just as we get to the Cudgegong River, we'll jump off. There's a nice sandy bank.' We were ready and waiting to jump as we approached the river.

'Not yet, not yet,' I said. 'I'll tell ya when to jump. I know this place well.'

As we come through the railway gates I thought we should be just about right. The train was only going slow.

'Jump!' I said.

Away we flew over the side of the truck. Splash! We landed right in the middle of the Cudgegong River. I'd misjudged it by about twenty yards.

I was working around Rylstone a short while after that, and I was getting to the age where I could get me driver's licence. The mailman that had the Glen Alice and Bylong mail runs needed a hand, so I went to work for him. We used to go to Glen Alice on Mondays, Wednesdays and Fridays, which was the hardest run. Then the other days we'd do the Bylong run. It was an easier run—not so much getting in and out of the ute. So on those days he taught me to drive. That's how I learnt to drive.

I was on the mail run a fair while. One evening, coming back from doing the run, I ran into a mailbox. I just got too close and splattered it. I went home and told Dad I'd run into Farrow's mailbox.

A couple of weeks went by and then one day Dad said, 'Come here, Johnny. Listen to this. The ironbark started to shiver and the white box started to shake, when Johnny hit the mailbox outside Farrow's gate.' Dad used to write a lot of poems. He was always making up a rhyme about something.

I used to drive the mail ute around and run all the errands while the boss was in the post office sorting the mail. I'd go here, there and everywhere. Then one day, I was driving up the street in Rylstone and a bloke stopped me. 'Hey, Jack!' he said, 'The policeman said to come down to the police station and get ya licence before ya get into trouble.'

I didn't think anyone knew that I didn't have one. Down I went to the police station. The copper said, 'There's no good askin' if ya can drive or takin' ya for a test.' And he just give me the licence. I was set then. I did all the mail driving after that. Then I got a job driving for all the carriers around the place. I thought I had it made.

Chapter Thirteen

Bloody Unlucky

As soon as I turned eighteen, in December of '44, I enlisted. I got the enlisting papers from the police station and sent them off to Sydney. A while after, I got me call-up papers and had to report to the barracks at the Sydney showground. I was only there two days. As soon as they found out I was a shearer, they packed me up and sent me straight out to a shed in Bourke, shearing. They were really short on shearers at the time. One of the publicans in Bourke used to get a quid a head for shearers. The cockys round the area would pay him to get them shearers. Any shearer he could get drunk, he'd throw him in his truck and take him out to the shed of the cocky that needed him. They'd wake up out at these sheds wondering where the bloody hell they were. I shore at sheds round Bourke till the season finished.

I come back to Rylstone then and got a job at a sawmill at the foot of Nullo Mountain—me and three or four other fellas from Rylstone. We'd go out into the scrub in an old truck and cut down the trees we wanted with an axe or a crosscut saw. Some of the trees were bloody big. They'd be four or five foot across. Then we'd cut them into logs with a crosscut saw. When there were enough logs cut, we'd cart them to the mill. I'd help them at the mill to cut the timber into four-by-twos, or three-by-twos, whatever size they wanted. I was the handle man. I'd wind the handle to help feed the timber through the saw.

There was a big bunkhouse that we all used to camp in—beds everywhere and big wide windows. At night, we'd go possum shooting and roo shooting, and shooting any bloody thing we could see, me and this other bloke. We were a pair of bloody ratbags. One night, we come back to the hut and everyone was asleep. He had a shotgun and I had a .22 rifle. 'What about we have some fun with these fellas?' he said to me.

There were two windows on each side of the hut, opposite one another. There was no glass in the windows—they were just made of wood that we propped open. He went to one side and pointed his gun through, aiming at the opposite window, and I went to the other side and aimed mine through to the other window. Then we let out a bellow and started shooting. Well, holy, bloody hell! What a racket! Gee, they got a fright.

I always had a set of boxing gloves in me swag. Everyone knew I was pretty smart with me fists and this other bloke that was with me was a real good fighter and a fair sized bloke, too. I think that might have been the only thing that saved our bloody hides.

While I was at the mill, we heard the war was over. One of the blokes had a wireless. He heard the news and come out yelling, 'The war's over! The war's over!'

A steam engine drove the plant at the mill. When he heard the war was over, the engine driver opened the whistle up and just let her go. It echoed for ages around the mountain. Every bloody roo knew the war was over, too. The boss declared it a holiday and we packed up and headed to town.

The car I was in was a little '34 Ford coupé. She had a crook battery but we could start her with a crank handle. This little car got halfway up a real steep hill on the way to town and stopped. There was something wrong with the motor but we didn't know what and we couldn't get her started. All the other trucks and cars had left before us. There were only four of us in this car. One had to steer and the other three couldn't push her up the hill cos she was too heavy. Someone got a bright idea and said, 'We'll wind her up the hill using the crank handle.'

We put her into gear and wound the crank handle. If a car's in gear when you turn the crank handle, as the motor goes over, the wheels will turn. We took it in turns. When one bloke couldn't turn it any more, we'd chock the wheel and then another bloke would have a go at winding it. It was a slow process but we got her to the top of the hill. When we got to the top it was a good two-mile run downhill straight to the post office. We were lucky the mailman was at the post office and he give us a lift into town.

One of the blokes I knew from Rylstone who went away to the war was a prisoner of war. When the war finished he come home. He had two young daughters. When he got out of the army he took his two daughters and his wife to Sydney for a holiday. He'd only been back a few weeks. They were walking along Pitt Street. There was a garbage truck on the side of the road. It jumped out of gear, raced down the hill and run over him. Killed him stone dead, the poor bugger. How's that for bloody luck?

I left the mill soon after the war finished. The bloke opposite us in Dawson Street was a ganger on the railway and he got me a job as a fettler.

So I worked on the railways for a while and met up with this bloke from Mudgee called Athol. He was working as a fettler, too. He'd been a prisoner of war. I was talking to him once about me cousin, Ralph. I told him he'd died in a prisoner of war camp—in a Jap camp. Athol had been in the same camp. He said to me, 'I seen Ralph die. But they wasn't gunna kill me. I was gunna die in Australia.'

We were working at Lithgow on the railway. We'd live in the fettlers' huts down there during the week and go home by train for the weekend. He lived in Mudgee and I lived in Rylstone. We'd go home on the Friday evening and get the train back down on Sunday night. So this Friday evening coming home, I got off the train at Rylstone, and Athol said, 'I'll see ya on the way back, Turner, on Sunday night.'

I said, 'Righto, mate.'

Sunday night, I went down to get on the train, and I was looking everywhere for Athol. He said he'd stick his head out of the window so I'd know which carriage to get in cos they were all box carriages. Anyhow, I couldn't find him so I got in a carriage and went down to Lithgow. Next morning, the boss said to me, 'Athol's dead. He fell out of the train.'

He was drunk, and he thought he was going into the toilet. Some of the carriages had a toilet in them. He opened the door and walked straight out of the moving train at Mortonmain cutting. That's between Lue and Rylstone. He must have been in a carriage on his own cos no one even knew till the next day.

There was another Rylstone fella who lived on a farm opposite us when we were on Misery. He went to the war and got shot by a sniper. He'd married one of Billy Mills's sisters. He'd just got a Rhode Island Red poultry farm going when he went away to the war. His daughter wasn't even born when he left.

Poor bugger, he never come back and he was only young, too. There was a bloody heap never come back.

I was only working for the railway for four or five months and then the shearing started again. Dad and I got a shed down around Glen Alice, so away we went in the horse and sulky. It was a two-stand shed and we had to do our own cooking there. We got another two sheds after that where we had to do our own cooking and I was getting pretty sick of it. After we'd finished around Glen Alice, Dad said to me that we should go up to Coolah and see if we could get some shearing up that way. He still had old Roany. We hooked the sulky up to her one morning and did the one hundred and four mile up to Coolah that same day. That's a bloody long way for a horse to go in one day. Trot a mile, walk a mile. You don't knock your horse up that way. That's what Dad always said.

Dad's sister had a couple of sons that lived up that way, so we went and seen them and stayed a day or two. There was no shearing work around at the time, though, so Dad decided to go back home. On the way back, we pulled up under the bridge near Mudgee, on the Cudgegong River, to give the horse a rest and a drink and have a feed ourselves. Dad told me to take the harness off Roany and take her down to the river for a drink while he lit a fire. So down to the river I went with Roany.

'Hey, Jack! Come here,' Dad called out to me.

I went up to see what he wanted and there was a bloke lying on his back over a rock. His mouth was wide open and there were flies all over him, even in his mouth.

'This bastard's dead,' Dad said, and walked up to him. 'I think he *is* dead,' he said and give him a kick. The bloke jumped up and staggered around. He was an old metho drinker.

'Do ya want a drink of white lady, boy?' he said to me. 'I get it because I got a sore bum.' He pulled his trousers down and showed us where he had some skin off on his hip. He was getting the metho and supposed to be putting it on his hip but he was drinking it instead.

The next shed I got was down near Lue, at Monivae again, for the same contractor that took us out there the first time. He had some good sheds, that contractor. He had Monivae, Rawdon and Dabee. Gee, he had some good shearers, too. It was a bigger shed, six-stands. I saw how much better the conditions were for shearers at this bigger shed, and I thought to meself, these little sheds are no good to me, I'll have to stay out amongst the big sheds. That contractor was going to Charlton Station next, out near Brewarrina, and he give me a pen at Charlton. So I went out there. It was a big shed, eight- or ten-stand, and was great experience. And I didn't have to cook there.

The shearing contractor's name was Bob. He had a real good sheepdog called Larry. He'd work in the yards and the pens. In each run, when you stopped for smoko, Bob would count the sheep out of each shearer's pen. The chutes at Charlton were underneath the catching pen. You'd have to crawl in under and hunt the sheep out, so the dog used to do it instead. Old Larry would go down the chute and hunt them out, come back up and go down the next one. If there was a shearer away or one stand never had a shearer, he wouldn't go down that chute.

If any shearer had a break down—broke his handpiece or something went wrong with it—he'd yell out, 'Expert!' and old Bob would come up and have a look at the handpiece. He'd take it back with him and get the shearer another one while he fixed the broken one. He'd go down to the engine room where he done all his work and get another handpiece. He'd tell Larry to take it back to Jim or Jack or whoever it was, and the bloody dog would bring the handpiece back right to the joker who needed it.

One day, Bob come down to have smoko with us but he'd left his tobacco in the engine room. He had a big bench in the engine room where he done all his work and fixed everything. There was a forty-four gallon drum cut in half and full of water that he used to cool things in. So Bob sits down and feels his pocket and he's not got his tobacco. He sings out, 'Hey, Larry! Go get me tobacco.' Away this dog goes to the engine room and after a while Bob says, 'By Christ! He's a long time. What's up with this bloody dog? Has he gone walkabout again?'

So he walks down to the engine room and has a look through the pigeonhole. That's where you'd put your combs and cutters, and you could see into the engine room through it. He could see Larry with his head and front legs down in the drum, scratching around.

He said, 'Come here, Jack, and have a look at this. Larry's in trouble here.'

He'd jumped up to get the tobacco off the bench but dropped it in the drum. It went straight to the bottom. He ended up getting it out and brought it back to Bob but it was as wet as buggery.

Bob told me that he had a better dog than Larry once. He said he was a real good dog but the army took him during the war. When the war was finished, they wrote to Bob and told him that they were bringing the dog back to him. Bob lived out at Coonabarabran on a property. They told him what day they were coming with the dog so Bob was outside waiting for him. The dog knew the property as soon as they got onto it. As they opened the car door he raced straight out. He was in that big a hurry to see Bob, he jumped the fence. There was a splice in the wire and a piece of it was sticking up. As he jumped over it, this piece of wire went straight in his guts and tore him open. They had to destroy him, poor bugger.

We did that shed at Charlton and a couple of others. They were fairly big sheds, thirty-two-stand and eighteen-stand—good sized sheds. Then we headed back to Rylstone. Old Bob had a little car. I think it was a Pontiac—a two-seater, with a dickie seat in the back where we used to throw our swags. It had a running board on it. On the running board he had a little frame built near where the spare tyre went, with a bag in it for Larry to sit in. Larry used to lie down or sit there while he was driving from one shed to another. Anyhow, I got a lift with him coming back.

'We'll go and have a couple of beers in Mudgee,' he said.

So we pulled up in the main street. It was forty-five degree parking and you had to back in. We left the car there. Bob said, 'You stay there, Larry.' We went over to the Mudgee Hotel and had a couple of beers, then Bob said, 'All right, we'll go.'

We were on our way to Rawdon to start shearing. Anyway, we go out and get over to the car. 'Hello,' he said, 'that bloody Larry's gone touring. Where in the name of Christ would he be?' He put his fingers in his mouth and give a whistle.

We were standing next to the car waiting for him. There were two women standing talking on the opposite corner, outside the Sydney Hotel. They had parcels on the ground between them. Around the corner come Larry, flat out. He skidded, hit these parcels and scattered them everywhere.

'Bloody hell!' Bob said. 'Let's get out of here.' We jumped in the car and took off. We were going down the street with Larry flat out beside us.

He jumped onto the running board, and out towards Lue we went. 'You bloody mongrel!' Bob said, 'You'll get us shot.'

Anyhow, we went out to Rawdon and the next day we were getting ready to start shearing. We were all over at the shed. It was about a six or eight-stand shed.

Bob comes in, 'Oh, Jesus!' he said, 'I forgot to bring the bloody handpieces over.'

The shearers' huts and quarters were only a couple of hundred yards from the shed but there was a little creek that used to run between them. It was a couple or three foot deep when it was full, and about ten foot wide. It had a big log across it for a bridge.

So Bob says to Larry, 'Come here, Larry.' He got a piece of cardboard and he wrote a note on it. Claude, our bookkeeper, was still over in the shearers' huts. 'Here,' he said, 'take this to Claude.' He put the note in the dog's mouth and away he went.

Claude give Larry the handpieces. There were six or eight of them in a sugar bag. They were too heavy for Larry to carry in his mouth, so he turned around and backed down the track, dragging them. He got to the log and backed onto it, pulling the bloody handpieces up onto the log. When he got to the middle, they fell off into the water. Geez! He was battling then.

Bob was watching him. 'Jack, come here,' he said, 'look at this. Larry's in bloody trouble here.'

I went to the engine room door to have a look and here's Larry, struggling and pulling. He was still on the log and trying to drag these handpieces across.

Bob said, 'Ya'd better go and give him a hand.' The poor bugger was in trouble there for a while till I give him some help.

Chapter Fourteen

Horse Sense

After the shearing finished, I went to Sydney for a holiday and stayed with me Aunty Min, Mum's sister. Her husband, Uncle George, was a confectioner. They lived out the back of his shop in Annandale. He taught the trade to his eldest son, Billy, and he made sweets for Luna Park.

One night her other son, also called Jack, and I went over to Luna Park. We were walking around there and we saw a rat running along the footpath up close to this wall.

I said to Jackie, 'Look at the rat! Get him! Race after him!' So we run after it.

Jackie was following me singing out, 'There's a rat! There's a rat!' Around this big cement building we went, chasing this rat.

The Yankee sailors were in town from a war ship. There were heaps of them in Luna Park. They started following us singing out, 'There's a rat! There's a rat! Chase him! Get him!' They were all running and following Jackie and me around this building chasing this rat. Well, we lost track of the rat at one part and eased off. But these sailors kept going. So Jackie and I stopped. We were standing there watching these sailors going around and around the bloody building singing out, 'There's a rat! There's a rat!' Geez, it looked funny.

While I was in Sydney I bought a pair of Mexican spurs. Fancy things they were. I brought them home and used them to show off. One day, I was down the street on Rainbow, riding bareback. I'd trained him to stop when you jumped off him, but I retrained him to keep going when I jumped off. I'd run along beside him and jump back on him while he was galloping, and then jump over him from one side to the other, like I'd seen them do on the cowboy pictures. I was coming up the street this day and there were a couple of sheilas that I wanted to impress walking down the street. So I got Rainbow cantering along up the street. I swung me leg over his neck to jump off him and run along and jump back on him. But as I threw me leg over, me spurs got hooked up in his mane and down I went with him still cantering along up the street and me, with one leg hooked up in his mane, getting dragged along on me back. I reckon that might have impressed them, but not the way I wanted. I had bloody hide off me everywhere.

Around that same time, I was in town poking around, not doing much, when the stock and station agent said to me, 'Hey, Jack! Do ya want to take a few head of cattle up to Cox's Creek for me?'

'Righto, mate!' I said.

I took a mate of mine from town to give me a hand. Johnny he was called. It took us nearly all day to get the cattle up to Cox's Creek. On the way up we went past a farmer's joint. His house was on the right-hand side of the road and on the left-hand side he had a paddock full of watermelons.

Johnny said, 'We'll have some of them on the way back.'

'That's a bloody good idea,' I said.

I was breaking in a horse that was a bit flighty for a fella at the time. I was riding him cos I thought the trip would do him good. We took the cattle up to the foot of Wheelbarrow Mountain and left them there. Coming back we stopped at the far end of the paddock where the watermelons were and jumped off our horses. We grabbed a watermelon each and run back to the horses.

The old fella who owned the paddock must have spotted us and got out his shotgun. He let drive in the air with this shotgun. 'Get outta there!' he yelled.

Johnny dropped his melon and took off on his horse. I got on my horse with the melon but just as I got on him, the farmer fired again and frightened the horse. The horse started to buck and took off and I had hold of a watermelon. I had no chance of holding the horse and the melon so I dropped it and finished up with nothing. Johnny was about a mile in front of me, spurring his horse on. Gee, we got a fright. We thought he was going to shoot us.

I was still in Rylstone not long after that, and I run into an old bloke from down the road. He said, 'Will ya quieten me horse down for me, Jack? He's a bit flighty.'

'Righto, mate,' I said, 'bring him up home.'

We had a round yard out the back at home. I thought, I'll have a go at this fella in the yard. So this old bloke leads him up. 'Leave him here,' I said. 'I'll have him for a couple of days.'

Anyhow, he went away and I got me saddle and put it on the horse, and a bridle.

Dad said, 'Ya better watch him. These bloody horses that these fellas bring ya, ya don't know what they're gunna do.'

I snuck on him and let him walk around the yard for a while, then I let his head go a bit. I dug the spurs in and he give a grunt. I thought, this bastard's going to buck. He shot his head forward and bent down. So I lay down over his neck to get a better hold of the reins. Well, he threw his bloody head back and bucked, and hit me fair in the forehead, and me stones hit the pommel of the saddle, and the bloody spew flew out of me.

I had a plate with four or five front teeth on it and a wire hook on either side to hook round the back teeth. It shot out of me mouth, too. I got off him, took the saddle off him and turned him out in the yard for a rest, and went inside. Geez, I was crook. I went and lay on the bed and had a spell for a while.

I got up later, went out, looked around the yard everywhere for me teeth, and couldn't find them. I thought, he's smashed me teeth for certain with all the bucking and jumping around the yard he did. Anyhow, I give him a feed and a drink.

Next day, I thought, I'll have to have another go at you, mate. I got the saddle and bridle, led him around, put the saddle on him and tightened the girth up. I went to get hold of the reins to get on him and as I did I felt his mane and thought, what the bloody hell's this? And here's me teeth hanging in the bloody mane. How was that for luck?

I rode him around for a couple of hours and he went all right. So I cantered him down the street back to this fella.

This same old joker, Harry his name was, he had another young horse he wanted castrating. The next corner down from him, a woman had yards and her brother had a stud out of town and he used to castrate horses. So he asked this woman's brother would he come in and do the horse for him. He said he would, so they made arrangements to get the horse in. The bloke doing the castrating was called, Harry, too.

When he come into town he said to me, 'Would ya come down and give me a hand to handle this horse?'

I said, 'Righto.'

He said, 'Ya want to get a couple of blokes.'

So me and another young fella went down. We put the rope round the horse's neck and the kicking straps on him, and Harry put a rope behind his legs. What you do is push him back and trip him. Then pull the ropes tight and it lays him on his back and keeps his two back legs up in the air so the bloke can get at him and take his stones out.

This bloody old Harry that owned the horse was a bit of an old fusspot, and he was there fussing around and getting in the way.

The other Harry said, 'Get outta the way, Harry. Get outta the way. I won't tell ya again.' But Harry was still there in the way. 'Righto, boys,' he said, 'Pull! Wrap him up, too.'

One of us had to go one side of the horse and the other one went the other side. We had to cross over. Old Harry was in the middle and we tied him up with the bloody horse. He stayed there too, be Jesus. Harry wouldn't let him go till he'd finished cutting the horse.

Another time, there was a joker down at the pub that had a pretty skewbald pony. A fairly big pony he was, and he couldn't do anything with him. He told Dad the horse was a mad bastard and he didn't know what to do with him.

Dad said, 'Jack's doing nothin'. He'll have a look at him for ya. He'll steady him down.'

Dad come home and told me and I said I'd go down and get him. Dad said he'd come with me on Rainbow, just in case. So I went down on me horse with Dad on Rainbow and we led the pony back to our place. I put him in the round yard, put the saddle on him and rode around on him.

'He's not gunna buck, anyhow,' I said to Dad.

'This fella said he's nasty,' Dad said. 'He said he can't do much with him.'

'Well, I'll get him out on the flat,' I said.

Dad rode along with me on Rainbow. Out we rode onto the flat. That's what we called the five or six acres of flat ground next to the common near our place. The house on the opposite side of the laneway to where we lived had a big paling fence about six foot high that ran for a few hundred yards along the side that the flat was on.

We got out onto this paddock and I stuck the spurs into him, and he took off, going like mad. He had his head in the air and I couldn't steer him. So I leant over his neck and pulled his head around till I had him heading for the paling fence, and I upped him with the spurs, heading straight for the bloody fence. Dad was yelling at me but I was spurring him on straight at the fence. About two yards from the fence, I slipped me feet out of the irons and he hit the fence and down he went. It took him a minute or two to get his bearings back. He staggered to his feet and I yanked the reins left and right. Then I dug the spurs in again and raced him down the paddock, yelling and spurring him, steering him left and right. Then I yelled out, 'Whoa!' and yanked the reins back and he stopped stone dead. I turned him around and raced him up the flat again, pulling him right and left, steering him around and around. I yanked the reins again and he stopped stone dead again.

I galloped him up to Dad. 'Ya bloody lunatic,' he said, 'ya could've killed ya bloody self.'

'I knew what I was doin',' I said, 'but the horse didn't.'

I raced him up along the Cudgegong road for about ten mile, sometimes flat out, sometimes cantering him and sometimes walking him. I raced him and stopped him, jumped on and off him and turned him this way and that for about an hour and a half. In the finish, as soon as I'd touch the reins he'd stop dead. I rode him home and put him in the paddock and took off the saddle.

'What are ya gunna do with him now?' Dad said.

'I'll leave him till morning, then I'll give him another go and if he's all right, I'll take him back to the bloke.'

The next day I saddled him up and rode him all around the flat. He stopped and turned as soon as I touched the reins, so I rode him up to the pub and tied him up outside. I went in and saw the bloke. 'How'd he go?' he said.

'He's all right,' I said. 'He's a bit cheeky but if ya give him plenty of work, he'll be all right. I knocked the sense into him, you keep it there.'

He went out to have a look at him, got on him and rode him up and down the street. When he come back he said, 'Mate, what a bloody difference. What'd ya do to him?'

'I just educated him a little.'

'How much do I owe ya?'

'About thirty bob.'

'That's bloody cheap,' he said.

Chapter Fifteen

Playing Up and Playing Tricks

Our house in Dawson Street had a spare block of land beside it. Dad dug it up and thought he'd grow veggies in it. After he'd dug it all up, he discovered it was all sandy, rubbish dirt and he couldn't grow anything in it, so he left it. Us kids used to play on it. It was soft going if we fell, so we used to do acrobatics. We put a rail up and used to turn somersaults over the rail, backwards and forwards. Anything up to four or five foot high, we'd leap straight over it and land on our feet.

We'd built a straight ladder, eight or ten foot high, to go down into our underground water tank when it was empty, so we could clean it out. Me, Tony, Larry and Billy would get this ladder, stand it straight up, and climb up it without anybody holding onto it. We used to balance on it and stand on our hands.

Dad used to show us lots of tricks to do. When he was home, if he had nothing to do, he'd go down to the river flat near the old bridge across the

Cudgegong River and take the kids with him. When someone was coming, he'd have us all turning somersaults and doing tricks. People would watch us as they were going past. He got a real kick out of that.

He would have been in his fifties and could still turn somersaults and stand on his hands. He was a pretty smart joker. He taught us some fancy tricks. We used to put a hat on the ground and turn a somersault over it and come up wearing the hat.

When Billy and Larry were older, they used to turn somersaults and do tricks outside the pub in Rylstone and blokes would throw them a penny. Mum would go mad if she found out about it. She didn't reckon they should be earning money outside a pub. It was a disgrace for kids to be anywhere near a pub in them days.

When Dad was home of a night, he'd tell us stories before bed. He called them gypo stories. A gypo was a make-believe sort of monster that Dad thought up. He would describe gypos in lots of ways—anything that would frighten the kids—but they always had big horns. One night, I dressed up like a gypo. I put the cow's tail on as a beard. Dad had the young kids in bed, telling them one of these stories and scaring them out of their wits, when in I walked dressed up like a gypo. They screamed their heads off and hid under the bed. After that, we all called the cow's tail the gypo's beard.

Dad would get all the kids huddled up in bed with him and tell them a gypo story. He'd tell stories like this: *One day, a big gypo was coming along and he saw Billy playing out in the yard. He grabbed Billy and was going to take him down to his cave on the common. So he got hold of Billy and Billy was singin' out and squealin'. Larry spotted him and come running after him but he couldn't get Billy off the big gypo, so he raced back and got Tony. Tony grabbed a lasso rope and away they went. They tied the rope to the gypo's leg, tied him to a tree and tried to get Billy off him but he wouldn't let him go. So they run back to get Dad and Jack. When they come back with Dad and Jack, the big gypo was gone. There was just a huge hole in the ground. He'd pulled the tree out of the ground and was going across the flat towards the common, still hanging on to Billy. Dad and Jack grabbed him, tied him up and got Billy off him. Then they went down to the police station to tell the police where he was tied up. After that they all went back home. Dad said, 'Come on, we'll go to bed.' As he goes to get into bed ... he finds the big gypo in the bed!* Well, the kids used to squeal their heads off.

Sometimes, when he was telling them a gypo story, I'd sneak in and crawl under the bed and start moaning and lifting the bed up in the middle. The kids would get a fright and yell out for Mum to come and help them. Dad wouldn't let them get out of the bed and run away. He'd hang onto them.

Dad's twin brother, Arthur, and I were good mates. We used to drink together and play up something bloody terrible. We were mad, the pair of us. One Saturday, Uncle Arthur said to me, 'Why don't we hold a party down at my place.'

He used to live on the corner of the main street and the street that went up to the railway station. He rented a little two-roomed shop there. He worked for the council. He'd camp out through the week and had this little shop to keep his gear in and live in on the weekends. It had an old table and a few chairs in it.

'We'll have a party,' he said, 'and we'll get Smithy down. We'll have some fun with him.' Smithy was a grader driver for the council, and a frightened bugger he was, too. He'd scare real easy.

So I chased up a few other blokes from the pub to come to this party. The pub shut at six, so I told them to come down to Uncle Arthur's at about seven. I asked Smithy to come as well. I picked up some grog and went down early to Uncle Arthur's. He and I were sitting there having a drink. Uncle Arthur looked out the door. 'As soon as we see Smithy comin',' he said to me, 'I'll lie down on the table and you pretend to be cuttin' me hair with a squaring axe, and we'll give him a bloody fright.'

So I got a squaring axe and we waited for Smithy. 'Here comes Smithy,' he said. He jumped up on the table and laid his head down. I stood on a chair beside the table with the axe in me hand. Smithy walked in.

'Just a minute,' I said, 'I'm just cuttin' Uncle Arthur's hair.' Whoosh! Whoosh! I went, and banged the squaring axe down on the table right next to Uncle Arthur's head.

Well, poor old Smithy's eyes stood out and he turned and bolted back up the street as fast as his legs could carry him. He passed Walter, one of the blokes coming to the party, on the way. 'Don't go down there,' he said to him. 'Jack's cutting Arthur's hair with a squaring axe. He'll end up cutting his head off. They're bloody mad.'

Walter come down. 'What are you mad pair up to?' he asked. 'I just passed Smithy and he's as white as a sheet and shaking. You bloody lunatics. He won't be back.'

'We're not mad,' said Uncle Arthur, 'we just like havin' a bit of fun.' And the next minute I looked around and he had a pushbike up on the table and was trying to climb onto it.

'What are ya gunna do with that?' I asked.

'I'm gunna ride the bike around the table.'

'I'm off, too,' said Walter, 'you bastards *are* mad.' And he left.

Another couple of blokes ended up coming down and I'm there pouring beer into a colander and Uncle Arthur's trying to drink it. Well, the other blokes left, too.

All Dad's brothers used to be good at playing up and acting the goat. Uncle Arthur had a screwed-up left hand because when they were kids on the farm, they'd try and see who was the toughest. They used to pick up handfuls of red-hot coals and see who could hold them the longest. Uncle Arthur held his so long that it burnt all the sinews in his hand and it stayed shrivelled up.

Years before I was born, Dad's younger brother, Syd, owned the cordial factory in Rylstone. He and Dad used to carry water in a 100-gallon tank with a horse and cart from the well on the common to the factory. When they were coming up the street, one of them would grab the other and tip him head first into the tank and pretend to drown him, and then keep driving up the street. The tank had a splash rim around the inside of the opening to stop water spilling and they used to stick their heads up there and get air cos there was no water in that bit. They could stay there all day but it looked as though they were drowning. People would race up and tell the police that one of the Turners was drowning the other.

One time, at Bogee Hall, there was a cricket match on. Dad and Syd were going past Bogee to Glen Alice in Syd's old car. When they got near the hall and cricket field, they stood up in the car and started belting one another with sticks. Then Dad fell down. Syd stopped the car, dragged him out to a big heap of dead timber that was beside the road and threw Dad into the timber. He threw bushes all over the top of him and set fire to it.

While Syd was getting the bushes, Dad had snuck out and gone back to the car to lie on the floor but the people at the cricket match didn't see him sneak out. So Syd set fire to the bushes and timber, and stoked it up good and proper, then went back to his car and drove off to Glen Alice. The people at the cricket ground charged off to Rylstone and told the police that Syd Turner had just killed his brother and burnt him in a heap of timber near the Bogee sports ground. The police were a wake-up to the Turners by then and just said, 'Don't worry about those bloody Turners. They're always doing things like that.'

Gee, they were a wild lot. They were always playing tricks and pretending to kill one another. It was a bloody shame how Uncle Syd did die. He shot himself in the head out the back of Grandma's house. He was thirty-eight. It was only about six months after Grandad died, too. Uncle Syd lived with Grandma and Aunty Em. Uncle Bob was staying there too at the time. I don't know how he knew something was wrong with Syd, but he'd come to stay at Grandma's to keep an eye on him. They slept in a double bed on the verandah. Uncle Bob was watching him all the time, but Syd snuck off early one morning while Bob was asleep. He walked around the back of the house and shot himself. The gunshot woke up Uncle Bob.

Uncle Syd was a clever bloke though. One of the tricks he used to do was to get a heap of tea chests and stack a couple on top of one another. Then he'd sit on them and get Dad to throw him up some more. He'd catch the chest, stand on a corner of the top one, and flick the other one under him till he had about a dozen all stacked up and him on top. Then he'd get Dad to throw him up a newspaper. He'd sit on the top one and pretend to be reading the paper. Then he'd start laughing like he'd just read something funny, and he'd rock back and forth with laughter. He'd get the whole stack swaying back and forth until it fell over. He'd turn a somersault just before it hit the ground and land on his feet.

Another trick he did was to put a needle sticking up in a little pile of sand, do a handstand, and pick the needle up between his eyelids. A travelling circus come to town one time and one of their performers did the same thing. The ringmaster was shouting out, 'Now we've got a very clever and dangerous act, you'll never see it done anywhere else.'

And the whole town yelled out, 'Syd Turner does it every Sunday at his place up on the hill.'

Chapter Sixteen

'You'll Shear a Few One Day'

Bob, the shearing contractor I'd worked with the year before, saw Dad in town one day. He asked, 'Does Jack want a pen on Rawdon?'

Dad said, 'Yeah.'

So I went to Rawdon and shore out there for him. I was shearing a hundred or so a day there. Bob had some good runs out in the west. From Rawdon we went out to Brewarrina, amongst the big ones. Eighteen, twenty-stand sheds. Gee, I thought I was made out there.

This Bob said to me, 'I'd better keep ya under me wing. You do what I tell ya and I'll make a shearer out of you. Don't get this goin' fast business into your head. You just take ya time and learn.' I'd start rushing and he'd come up and tell me to knock off and go and have a look at so and so. 'See how he finishes that side off,' or 'Have a look at that bloke. See how he finishes the neck,' he'd say to me. 'I want you to be a bloody smart shearer by the time ya go back to Rylstone.'

He'd come up to me halfway through the shed and send me rouseabouting. I was chaffing at the bit to try and be a gun shearer. 'Go and watch that bloke. Go and see that fella,' he'd say to me. 'Now you'd better take a day off. You're gettin' too smart for ya boots. Go do some rouseabouting.' When that shed finished it was the end of his run for the year, so I went back to Rylstone.

Dad got a shed then, at Glen Alice, on Umbiella Station and I went with him. It wasn't a very big shed. I shore one hundred and sixty one day and thought I was going great guns. Dad was that pleased I shore one hundred and sixty that when we got home at the weekend, he went and saw the local paper and the bloke put it in the paper. Then that was the end of the shearing for the year.

The next year, when the shearing started again, I went out to Brewarrina with Bob and we done a few sheds out around there. 'That's enough,' he'd say, 'don't go trying to do any more than that. You'll shear a few one day.'

He'd say to me, 'Go and look at Roy.' And I'd go and watch Roy for a while. Roy was the gun shearer on Bob's team. He had such a graceful style of shearing. He made it look easy. I never saw the bastard sweat even though he'd shear two hundred a day.

Later on, blokes would come and watch me to learn. 'I don't know how ya make it look so easy,' they'd say. The last side was where I was prettiest. I learnt that from Roy. He went straight from the shoulder to the toe in one blow. It was real hard to do but it was much neater.

After Bree cut out, Dad, another bloke and I got a shed at Galargambone, Mt Tenandra Station. It was a bloody big shed but there were only six shearers when I was there. When we walked onto the board I looked up at the catching pens. The walls and the gates of the catching pens were about nine foot high.

On one of the gates was a ram's skull with the shape of a tension nut from a handpiece straight in the middle of the forehead. Some shearer must have hit the ram and killed it and it was there as a warning for us not to do the same.

There was me and Dad and a big redheaded bloke with us this day. The bookkeeper come up to us to take the tallies down. He was writing in his book. He had the stand numbers, one, two, three, etc., and then the shearer's name. The bookkeeper said to this redheaded bloke, 'There's S. Turner and J. Turner. Are they any relation to one another?'

'Yeah,' he said. 'They're father and son.'

'Shit!' he said. 'He must have married a white woman, that bloke.'

Dad laughed his head off. He thought it was the funniest thing he'd heard in a long time. He told every bugger about it. He was proud of looking black, even though as far as we know, he didn't have any coloured blood in him.

When we'd finished shearing in the Galargambone area, Dad and I and a couple of other shearers from around Kandos went out to Trangie, shearing. It was out on the flat country. One of the blokes out there wanted an emu for dog meat. He said he couldn't get up close enough to shoot one. Another fella said that if you make a funny movement, wave your arms around or wriggle around on the ground, the emu will come straight up to have a sticky beak and see what it is.

'Get ya gun,' Dad said. 'I'll fetch him up for ya.'

We walked out onto the clay pan away from the shed, out where this emu could see us, and Dad started waving his hat around. Then he got down on the ground and started turning somersaults and rolling and leaping. Well, this bloody emu stuck his head up and come jogging straight over.

All the other fellas were standing around watching Dad, too. They were laughing too much to shoot the emu.

We come back to Rylstone and it was time for lamb shearing and crutching. You shore sheep once a year, and six months later, crutched them. You might have eight or ten thousand sheep to crutch and three thousand lambs to shear. Crutching was where you took the wool off around the sheep's bum and down their legs because if they wee or anything and it dribbles onto the wool, that's where the flies strike. Then they get maggots all up and down their legs and they eat into the skin. It's no good for the wool or the sheep if they get fly blown.

Sometimes, if they're real woolly sheep with a lot around their faces, you have to wig them. Wigging was when you'd take the top notch off and a bit of wool from around each eye so they could see, to stop them getting wool blind. A lot of sheep are shorn just after they lamb but the lambs are too small to shear then, so you do them at crutching time, too.

A lot of the stations had Bathurst burr on them and it would get caught in the wool. It was a little burr, a bit bigger than a pea and as hard as buggery. It would break the comb on your handpiece and sometimes, if it didn't break the comb, it would lock your machine and throw it out of your hand. The machine would go flying around. I've had it cut me legs and me arms and me hands.

We were shearing lambs on Dabee one time, and one of the other shearers was going up the neck of a lamb, when he hit a burr. His machine locked on him, flew up, and cut his bloody throat. Just missed his jugular but put a bloody big gash in his throat. He bolted. He wouldn't let anybody have a look at it. He took off straight down to the hut to get a mirror and see how bad he was cut. They had to take him to hospital and get it stitched up.

Dad told me that in the early days the shearers had to wash the sheep before they shore them. There was a big sort of a drain thing they used to wash them in. They had to wash them and then shear them. He also told me that they had what they called 'dab and raddle'. The cocky used to raddle—that's put a mark on—the sheep they were going to pay you for and put a dab on the ones they didn't think were shore good enough. The cocky would come round and if he didn't like the way you shore them he wouldn't pay you for them. He'd put a dab on them. Then when they were counted out, you wouldn't get paid for the ones with the dab. That was before the big shearers' strike in Barcaldine, when all the shearers went out. It was tough on the poor bloody shearer in the old days.

When I first started shearing, it was only seventeen and sixpence per hundred sheep. That's $1.75. Then it went up to a pound and sixpence and we thought we were made. It stayed at that for a good while. When I finished shearing in 1956 it was eight pound per hundred.

Before I'd started shearing, they used to do a run before breakfast. They'd start earlier and shear for two hours before they had their breakfast, then still do the four runs after that. We used to do two runs on a Saturday morning when I first started shearing. It was some time after the war finished that they brought in the forty-hour week.

One shed we were shearing at, the cocky was real fussy. He'd go along and say, 'Tell that bloke on number three not to leave so much wool on them. Tell the bloke on two not to cut them so much. Tell number four to clean up around the ears better.'

When a cocky complained about the way you were shearing, it was called a chip. Bob, the contractor, come up to us and said, 'Ya'd think it was a bloody wood heap the way the chips are flyin' in here.'

We'd do the three sheds—Dabee, Rawdon and Monivae—at crutching time. They were the three biggest sheds around Rylstone. We went out to Dabee crutching, then Rawdon and out to Monivae. Then Bob said, 'That's all I got for ya till next year.'

'Righto!' I said.

Dad and I went back down to Glen Alice to a shed and shore down there. The bloke we were shearing for got an old drunk out from Rylstone to help in the kitchen. After he finished of a night, one of us had to wait around for him after tea and take him back to the shearers' hut. He'd have got lost in the dark otherwise, being a town bloke, and a drunk. A couple of hundred yards off the main track back to the shearers' hut, on the left-hand side, was a dam. This night, Dad said to me, 'You wait and bring old Bill back and walk on the left-hand side of him when you're coming back, cos I'm gunna frighten him.'

So we were walking back and I got on the left-hand side of him. Halfway back to the huts on the right-hand side was a big ironbark tree. As we were getting up towards it, this figure draped in a white sheet walked out from behind the tree and flames flew out of its mouth. Well, old Bill took off. I was young and fit, and I was flat out catching him before he hit the dam.

Dad had put a sheet off the bed over himself and got a mouth full of kero. As he stepped out from behind the tree he'd squirted the kero out of his mouth and lit it with a match. Dad used to do that a lot with the kero. He could shoot out flames two or three foot. I got into the habit of doing it too, to scare people.

While we were at that shed, I got a lot of boils all down me shearing arm. It was bloody painful. At this shed, the cocky had a son around my age.

A big bugger he was, too. As usual, I had me boxing gloves with me. Dad said to him, 'Come down to the hut of a night and Jack will have the gloves on with ya.'

By Christ, it was bloody painful sparring with boils all down me arm. But if you've got a set of boxing gloves with you, you've got to be prepared to put them on with all comers. We went onto another shed and the boils got worse. One night, I was lying there moaning and I said to Dad, 'I can't cop this bloody pain anymore.'

Dad said, 'Come here, I'll fix it.' He tore a lump off the end of his flannel shirt and soaked it in kerosene and wrapped me arm up in it. 'There ya are,' he said, 'that'll fix it. Now go to sleep.'

I couldn't sleep. It was too bloody sore. After a couple of hours, I thought, I can't cop this anymore, and I took the bandage off. All the skin come off with it and all the guts out of the boils, too. It left me arm sore but clean as a whistle. It wasn't aching and throbbing anymore, at least.

Dad used kerosene to cure a lot of things. A teaspoon of sugar with a few drops of kerosene, he'd use to cure a cough and a sore throat. I remember he come home from rabbiting once. He'd cut his finger and it was infected so he wrapped it up with a bit of kerosene soaked rag. He sat up in bed to have a smoke and lit his pipe, but he caught this kerosene rag alight, too.

He come flying out of the bedroom yelling, 'I'm alight! I'm alight!' and flames were shooting off his finger.

I'm buggered if I know how he put it out now, cos we were laughing so much. He never had any pants on, just his shirt.

Chapter Seventeen

Shearers' Yarns

During the mid-forties, when I was shearing at Charlton Station, some of the older shearers that were there were telling us yarns around the campfire one night. They said that one of the old time shearers was going from Bourke to Sydney on an old steam train. They used to have the dog box carriages and above each door there was a bottle of water and two glasses in a frame. There was a luggage rack above the seats where the shearers put their swags. This old shearer was on the train with some of his shearing mates, when a governess got on at one of the stops. She sat down in their carriage and they started talking about shearing. 'I've never seen shearing,' she said. 'I'd love to see how it's done.'

'There's nothing to it, lady. I'll show ya,' this old fella said. He stood up and got one of the glasses from above the door. 'This is the handpiece,' he said. Then he grabbed his swag down off the luggage rack. 'This is the sheep. Ya put him between ya legs and go down the belly like that and take the belly wool off. Then ya go in the crotch, then ya turn him over and do the first hind leg, then ya go up the neck, then onto the shoulder,' he said, all the while showing her how it was done with the glass and swag. 'Then ya work him round onto the long blow and ya do that. Then ya get up round the head and then ya go down the whipping side, down over the last shoulder. Ya go down there, then ya finish the last leg off, and when ya finish that off, ya just throw him down the chute.' And with that he threw his swag out the train window. So the story goes.

Years ago when I was a young shearer, all the shearers used to meet at the Campbell Street Bar of the Sydney Hotel in Sydney. That's where you'd meet shearers from all the different towns and states. They'd all congregate down there when they went to town. I'd walk in there and the barman would say to me, 'How long are you down from the bush?' I must have still had gum leaves in me hair or maybe he could still smell the sheep shit but they always knew I was from the bush. Didn't matter how I was dressed.

There was a big, redheaded barmaid there that everyone was trying to pitch for. I asked her to come out with me one day. She said to me, 'No, Jack. All you shearers are the same. You're either too drunk, too tired or too bloody far away.'

A shearer used to reckon if he was twenty-five mile or more from home, he was single. I was working with a shearer once and he was pitching for this girl.

'You're married,' I said to him.

'Jack, twenty-five mile from home, nobody's married.'

I used to say to Mum, 'The day I get married, I'll throw me handpiece away.' I wouldn't get married while I was shearing.

Anyhow, this big, redheaded barmaid was telling us that she had a young woman in the bar with her this day, learning the ropes. There was a group of shearers in there, too. The young girl said that she would like to know how to shear a sheep.

So one of the old shearers said, 'Here, I'll show ya, love. It's no trouble.' He grabbed his beer glass, 'This is the handpiece,' he said. There was a rouseabout there with him having a drink, so he grabbed the rouseabout. 'Get down on the floor,' he said to the rouseabout, 'and this fella's the sheep. Ya put him between ya legs and take the belly wool off and then ya turn him over and when they kick this is what ya do. Kick! Kick!' he said to the rouseabout. The rouseabout kicked and the shearer hit him in the head with the beer glass.

There were always plenty of jokes and yarns floating around in my day about shearers and rouseabouts. Like the one me stand mate told the barmaid one weekend when we were in town. Me stand mate was drinking with me and he said to her, 'Come here, love, and I'll tell ya what Turner did through the week. He was shearing away there and was chasing the ringer, goin' like mad, flat strap he was. I said to him, 'Ya got one sheep around the ringer, keep goin'. So he took off into the pen, grabbed another one, flew down the belly and done the leg and flew up the neck. He was going that fast when he went up the neck that he went straight past the neck and cut the sleeve off a rouseabout that was walkin' past.'

There was a shearer I knew called Big Angus. Every bugger in Bourke knew him. He had a big, waxed mo sticking out and smoked a pipe shaped like a torpedo. He was shearing lambs one day and he was going that quick he got sick of walking in and out of the pen to get them. So he emptied out a wool basket, scooped up a heap of lambs, and set it by his stand so he could just grab the next lamb when he'd finished.

They tried to sack him once for shearing rough and he refused to go. So they pulled his overhead gear down so there was nothing for him to attach his handpiece to. He went up to a learner, who was shearing next to him, and said, 'You get out of the way. I'll shear enough here for the two of us.'

He used to cause a lot of trouble for the coppers, too, if they come to pinch him. I heard that one time the coppers went to get him in Bourke. They pulled up on a motorbike and sidecar to arrest him. 'I'm not gettin' in that,' he said. 'That tyre's nearly flat. It's dangerous.' So the poor copper had to go and pump the tyre up before Angus would get in. There were plenty of shearers that were larrikins in my day. I don't suppose that'll ever change.

Chapter Eighteen

Carrying On

In between shearing and rabbiting, I'd go back and work for a carrier in Rylstone. While I was working for him this time, me and his son, Ross, were carting marble from Cudgegong to Rylstone. We'd load the lumps of marble from the quarry onto our truck by hand, then take them the fourteen mile to Rylstone and unload them by hand onto the railway truck. There was about five ton in a load. We'd already done three loads this day. It was a Friday afternoon and we were going back for the fourth.

'Come on, Turner, hurry up,' Ross said. 'We'll go down and get this load, then we can go home and get ready for the dance.' There was a ball on that night.

Away we went and loaded up the truck. We were just backing out of the quarry when … Bang! We snapped an axle. 'Geez,' he said, 'this is good. We gotta get home and unload that railway truck before nine o'clock tonight, otherwise we gotta pay demurrage on it. Fifteen quid a day.'

If the railway truck wasn't ready to go when the train come to get it, the carrier would have to pay extra to keep it there. So we run the fourteen mile back to Rylstone. Run straight down to the railway yards, pushed the truck up to the goods platform and unloaded the fifteen ton of marble we'd already put on it. Then the truck was free to go whenever the train come. After that we raced home, had a bath and a feed, got ready, went to the ball, and danced till about three o'clock in the morning, and thought nothing of it. I wish I was still that fit.

This carrier, Pat he was called, also had the contract to cart gravel from up the head of the Cudgegong River out to the Kandos and Charbon cement works. He had a semi-trailer that we'd shovel twenty-two yards of gravel onto and take out to Charbon or Kandos. Then we'd shovel it off and go back and get another load. Sometimes, we could get three loads in a day. When the cement works wanted a lot more gravel than what we were carting, Pat went to Sydney and bought a tip-truck. We used to shovel it onto that then and he'd drive it out to the works and tip it.

After a while he got an idea to build a 'chinaman' to make things quicker. That's a wooden ramp that leads up over the side of the truck. It has two supporting posts on the other side making an A frame. You'd back the truck in under it. There's a gap at the top of the ramp so the gravel can fall through onto the back of the truck. You have a horse on one side of the truck and a scoop on the other side, with a wire cable that goes across the top of the 'chinaman' on a pulley. One bloke rides or drives the horse and backs him back to the truck. The other fella pulls the scoop back to where the gravel has been piled up and then he pushes down on the handles at the back of the scoop, tilting it downwards into the gravel, while the other bloke makes the horse walk forward. The scoop drags along and fills up with gravel, which goes up the ramp and tips into the back of the truck. When the truck was full,

Pat would drive it out to the works while we piled up gravel ready to load again. We'd take the scoop off the ramp while the truck was away.

Les, Pat's youngest son, was working with me this day. He was sitting on the horse while we were waiting for Pat to come back with the truck. He was too little to drive the horse, so he was riding him. I walked over to the water bag to get a drink and this Les sang out, 'Pass the water bag up here, Turner.' He had a drink and said, 'I wonder does Dick want a drink.' That was the name of the horse.

So he leaned over to tip a bit of water down the horse's forehead but ended up tipping it in the horse's ear by mistake. Well, the bloody horse give a snort and took off, and completely wrecked the 'chinaman'. When Pat come back, he couldn't believe it when he saw the ramp scattered all over the riverbed.

Pat had three sons. Ross was the middle one. He and I were going down The Gulf to Bylong one day. That was a big, steep, windy hill going down to Bylong from Rylstone. We were coming down empty when we come up behind a truck fully loaded, going down in low gear. He was sneaking along round the bends, going down this steep hill nice and steady.

I said to Ross, 'I'll give this fella a fright.' So I got out on the passenger side, run down to this truck and jumped onto the mudguard of the passenger side. I stuck me head in the window and yelled, 'G'day!' The poor bloke nearly jumped out of the bloody cab he got such a fright.

Pat and I were going out to Growie another day, that's down at the foot of The Gulf. We were coming out from Rylstone, but before we got to the top of The Gulf, there was a bloke on a pushbike riding along. Pat pulled up and said, 'Do ya want a lift, mate? Where ya goin'?'

He said, 'I'm goin' down to Bylong.'

Pat said, 'We're goin' down that way. Throw ya bike on the back and get on.' This bloke got on and away we went. We got to the top of The Gulf and started to go down.

This bloke knocks on the roof. 'Pull up,' he said, 'I'll get off here.'

'Why?' said Pat, 'We're goin' right down.'

'No, mate,' he said, 'I'm in a hurry.'

So he gets off with his bike and away he went. He went down the hill that bloody fast on this pushbike he was out of sight by the time we got to the bottom of The Gulf. No sign of him anywhere, and it was all gravel road, too.

Pat had to cart lambs from Glen Alice up to Rylstone to put on a train for Sydney. He had to go through the stock and station agent in Rylstone. Pat and I went out, got the load of lambs and brought them up to the railway trucking yards. We unloaded them off the truck and put them in the yard. Then we gave the stock and station agent a hand to load them onto the railway truck.

This stock and station agent had a sheep dog called Rowdy. He was as useless as the bloody stock and station agent. Anyhow, we were trying to load them and he's yelling, 'Speak up, Rowdy. Speak up, Rowdy. Here, Rowdy.'

The bloody sheep would have still been in the yard if it hadn't been for me and Pat. *We* loaded them. They had to go up a ramp onto the railway truck. We had what you called a tin dog. That's a heap of little tin lids all put on a piece of wire. When you shake it, it rattles and frightens the sheep. We loaded them with that, but this bloody stock and station agent with his, 'Here, Rowdy, speak up, Rowdy'—I got sick of that.

I started rattling this tin, yelling out, 'Here, Rowdy! Pick up, Rowdy! Speak up Rowdy! Come on, Rowdy! Speak up, Rowdy!'

Pat said, 'Turner, if you don't shut up, you'll send me bloody mad.'

They were harvesting on Rawdon just after that, so Pat was carting the bags of grain up to the sheds for them. I was working for him this day and there'd been a bush fire on Rawdon. They'd put the fire out but right up in the hollow of a big tree, there was a limb still burning. Sparks from it were blowing all over and setting fires to the paddocks of grain.

I said to John, the owner, 'It's that tree that's settin' the fires. Get me a tomahawk and I'll climb the tree and cut the limb off.' Now you shouldn't climb a tree carrying a tomahawk, it's too dangerous. So you climb up and get someone to throw it up to you.

'Ya can't climb that tree,' he said, 'it's still on fire.'

'Yes I can,' I said. 'You just throw the tomahawk up.'

So I climbed up it, someone threw me up the tomahawk, and I cut the limb off. That was the end of the fires. I got a bit black but I didn't get burnt. The trunk wasn't hot by that time. I just had to be careful not to climb on any branches that were burnt too far through. Every time he saw me after that, old John called me 'The man that climbed the tree of fire.'

I was working for Pat in 1947 when there was a big rail strike in New South Wales and they wouldn't cart any wool or anything on the trains. So every man and his dog that had a truck was carting wool to Sydney. Pat had two trucks and we were carting wool every day. Down, do a load, back, do a load.

One Sunday we had the two trucks going down loaded with wool, me driving one and him driving the other. Crippled Jack Turner asked us if he could come with us to Sydney. He used to get around on crutches. 'Righto,' Pat said. 'Ya can come with us.' So we got him up into Pat's truck.

On the way down we both pulled up at a café in Lithgow to have a feed. In we go and sit in this four-seater booth. We put Jack in first, and we had a job to get him in there and sit him down. I sat next to him. We ordered our meals, steak and eggs, and whatever else. The waitress come along with our meals and put me plate down. Then she leaned across and went to put Jack's down. Just then, I stuck me knife and fork into me steak and let out a bellow like a poddy calf. Well, she screamed and dropped the bloody plate. And Crippled Jack laughed that much he was helpless. He slid down under the table and we nearly had to wreck the café to get him out. Geez! He was in a pickle.

While I was working for Pat, there was a kid used to keep wagging school all the time and he'd come on the trucks with us. He'd come along for the ride out to get hay, or cart sheep, or whatever. Ned he was called. I had a load of super-phosphate on the truck this day and Ned come poking around. I said, 'Are ya comin' for a ride, mate?'

He says, 'Yeah,' and gets in the truck.

We were going out along the Pinnacle Swamp road, out towards White Rock way. We were going down a hill and there was a gate across the road with a grid off to the side. I turned off to go over the grid. There was a big sign up and it said, *light cars only across this grid*. I'm heading straight for it and Ned starts jumping up and down. 'Stop! Stop! Where are ya goin'?' he yelled.

'What's wrong?' I said.

'Ya can't go across there. It's light cars only.'

'Geez!' I said. I pulled up just in time, backed the truck up and went through the gate instead. 'Ya goin' straight back to school, Ned, when I get home. Some bastard better have brains cos I got none.' I couldn't read the sign.

Chapter Nineteen

'You Bloody Near Died'

Whenever the shearing was back on, I'd leave the carrying job and go back shearing. So I left and went out to Brewarrina. I was shearing out there and a half-caste fella come along. We were having a yarn and he was talking about his father. 'Me father's as white as snow,' he said, 'but me mother, she's three shades blacker than a bloody crow.'

This same joker was in the army during the war. Back then it was illegal to give a black fella any grog. While he was in the army, when he come home on his final leave, the townspeople took him down to the pub and bought him beer. Even the copper bought him a beer. Then when the war finished, he was discharged and come back to Bree. He went into the pub to have a drink and they pinched him, the hypocrite bastards.

In one of the sheds I shore at in Bree, Charlton Station, I was the only white fella in an eight-stand shed of black fellas. We were shearing burry sheep and one of these black fellas hit a burr. His machine locked, flew up and cut his arm. Ripped a bloody great hole in it.

Old Bob, the contractor, said,' Geez, we better take ya to town and get that fixed up.'

His mate said, 'No, he'll be all right.' He just got an oilcan, squirted oil into the cut and bound it up with a bit of rag, and that's all there was to it.

One night, we were out around the galley. That was where they had big fires going under the forty-four gallon drums of water for washing and showering. The black fellas used to sit around there every night. This night, one fella looked up and said, 'Hear that. The death bird's calling.' It was a bird that made a sound something like the rainbird. I never seen it but you could hear it for a long way. They believed that meant someone was dying at the mission. All of them either came from the mission out near Bree or had relatives living there. When I got up the next morning, there wasn't a black fella left on Charlton. They'd all gone back to the mission.

I used to love sitting around the fire with the black fellas, having a yarn. They were the wittiest bastards you'd ever want to meet. They'd always have a laugh, even at their own misfortune. One night, we were sitting round the fire talking. They were telling me about a shed they were at. The owner of the shed was a real big man named Martin. He'd kick the sheep up the arse to get them in the pen. They said the sheep only had to see him coming and they'd tuck their arses in and run.

Then one of these blokes said to the other, 'Remember the time Martin kicked ya up the arse and ya had to run round like a giraffe with ya arse tucked in for a week.' Gee, they were funny. They could see the funny side of anything.

There was an old black fella rouseabouting with us at the time. I can't think of his name, but gee he was a nice old bloke. I was sitting in a wool basket in this shed one day and he come up and said to me, 'Move over ya little, white bastard and let me get in there too.'

He was telling me one time that he was in town with some of his mates and one of them got into a fight with another black fella, and he was getting a hammering. His mate had a white shirt on. He told me he yelled out, 'Take ya shirt off, ya silly bastard. He can see ya.'

When I was shearing out at Charlton the next year, there were two or three shearers and three or four rouseabouts that were Aboriginal. There was a rouseabout from Rylstone with me, a white fella. He had a sister living in Bree who was married to a policeman. She used to play the piano at dances. One Saturday, she told her brother that she and her husband would be going to the dance at Goodooga that night and if he and I wanted to go, to be at her place at five o'clock.

We used to catch the train Friday night from the Charlton siding and get off at Brewarrina. We'd stay at the pub Friday and Saturday nights and catch a goods train back some time Sunday. We were at the pub Saturday afternoon having a few beers before the dance. When I went out the back to the toilet, this black fella, Jimmy, who was one of the rouseabouts at Charlton, asked me to get him a bottle of rum. They weren't allowed to be in pubs back then.

'I'm goin' straight home. I won't get into trouble,' he said. So I got him a bottle of rum.

In the evening, we went round to this woman's place, her brother and I. We were waiting for her husband, the copper, to come home from work so we could all go to the dance. When he did get home, he said to me, 'I should lock you up, Jack. Givin' black fellas grog.'

'Not me!' I said.

'Yes, ya did,' he said. 'I just locked Jimmy up. I asked him who give him the rum and he said, 'Jack Turner's too good a bloke to tell on, boss.'

I was sitting around the fire one night, with these black fellas, yarning. They were talking about tickling yellowbelly.

'What's this tickling yellabelly?' I asked them.

'Oh, Jackie,' one said, 'we'll take ya down to the river at the weekend and show ya. We'll get ya a feed of yellabelly.'

The weekend come and we went down to the Bogan River. They stripped off and got into the river and started swimming along the bank, running their hands along the bank under the water.

'What are ya doing?' I said.

'You watch,' they said.

They went on down the river for about three hundred yards, all the time running their hand along the bank under the water. The next thing, one give a yell and whoosh, threw a yellowbelly up onto the bank. When the fish weren't feeding, they'd find a little hollow or ledge against the bank and lay there. These fellas would run their hands along the bank, nice and steady, and when they touched a yellowbelly, they'd softly run their fingers along him till they got to his gills. Then they'd shove their finger in his gill and pull him out. They got a couple while I was watching them.

'That's the smartest bloody way I've seen to catch a fish,' I told them. I tried heaps of times after that to catch one, but I never could.

There were two West Australian blokes shearing there with us that year and they were buggers for fishing. Every weekend they'd be down at the river.

They were down fishing one day and one fella said, 'Geez, I'm snagged.' He couldn't pull his line in. He said, 'I might strip off and go in and get this.'

He stripped off, walked out onto a log and got down to the edge. He stood on the log and started pulling at the line.

'Pull it a bit harder,' his mate said. 'Give it a flick.'

So he give it a big flick—and ya wouldn't believe it—the line flew back and the hook hit him on the end of his old fella and hooked in there. He had to cut the line off it and walk back to the shed to get some wire cutters so he could cut the eye out of the hook and pull the bloody thing through. He was sore for a while, I'll tell ya.

This bloke's mate was a bugger for sleeping sitting up. He'd sit down on the board in the shed for a spell, and he'd soon be sound asleep, sitting up. At night he used to sit in bed and read, then he'd go to sleep sitting up. He'd sleep all night like that. Specs we called him cos he wore glasses all the time.

One weekend, we went into town and got on the booze. The bloke who worked the wool press come with us. He was a big, mad bugger. Anyway, we all got drunk and come back home to our huts. There were two big rows of huts made out of corrugated iron. The presser bloke was in one of the end huts and he got arguing with another fella. He grabbed a .303 rifle and took a shot at the bloke he was arguing with. The shot went right through the walls of all the huts. It was the middle of the night and every other bugger was in bed asleep. The bullet come through the wall only six inches from old Specs' head, where he was asleep sitting up, and finished up out in the paddock. If he'd been sitting six inches over, it would have blown his bloody head clean off. There was hell to pay after that. We all grabbed the presser bloke and wrestled the gun off him before he could do any more harm, and held him down till the coppers got there and took him away.

After that first year I shore at Charlton, in 1947, I come back to Rylstone and Dad and I got a shed down in Glen Alice. While I was there I picked up a disease, so Dad brought me home. I was lying in bed, really crook, so Mum got the doctor. Next thing I know, I'm in an ambulance being sped off to the hospital in Mudgee. They didn't know what it was but they filled me up with penicillin. It was one of the first times they'd used penicillin in Mudgee. After a few days I come good. That's when Mum said to me, 'You bloody near died.'

They reckoned I'd picked up a fever from shearing wet sheep. They never said exactly what it was but I needed to recuperate. I'd lost a lot of weight. I was as poor as a crow, and not just in condition but in me wallet as well. The doctor told me not to do any work for a while. So I stayed around Mudgee with one of me aunties. About a week out of hospital, I went wood cutting. That's not what you'd call recuperating. It bloody near killed me.

Soon after that, the bloke next door to me auntie said, 'Can ya drive a truck, mate?'

'Yeah!' I said.

'Do ya want a job? I need a truck driver for carting wheat. Nine pence a ton. Load the truck, cart it to wherever it's going and unload it.'

'That'll do me,' I said.

I did that job for a month or more. Then he was getting near the end of his contract and he had hardly any wheat left to cart, so he asked me to go and get a load of furniture from out Cooyal way. It was on me birthday, two days before Christmas.

Out I went to this place and got the load of furniture. It had been raining like buggery. Coming back, I got bogged. The four wheels went straight down to just below the tray. I had to climb out the window cos I couldn't even open the door. I walked about half a mile to a farm and got in touch with me boss. He come out in another truck. He couldn't get too close to where I was cos he'd have got bogged too. We had to cut the ropes cos we couldn't undo them—they were underground that much—then cart the furniture through all the mud, over to the other truck. We took the furniture to town but we had to leave the bogged truck there till after Christmas. That's how I spent me twenty-first birthday. When the ground had dried out we had to go and dig the truck out.

There was no more work driving after that but I got to be mates with one of the wheat lumpers, and his father was the boss of the wheat lumping machines in Mudgee.

He said, 'Do ya want a go at stack building, Jack? Working on the stack with me son.'

So I got on wheat lumping, stacking the wheat. That was thirteen bob a thousand bags. That was big money, good money. Bloody hard yakka, though. I worked with him for six to eight weeks, lumping wheat.

Every weekend, we'd go about eighteen mile out to a place called Gulgong and lump wheat there for the cocky. We'd make a stairway with the bags there, but in Mudgee we had an elevator. You fed the bags from the truck onto an elevator that took them up to the top of the stack. It could go up to twenty-four bags high.

One day when we got back to Mudgee from Gulgong, there was a queue of trucks waiting to be unloaded. A bloke asked us if one of us would move his truck up when it was his turn and unload it for him. When his turn come,

I climbed down and moved his truck up for him, and started loading the bags onto the elevator. The stack was twenty bags high by the time he come back. I climbed onto a bag that was going up the elevator to continue building the stack. It was pretty steep and I lost me footing and I fell backwards. Down I went but me foot got hooked in the cogs of the elevator. The bag of wheat I was standing on followed me down, hit me in the head and knocked me out of the cogs. If it hadn't, I'd have lost me leg. I finished up in hospital with fourteen stitches just under me ankle. I was a week in hospital.

When I got out, I was hobbling around on crutches. The same truck driver I'd worked for before said to me, 'How are ya goin', Jack? Can ya get around?'

I said, 'Yeah, mate!'

'Can ya drive this truck out and get a load of hay for me?'

I said, 'Oh, yeah. I can drive okay. Me left foot's all right, I can change gear, and I'll just use me crutch for the accelerator.'

It was an old blitz wagon he had. So I went out and got a big truckload of hay and brought it back into town where they unloaded it. Out again I went for another load. Coming back the truck caught fire. Well, I pulled over, flew out of the truck, and raced over to a dam not far away, wet a bag and flew back with it. But I tore the stitches out of me foot in the process, so I had to go back to the hospital and get it re-stitched.

Just after me foot healed up, I was in the pub in Mudgee when a bloke come in and said, 'G'day, Jack. Gee, I know a bloke in Rylstone who'd like to see you—ya Dad. He's at home with the family and every bugger's sick bar him.'

'I better get home,' I said. I got the next train back to Rylstone.

When I walked in the house, Dad said, 'By geez, I'm glad to see you.'

Mum and all the kids had got whooping cough and they were all as sick as buggery. Mum had buckets and billies, even jam tins, anything she could get her hands on for every bugger to spew in. Dad had been away when they first got sick and poor Mum had to stagger out of bed to try and look after the kids. She had a rough time, old Mum did. When Dad come home, he took over the reins and give Mum a bit of a spell. Then when I got home there were two of us to look after them.

I'd joined the Buffalo Lodge in Rylstone a while before this. When they heard that everyone was sick, they provided tucker for us all while Dad and I were looking after the family and couldn't work. I stayed home till everybody got right.

While I was back in town a bloke called Les come up to me and said, 'What are ya doing?'

'Nothin'.'

'Do ya want to have a go at painting roofs?'

'Where we gunna do that?' I said.

'A bloke's lent me his compressor. He wants it back in a couple of weeks but there's a bloke I know in Rylstone wants his roof painted.'

'That suits me.'

'Okay,' he said, 'we'll have a go at it.' We got the paint and sprayed this roof.

While we were spraying it, another bloke come along and said, 'Will ya spray my roof?'

Les said, 'Yeah.'

He worked out a price by the square foot, or whatever, and told this bloke it would be so much. He was happy with that, so we done his roof.

Another woman said, 'Will ya paint my roof?'

I said, 'Yeah.'

Les worked out a price and we sprayed that roof, too. Then the bloke that had loaned him the compressor come and got it. One of the stores had a brand new, little air compressor for sale, sixty quid, so Les bought his own. 'We can make a living out of this,' he said. 'We can do all right.'

We did a shop roof for a bloke. Then he said, 'Will ya paint the front of me shop too?'

Les said, 'Yeah.'

I said, 'What about we spray it?'

'Oh shit,' he said, 'that'd be the idea. It'd be quicker.'

Just up the road there was a stock and station agent. He'd just bought a brand new Dodge car. You had to wait bloody months to get one. He'd only had it a little while. Black it was. It was parked at the kerb out the front of his shop, only about two shops away from where we were painting this shop front. We got the spray gun going with a bluey-coloured paint, spraying away, climbing up on the balcony and spraying, going good guns. Next thing this stock and station agent comes down bellowing his bloody head off. The drift of the paint was going all over his brand new car. We had to go and wash it off. It took us two days to clean it up properly.

After that, there was a bloke down the bottom end of town that had a garage. He said, 'Will ya paint me roof, Jack?'

'Yeah,' I said.

'How much?' So I asked Les and he give a price. 'What do ya thin the paint down with?' he asked.

'Oh,' I said, 'we got special stuff we get to thin it down so it'll go through the gun.'

'Oh, that's good,' he said.

But we thinned it down with petrol. You were supposed to use turps because it wasn't as explosive but it took longer to dry and cost more. So we get to this bloke's garage and I go round the front and get a gallon of petrol off him.

'What's that for?' he says.

'For the motor,' I said.

'Oh, is it a motor one, is it? Oh, that's good.'

We mixed the paint up and sprayed his joint. Put a couple of coats on it, got our money and away we went.

We done a couple of houses. Then one woman wanted the inside of her house painted. 'What about we spray the inside?' I said.

'Oh, geez,' Les said, 'I don't know whether we can.'

'Yeah,' I said, 'we'll try it.'

So we sprayed the inside of her kitchen. We just masked everything up. We did a good job on the walls but we finished up having to paint the ceiling again by hand cos the drift from the walls got all over it. Then we had to paint her gutter. We done another house for a lady up the street.

After that, I'd had enough painting. It was crutching time again so I said to Les, 'I'm goin' back shearing.'

So Dad and I went crutching—down to Glen Alice—and did a few sheds down there.

When we finished there I said to him, 'I'm gunna buy a car.'

'No, no, ya don't want a car. Buy a utility or a van, so ya can camp in it instead of living in pubs,' Dad said.

So I bought a little Fordson panel van, a new one, from the garage out at Kandos. I had to pay it off. I thought I was made then. Dad had gone back down to Glen Alice rabbit trapping and I was working around the town. The panel van I'd bought only had one seat in it, so I made up a little box seat and fitted it in next to my seat.

I said to Mum, 'I'll take ya down to see Dad.'

Away we went, down the mountain. Mum thought it was great, better than a horse and sulky. Anyhow, we went down and seen Dad and had a feed with him, then we come home. We were coming back up Mt Marsden. It was pretty steep and rough, and I had to change down gears. When I changed down, I took off fairly fast and it tipped Mum's seat over. She went arse over head backwards, rolling down the back of the van yelling, and her legs flying everywhere. I had to pull up and straighten her up. In the finish, I got a seat put across the back of it.

When Dad come back from rabbiting, it was shearing time again. 'We'd better go and get a shed in the west,' he said. So we packed up and drove the panel van out to Bourke. We got a shed at Hungerford, about a hundred mile the other side of Bourke. They wanted a shearer and a rouseabout.

The contractor in Bourke said, 'Leave ya van here, Jack, and you can drive me truck and take the rest of the shearers and the tucker and the cook out.'

'Righto!' I said.

I had all these blokes in the back of the truck and a forty-four gallon drum of petrol. It was only a week or two after Christmas and it was hot. We got out to the other side of Ford Bridge and I had to fill up with petrol. I got up on the truck to undo the bung in the drum of petrol. I got it half undone when it blew out with that much force, we never found it. If it had hit me in the head, it would have killed me stone bloody dead, no doubt about it. We had to cut a stick and shove it in the hole.

We got out to the shed and it was bloody hot. Dad said, 'I'll be the rouseabout and you can shear.' We were going along doing all right and Dad said to me, 'You can ring this shed.' To ring a shed, you have to shear the most sheep.

'Geez, no I couldn't,' I said, 'They're too good a shearers for me.'

'Yeah, they're better shearers than you, but they're not as tough,' Dad said. 'When it gets too hot, they'll stop for a spell, so you keep goin'. I'll splash some water on ya to cool ya down. Ya can shear half a dozen while they're having a rest.'

He was right. I rung the shed. They might have been faster than me, but they couldn't cop the heat. When we got back into Bourke we were told that it had reached 121 Fahrenheit—that's 49 Celsius.

After that, Dad said, 'I'm goin' back to Rylstone. I'll catch the train.' So I got a shed with another fella then, out the other side of Bourke. We drove out in me little Fordson. On the way, we pulled up at a government tank. That's a real big dam on a stock route for watering stock. We went to have a look and see if there were any ducks on it. There was a mob of goats hanging around, too. While we were looking at the dam, a couple of them jumped up onto the bonnet of me car. When I spotted them, I was that wild I raced up to chase them off it. When they jumped off their hooves scratched the bonnet. It was only a couple of months old, me car. Gee, I was savage over that.

When I was younger and first started shearing away, Mum used to give me a few stamped envelopes and write her address on them for me. I used to get one of the other shearers, or somebody, to write a line or two just to let her know where I was and that I was okay, and I'd post them home to her. Over the years, shearing mates here and there persevered with me and taught me enough to be able to scratch a letter home to Mum. Sometimes I'd go from hut to hut asking them how to spell this or that. They taught me enough to be able to write a little. So I scratched a letter home to Mum to tell her where I was. She sent a letter back. I got someone to read it to me and it said she'd got a letter from Bob, the shearing contractor, and he was starting at Charlton Station again on such and such a day, and did I want a pen? So I wrote and told her to tell him I'd be there. I finished the shed I was at, and me and this other fella, Claude, who was the bookkeeper for Bob, went over to Charlton and started there.

When that shed finished, we did Rawdon, Monivae and Lue and went on to Dabee. I had me little van and it was only five mile into Rylstone from Dabee Station. I hooked up with a sheila and I was in town all night, every night.

Bob, the contractor, come into town and said to the policeman, 'If ya see that bloody Turner or his wagon in town after half past five at night, lock the bastard up until seven o'clock the next morning.' They locked the station gates and I tore a hole in the fence to go into town to this sheila. We went all over the place, up to Lue and Cudgegong, out having fun.

When we finished the shed, old Bob said, 'I don't believe this.' I'd rung the shed and still ended up owing him five pound. Gee, I spent some money. 'We'll have to get it out of ya at the next shed,' he said. 'I'll see ya when we go back to Brewarrina.'

After that I went down to Crookwell, shearing. That's where I met the George brothers. They were shearers as well as shearing contractors around Crookwell at that time. I shore in three or four sheds down there with them. They were real good shearers, the lot of them. One of them shore three hundred and three one day, at Wyacaroy. I shore one hundred and eighty and thought I was doing a good job. By geez, he could shear. I done about three other sheds after that, before I come back to Rylstone.

Then I got another shed out at Brewarrina with Bob. I took me younger brother, Bryan, and another young fella out with me as rouseabouts. There were ten shearers and two rouseabouts. One rouseabout picked up the wool for five shearers. This other rouseabout got sick one day and couldn't work. Bob said to me, 'You'll have to knock off or go steady two or three of you fellas, or one of these kids won't be able to pick up for the lot of ya.'

'Course he will,' I said. And Bryan picked up for the lot of us. He was busy all right. He started whinging and I said, 'You can do it. No trouble at all.' He picked up all day. Bob said he was the best rouseabout in the world.

After that, we come back home for a while. Then we went down to Crookwell, near Goulburn, me and Bryany and the shearer's cook from Charlton that I'd met in Rylstone. I knew a few shearers around there. I went into the pub and saw a couple of blokes. One of them said, 'Yeah, we want a rouseabout, a shearer and a cook.'

'I got the bloody three,' I said.

We went out to this shed at Bungendore. There were four shearers there. One Saturday afternoon they were saying, 'Take us to town Jack, take us to town.'

So we all got in me little van and into Bungendore we went—the cook, the other shearers, me and Bryan. We went into the pub and got drinking. Then we went for a feed and I got on to a sheila at the café. Just on dark she knocked off, so I picked her up and took her out for a drive. I was out with her till about two o'clock in the morning. I forgot all about me mates and me brother.

I got back to the pub and Bryan's running around the street. 'I'm gunna tell Mum on you. I'm gunna tell Mum,' he's yelling. He was only about fourteen at the time.

'Where is everyone?' I said.

'They're all in jail.'

They'd got cold and had nowhere to go, so they'd broken into the pub to get blankets. I had to go and bail them out. Gee, they played up. They reckoned they were going to shoot me.

After we finished there, I took Bryan back to Rylstone. We were only there a few months and I got word Charlton was starting. I got in touch with Bob and asked him if he wanted a rouseabout. He said he needed two, so I took Bryan and another bloke from Rylstone, as well as a bloke who was a penner-up. Out we went to Charlton.

We got there and it started to rain. We shore two sheep and they voted them wet. We didn't shear any more. After two weeks it was still raining. So they declared it a cut out. Bryan said, 'I'm not goin' home. I've got a job as a jackaroo on the station.'

'Well, I'm bloody goin' home,' I said.

'Ya can't get out,' he said. 'Ya can't get anywhere.' Everywhere was flooded. The Bogan and the Barwon rivers had joined, a hundred mile wide they were.

The other blokes had left their cars and trucks and got out by train. Bob had left his there, too. Another bloke had a little Austin A40 car that he drove up into the wool room in the shearing shed and thought it would be safe there.

'Not me,' I told them. 'I'm taking mine home.'

So me and the other two blokes I took out there got in me van. We only went a little way and we got bogged. So we Spanish-winched me car for a mile and a half, with a lump of fencing wire and two sticks, till we got down to the railway line at Gongolgon. The train only come along that line every second day. So I drove the van from Gongolgon to Byrock—about fifty mile—on the railway track with one wheel inside the track and one out of it. When we crossed the Bogan River, the water was lapping the top of the sleepers. The other two fellas were too frightened to ride in the car across the bridge—they walked behind.

When we got to Byrock, I pulled off the railway track and drove down to Nyngan. At Nyngan they said the main road was closed but there was a bypass road. The water was fairly high across it, too. We camped the night there because the road was covered. We looked up in the night and saw lights bobbing along where the road was.

I said to the other fellas, 'Who can that be? I walked through there not long ago and the water was up to me shoulders.' When the lights got up to us we saw it was an army duck.

'Do ya want a tow through, mate?' the bloke said.

He hooked on to the front of me van and towed us through. The van floated all over the place going through—water everywhere. We got home a couple of days later. Then we got word to go back in two months' time to shear them out at Charlton—when the flood had dried out.

Bryan stayed on as a jackaroo at Charlton. During the flood he wrote to Mum and told her they were having to row boats out to feed the sheep that were stranded on little islands by the floodwater. I didn't see Bryan for four or five years. He never come home after that. He stayed on Charlton and became station manager. Then he went on to manage other stations for A.L.M. & F. It was an English firm. I forget what it stands for now. He ended up being their last manager. He sold their last station for them.

(top photo) Camping out in me swag. Me little Fordson van in the background.

This photo of me was taken at the Rylstone Show in 1946 or 1947. It was taken on me box Brownie camera. I can't remember who took it.

Chapter Twenty

Motorbike Madness

When the shearing was over once more, Dad and I went back down to Glen Alice, rabbiting. We come home one weekend and a cousin of mine, Billy Mac, was up from Sydney, visiting. He told us that they were paying big money in Sydney for rabbits for the coursing dogs to kill.

'I can see meself making a fortune here,' I said.

'What do ya mean?' he said.

'Come with me down to the bush and we'll get a load of rabbits and we'll take them to Sydney.'

We went and told Dad. 'Geez, that sounds all right,' he said. 'You'll get more than ya would for a skin.'

We went back to Glen Alice where we'd been trapping and took a couple or three ferrets and a heap of nets. We caught about two hundred rabbits and stuck them all in the back of me van. We fenced them in with bits of trees and put grass in there for them and set off for Sydney. Well, half the poor buggers had died before we got there. They'd died of fright, I think.

In Sydney, we went around to see different fellas about the rabbits and no one wanted them. I ended up giving half of them away but I got a few bob for the skins of some of them.

Billy Mac's brother-in-law had a coursing dog. He said to me, 'I'll tell ya where ya could make a quid, Jack. Carting coursing dogs around. You'll get a quid or more to take them to Goulburn and Daptow.'

'That'll suit me,' I said.

I stayed in Sydney for a little while, carting coursing dogs about. I'd take a couple to Goulburn for a race, then a couple to Daptow for races. I took a heap of them out to the trials at Wentworth Park. All around the place I carted them. Then I was offered a job at Exide Batteries in Sydney, where two of me cousins worked. That sounded all right to me. So I stayed in Sydney and worked there.

While I was working at the battery factory I met up with Dave, the bloke I'd been splitting posts with at the foot of the Nullo a couple of years before. It was getting on towards Christmas. The factory closed down for a couple of weeks over Christmas, so we'd been given our pay packets just after dinnertime. I put mine in me pocket but sometime during the afternoon I lost it. I looked around everywhere and couldn't find it. I told this Dave that I'd lost me pay packet.

'I'll have a look round and tell everyone to keep an eye out for it,' he said.

When knock off came, I still didn't have me pay packet. I told Dave and he waited outside the door with his hat, and as everyone bundied off, he said, 'Jack's lost his pay packet. Some bugger's kept it. He'll need some money for Christmas.' And he held his hat out to everyone.

Nearly everybody put some money in it. I finished up with a lot more than what me pay packet had in it. So Dave give me what had been in me pay packet and took the rest out to the home for old men in Lidcombe.

There was another fella who'd come from the bush that worked at the battery factory. John Osborne he was called. I got to be mates with him. He was a showman. He'd just come to Sydney for a few months while the shows were quiet. We got to be real good mates, him and me. I was staying at a boarding house in Annandale. He lived in a boarding house in Burwood. There were eight in his boarding house. When one of the other fellas left, he got me into there. We used to have great fun. We'd go to the races on Saturdays and the dances Saturday night, and then to the beach, swimming, on Sundays.

While I was at the battery factory, I thought, bugger this van, I don't need it. There was a dry cleaner I'd met who wanted a van, so I sold it to him. Then I bought meself a motorbike. A red tank Matchless it was. I'd go home to Rylstone on the bike now and again, on a weekend. I acted like a bloody lunatic on it. Gee, it could go.

One day, I was coming up through Bell, going like a rocket on this thing. I looked down and I could see a shadow beside me. I thought, gee, this fella's travelling. Let's see how good he is. So I opened this bloody bike up ... he was still there. After a minute he came up alongside me and pointed to the side of the road. It was a copper and he was on one of those Golden Flash BSA bikes. They could go—do a hundred and ten mile an hour straight out of the shop, and the coppers used to boost them up.

He pulled me over. 'G'day,' he said.

'G'day.'

'Where's ya licence?'

'Mate,' I said, 'I'm just goin' home to get one.'

'What?' he said. 'Where do ya live?'

'Rylstone,' I said, 'I'm knockin' around with a copper's daughter up there. I'm going up to see her and ask Alan for me licence.'

'Say g'day to Alan for me,' he said. 'But if I catch ya without a licence or riding like that again, I'll have ya.' And away he went.

When I got to Rylstone, I went straight to the police station and said to Alan, 'I've bought a motorbike and I've come up to get me licence.'

'Ya didn't ride it up, did ya?' said Alan.

'I did and got pulled up. But the copper that pulled me up knew you.'

'You're bloody lucky, mate,' he said, and give me the licence.

Alan had two daughters. They used to come up home of a night and we'd all play cards and have the gramophone going. We'd have great sing-a-longs.

Not long after I got me motorbike, me and me cousin Billy were in Rylstone one weekend and Dad said to Billy, 'Can ya get me some sheets of steel? I'm gunna start makin' ash bricks.'

He was going to brick in the front verandah in Dawson Street. He used to make the bricks for other people, too. An ash brick was eighteen inches long and nine inches high.

'Yeah, I can get ya some,' Billy said.

He got seven or eight pieces of this light, flat steel, about nine inches wide and eighteen inches long, for Dad to sit the bricks on. One weekend he said to me, 'We'd better take this steel up to ya Dad.'

I put the sheets of steel in a knapsack on me back and got on the motorbike. Away we went, with him as pillion. He was just learning to ride a bike, so we took the quietest road up through the Blue Mountains. After we got out past Parramatta, I got on pillion and let him have a ride.

'Give it to her,' I said to him.

We were travelling along doing about sixty mile an hour when we come to a right angle corner. 'What do I do?' he yelled.

'Just turn it,' I said. So he turned the front wheel, but he didn't lay the bike over as he did it. Away we went sailing through the air. These steel plates went flying everywhere. How one didn't cut me bloody head off, I'll never know. I was playing a mouth organ at the time, too. It's a bloody wonder I didn't swallow it. We never even found that.

We were scrambling around on the ground, when a bloke come running over. 'How many of ya are dead?' he yelled.

We'd gone over a fence and landed in a paddock which was a lot better than landing on the road, but we still had some skin off us. 'We're okay, mate,' I said. I got up and straightened up the handlebars. I said to Billy, 'Get on here again.'

'No bloody fear,' he said. So I rode it the rest of the way to Rylstone.

Billy bought his own bike after that and taught himself to ride. I think he thought that would be safer than me teaching him.

While I was still working at the battery factory, Billy said to me, 'What about we go to Rylstone for the weekend?' It must have been a long weekend because Monday was a holiday.

I said, 'Yeah, that'll do.' So on the Friday I said, 'We can't go tonight, it's too bloody late. We'll go Saturday.'

The next morning, it's pouring rain in Sydney. We waited around and waited around. A bit after dinnertime, it cleared up and looked all right, so I said, 'Okay. We'll go now.'

Billy's brother, Jackie, never had a motorbike at the time but he wanted to come, too. So I put him on behind me. Away we goes up the highway. We get to Penrith and down come the rain. It was wintertime, and it was cold and as windy as buggery.

We got to Lithgow and I said, 'Bugger this. We'll pull in here and try and get a room somewhere.'

Well, we tried everywhere and couldn't get a room. It was all booked out for the long weekend. So we got a couple of bottles of rum and got out onto the highway again, and come to a bus shelter. It had a tin roof and tin across the back and halfway down both sides.

'This'll do us,' I said. 'We'll get out of the wet here.'

We got in this bus shelter out of the wet and got into the rum. There was a rubbish bin beside the bus shelter. It was one of those round rings with the bin sitting in it. I pulled it out of there and tipped the rubbish out of it. Then, I scrounged around and got some rocks and put in the bottom, then got some bits of wood. It was all wet but somebody had left a newspaper in the shelter and a bit of that was dry. I got it, tipped the motorbike up and tipped the petrol over it, shifted the bike out of the way, put the paper in the drum, lit it, and up she went. We kept the fire going and got into the rum. We were having a bloody party.

It was getting late and we had to try and get to sleep. It was windy and cold and still raining, and traffic was going past cos it was the main road. Everybody got quiet and I thought, geez, they're asleep. I could hear a big truck coming. So I jumped up, snuck out round the side of the shelter and got hold of a big stick. It was corrugated iron running straight up and down on this shelter. I waited till the truck got bloody near opposite us, then I wailed the stick along the tin. Well, holy, bloody hell! They screamed like mad and flew out of the shelter. By the Jesus, it frightened them.

'Ya bastard,' they yelled, 'we should shoot ya.'

Anyhow, daylight come. 'Come on,' I said, 'we'd better get goin' and get to Rylstone.'

Me cousin, Billy, was a religious bloke and as we were riding along he yells out, 'It's Sunday! We gotta go to church, we gotta go to church.' We come to Ben Bullen and saw people going into church. 'That'll do us,' he said.

We pulled up on the side of the road near the church, brushed ourselves down, went into church and sat down on a seat along one side. What a bloody stink of rum and smoke there was on us! The people in front of us got up and moved to the other side of the church. We went to Rylstone after church and come back to Sydney on Monday afternoon.

Jackie, me cousin, got his own motorbike not long after that. He was just learning to ride it. We used to go out to Coogee and Bondi to the beach. We were coming back this day along Bondi Junction. There were trams everywhere back then and you had to stop when a tram stopped, to let the people get across. We were coming along and this tram in front of us pulled up at a stop. Jackie, who was still learning to ride, was in front on his bike. The conductor lady got down to help an old lady off the tram. Just as she got off and stepped back, Jackie went past and the bloody handle bars of his bike hit her money bag, and threw it up around her head and spun her round. He kept going but geez, didn't she give us a bloody tongue bashing. She went crook on us all right.

Another time, I was coming back on me bike from dropping a sheila off at Manly. I was coming back across the Harbour Bridge. There was nobody about—it was about two o'clock in the morning. I opened me bike up before I got onto the bridge and got up to about one hundred and two mile an hour going across it. The wind nearly took me to the other side of the road. I looked down and there was another motorbike wheel beside me. He waved me over. It was a copper.

'What the bloody hell are ya trying to do? Kill yaself?' he said.

'No mate,' I said. 'I was just seeing how this bastard would go. I want to try her out at the Castlereagh air strip.'

'Well leave it till bloody Castlereagh air strip. You'll kill yaself and some other bugger if you keep this caper up.' I was lucky I never got booked for that.

But I still didn't learn me lesson. Another wet afternoon, after I knocked off work from the battery factory, I was flying along up Glebe Road and hit the tram tracks. Arse over head I went and onto me back. I was skidding up the road on me back and I could hear a squealing noise like a siren. I thought, here comes an ambulance or fire engine, they'll run right over me. Then when I stopped, the noise stopped. It was me jacket scraping on the bitumen. I was fairly going all right.

Me and me mate, John, left the battery factory shortly after that. We went working at Lark Austin Motors, on the assembly line, putting motorcars together. We didn't stay there long, only about three weeks. Then we got a job out at Ryde, at Cooper's, where they made sheep dip. We were working there for a little while, then John's father got crook, so he went back working on the shows.

There was another fella at the boarding house, who'd come from West Australia. Duncan he was called, and he was nearly as mad as me. He used to knock around with John and me. When John left, we teamed up then and had some great fun together. That's when we used to get into trouble. John used to keep us straight. We'd get into the room that I was in and spar and wrestle. We used to nearly wreck the place. The old lady that owned the boarding house, Mrs Mac, she used to come up and say, 'Boys, boys, go steady now.'

We used to go to the races and the pubs and the dances at Paddington. He was a bit of a ratbag like me, this bloke. He come with me to Rylstone a couple of times and we'd go down to the pub and play up. Anyhow, one long weekend, he come home with me to Rylstone. We had a ball. I took him to the dance and the pubs. He thought it was great and got on good with Mum.

We got pinched one night at Petersham's Dance Hall in Sydney for playing up. They took us to the cop shop and locked us up. At two o'clock in the morning, the copper come in to me and dragged me out.

'What's ya name?' he said.

'Jack Turner.'

'All right,' he said, 'it'll cost ya ten bob then ya can get. Get home and don't play up again or I'll lock ya back up.'

'Okay,' I said. 'But what about me mate?'

'Don't you worry about him, you just get goin'.'

I thought, oh well, I'll wait outside for him. I was going out, when they brought Duncan in and asked him his name. He told them, but then he started to give them cheek, so they locked him back up again. A bit later on they went and got him again and asked him what his name was.

'The same as it was before,' he said. So they locked him back up and didn't let him out till daylight.

(top photo) Me Matchless motorbike. It didn't look much but geez it could go. This is the bike I was doing a hundred mile an hour on across the Sydney Harbour Bridge.

*Me and **Freda** at the Chinese Ball at the Trocadero Ballroom in Sydney. She was the neighbour of the lady who ran the first boarding house I stayed at in Sydney. She needed a partner for the dance. And me being an obliging sort of bloke agreed to take her. >>*

Motorbike Madness

(top, left photo) Larry doing tricks on the ladder in front of our house in Dawson Street, Rylstone. The three roofs in the background all belonged to our house. The first part of the house had Mum and Dad's bedroom and the lounge in it, the middle roof covered the two bedrooms the girls slept in, and the back roof covered the kitchen and dining room. All six boys slept on the verandah at the front of the house.

(top, right photo) Me doing a handstand and Dad standing on my neck. No wonder I've got a crook neck now.

(bottom, left photo) Me pulling **Tony** in the billy cart, Dawson Street, Rylstone. About 1950, before Tony went away to Sydney as an apprentice jockey.

Tony in his racing silks, *Larry* on left, *Billy* on right.

Dad and Tony on the verandah of our house in Dawson Street, Rylstone. Dad always wore a suit coat, summer or winter.

Chapter Twenty-One

Carpentry, Card Games, and me Little Car

I left the sheep dip factory after a couple of months. I got itchy feet. So I decided to go bush and go back shearing. I packed me swag and bought a train ticket to Brewarrina. It must be shearing time out at Bree, I thought. I'm bound to be able to get a pen out there. So out I went on the train. All I had left was two or three bob in me pocket, after I'd bought the train ticket. I walked down to Mrs Ives' pub, the Barwon Hotel.

'Hello, Jack,' she said. 'How are ya?'

'I'm all right. I'm lookin' for a pen.'

'Oh,' she said, 'there's none about. All the shearers left last week. There's no shearing left around here.'

'Fair dinkum. I'm broke. I thought I'd be bound to get a pen.'

Outside I went and there was a taxi driver sitting in his car. I got talking to him. I asked him if he knew of anyone who wanted a worker for a few days so I could get a quid for a ticket down to where the shearing was. He said there was a joker around the next street who'd been looking for a carpenter for a good while.

'That'll do,' I said.

'Oh, are ya a carpenter?'

'Well, I think I am.'

'All right, I'll take ya round to him.' He took me round to this joker and said to him, 'Here's a bloke lookin' for a job.'

'Are ya a carpenter, mate?' the other bloke said.

'Yeah, I am,' I said, 'I come out here lookin' for a shearing pen but the work's all gone and I got no money.'

'All right,' he said. 'When do ya want to start?' This was Friday afternoon.

'Any time.'

'Will ya work tomorrow? Saturday?'

'Yeah, any day'll do me.'

I thought, if I could just work labouring for him for a few days, he'd give me a few bob to get the train out to Nyngan where there would still be some shearing. I camped in the stables out the back of Mrs Ives' pub that night. The next morning, I met him and we went out to the house he was building. He give me a nail bag, a hammer, a ruler and a saw.

'You start here,' he said.

Well, I knew absolutely nothing about carpentry. It was a Nelson and Williams ready cut home he was building. It was already pre-cut and just had to be put together.

'You can start over that side,' he said. Well, I didn't know where to start. I just had bits of timber poked here and there. 'No mate,' he said, 'not like that.'

All day he was saying, 'Put that here, nail that there, do it like this. That's not right, do it like this. That's not the way to hold a bloody hammer.' At lunch time he said, 'Where's ya dinner?'

'I got none.'

'Here, have a bit of mine.' He give me one of his sandwiches.

The rest of the day he was saying, 'Here, carry this for me, do that for me.' Later on he says, 'Righto, knock off time. Come on, we'll go down the pub.' We only had to walk a couple of streets to the pub. 'Where'd ya leave ya swag?'

'Round the back of Mrs Ives'.'

'Come and have a beer.'

'No mate,' I said, 'I got no money.'

'Come in anyway and have a pot.' So in we went. 'Two beers thanks, Mrs Ives,' he said. She put them down on the bar and he paid for them. He took a long drink, then he said, 'Well, you're the biggest bloody liar I've ever met, but you're the gamest bloody man I've ever met. If ya stay with me, I'm ready to pay ya, and I'll make a carpenter out of ya yet. I'll give ya twenty-five quid a week and ya board. Will ya stay?'

'Bloody oath, I will,' I said. He reckoned if I was that game, there had to be some good in me.

We built three houses together. After we finished the one in town, we built one near the river just out of Bree. He had an old De LaSalle car. We slept in that. Eight cylinders straight, they had. We shot pigs and caught fish, and lived on that, plus potatoes. Once we got the house built enough so we could fix a room out, we'd work till twelve o'clock at night by a hurricane lantern. Saturdays and Sundays I worked for him, too.

He said to me one time, 'You got pinched in Sydney for drunkenness.'

'How'd ya know that?'

'I got the copper in Bree to check up on ya, just to see if you were fair dinkum,' he said.

After we'd built another house, I met Bob, the shearing contractor, in Bree and he told me he was starting shearing at Charlton the next week.

'Do ya want a pen, Jack?' he said.

'Yeah, mate, I'll be there.' I went back and told Don, the builder, that I was going back shearing.

'Don't leave,' he said. 'Stay another six months and I'll get ya a carpenter's ticket. You'll be a fully-fledged carpenter then.'

'No mate. Charlton Station's starting next week and I've been offered a pen there.'

I wish now I'd stayed with Don and got me ticket, after all the other jobs I've had to do to get a quid.

I went back to Charlton, shearing. It was getting around Easter time by then and we all wanted fish for Good Friday. The Bogan River run through Charlton, so we were poking around down there one weekend, near the railway crossing, when we spotted a fish trap that the fettlers used to use. We got the trap and drew straws to see who would go down to peg it on the bottom of the river, so the current wouldn't wash it away. I drew the short straw. Down I dived, but half way I ran out of air, so up I come again. On the way up, the river washed me false teeth out. We dived for hours and hours but we never found me teeth. I had to spend the rest of the time in that shed with no top teeth.

When we were kids, Mum was always on at us to brush our teeth, but we'd just run outside and play and bugger the teeth. Mum was busy, she had too many kids to keep track of so she didn't know whether we'd brushed them or not.

In the finish we all ended up with rotten teeth. When we got a toothache, we'd have to go into town and the dentist would say, 'It'll have to come out.'

The old dentist we went to in Rylstone used to come from Kandos. He'd come in a couple of times a week to Rylstone. He used to shake like buggery. When he come to give you a needle, it would be shaking coming at you. It used to frighten buggery out of us when we were young. I'd got me four front teeth out and got a plate when I was about twelve. By the time I was twenty, I'd had all the top ones pulled out and wore a denture.

When Charlton was finished, we all got our cheques and had to go back into Brewarrina to get them cashed. We stayed in Bree the night, so we could get the train back to Sydney the next day. You had to go to Sydney to get a train to anywhere else. The train only come through every second day. It left at seven in the morning and got to Sydney at eight in the morning the next day—travelled all day and all night. There were six of us that caught the train. A few shearers, a wool presser, a cook, and a station hand, who was going to Sydney for a holiday. Up to the station we went. Each of us shearers had a carton of beer and a bottle of rum.

The stationmaster said to us, 'You can't go on the train with that.'

'Listen, mate,' I said, 'don't you worry about us. We won't cause no trouble.'

The trains at that time weren't all the old dog boxes. They were starting to get a bit more modern and had a corridor along one side down the length of the carriage, with compartments coming off it. We commandeered one of these compartments. Before the train even left we started playing Slippery Sam—a gambling card game.

The conductor come along and said, 'You behave yourselves with that bloody grog or I'll have to put you off.'

I pulled out a bottle of beer. 'Here mate, go and have a drink, and don't worry about us.'

Away the train went. We got to Byrock and met up with the Bourke mail train there. They hooked it onto our train. Another guard got on and come down and told us we couldn't play cards or drink on the train.

'Here, have a drink yaself, mate,' I said, and poured him out a snort of rum and give him a bottle of beer.

Away the train went again, with us still gambling. At one stage there was three hundred pounds in the centre. Geez, that was a lot of money in those days. A bloody lot of money for six blokes. We kept playing all day and night. The guard come back just as we were getting around Orange and had another bottle of beer.

'I been on some big trains,' he said, 'and I've seen a lot of gambling, but I've never seen a bigger card game anywhere in me bloody life than the one you blokes have got going on here.'

The next morning, we got to Sydney about eight o'clock. The station hand was broke. He didn't have a penny left. 'I'm broke,' he said, 'I gotta turn around and go straight back.' I was a big winner, though. I'd made a bloody lot of money out of it.

'What did ya start with?' I asked him.

'About eighty pound. I was coming to Sydney for me holiday.'

'Here's a hundred pound,' I said. 'Go and have a good holiday.' He thought I was a great bloke.

Anyhow, I got off the train at Sydney. I thought, bugger it, I've got a few quid, I'll stay in Sydney for a week and have a holiday meself. I went and saw Mrs Mac at the boarding house I used to stay at and she said I could stay there.

Me mate, Duncan, was still there, so we got on the grog and were out having fun and playing up. After a few days, he run out of money.

'No, Jack, I can't go out with ya, mate,' he said. 'It's not payday till Monday and I got no more money.'

'That's all right,' I said, 'I got plenty. Here's a fiver.' I give him the five pounds and out we went again.

When the week was up, I caught the Mudgee mail train back to Rylstone. I got in at about six o'clock and walked the mile or so home. As I walked in the door, Mum said, 'Dad said ya'd be home today or tomorra.'

'How'd he know?' I said.

'I don't know but he always knows when ya coming home.'

At that time, the garage down the street had a little 1929 Triumph car, a two-seater. It was like a baby Austin, only smaller. It had a little canvas hood. The bloke at the garage wanted eighty pounds for it. So I went down to the garage and bought it.

Gee, didn't I have some fun in it. I'd wedge me brothers and sisters in it and drive around everywhere. I was a real lunatic in it, too—all these kids piled up in it and going like a bat out of hell. It used to frighten buggery out of poor Mum.

Dad got the kids to write on me car, 'The Boneless Wonder. The only one of its kind in the whole of Australasia. Imported at enormous expense all the way from Calcoola.' That was a mountain up near Nullo Mountain. It's actually spelt Kelgoola but we didn't know how to spell it at the time. So they painted that on the side of me car.

One night, I went to a dance in Rylstone. I had the car parked outside the dance hall. It was winter, and it was raining and cold. I got onto a sheila at the dance and she lived at Kandos, so I said I'd take her home in me car. There was only one door on the car. The spare wheel was on the driver's side. I got in first and she got in after me and shut the door. I had the hood up. I started it up and revved the guts out of it, and I was going nowhere. There were half a dozen blokes behind the car, holding it up at the back with the wheels off the ground. I revved and revved. Then they let it down and I took off like a rocket. I bloody near run over the copper who was walking down the street.

'What the bloody hell are ya doing?' he said.

'The blokes back there are playin' up with me,' I told him.

A week or so later I hooked up with another sheila at the pub in Rylstone. It was a Sunday, and the footballers from Kandos were playing in Rylstone. There was a double brick wall along the footpath outside the front of the pub. I parked me car near there and went upstairs with this sheila, who was the barmaid. Anyway, when the footballers come over to the pub after their game, the publican let them in and they all got on the booze. About two in the morning, I come outside to go home and me car was gone. Some bugger's pinched it, I thought. Then I looked around and saw it. The footballers had picked it up and put it up on top of the brick wall. I had to walk home. The next day, I walked back down the street and the copper come over to me.

'What's ya bloody car doin' up there? Get it down!' he said.

'How the bloody hell am I supposed to get it down?' I said. 'I can't lift it on me own.' There were no cranes in town so I had to wait till all the footballers had finished work that afternoon, so they could come and lift me car down.

In Rylstone they used to call me 'ten to six' because, when I wasn't working or away, I was at the pub at ten in the morning and I was the last one to leave at six at night. There were two pubs in Rylstone. The bottom pub was called The Globe Hotel. That was the workers' pub. That was where I used to drink. The other pub was called The Royal. It was further up the street on the corner almost opposite the Rylstone Hall.

There was an old drunk called Bill, who used to cut a bit of firewood for people around the town, to get a few bob. He was the one Dad give a fright to and he nearly jumped in the dam. He lived over the river in an old hut on the side of the hill. Of a daytime, people would fill him up with grog to make fun of him or to get him to sing.

One day, I was in the pub and the publican said, 'Jack, what about taking old Bill home?'

'Yeah,' I said.

There was a laneway beside the pub that went down to the street. Level with the laneway was the side entrance to the pub. There was also a set of steps that came off the top of the pub's landing, next to the laneway, and went down to the street. I drove me car right up onto the landing from the laneway and opened up the door. The publican staggered out with Bill and put him in. Then instead of backing up the laneway to get out, I drove straight down the front steps of the pub. Well, the publican let out a bellow. Just as I got down onto the footpath, the copper come round the corner. He just looked at me, shook his head and walked away.

Around this time, I got a letter from me showman mate, John, to say he was getting married, and asking if I'd go over for the wedding. I drove down in me little car, through Sofala and over to the wedding in Orange.

After John's wedding, I got some shearing around Rylstone and I hung around there for a while. Then the Rylstone Show come to town and I went down to that. Me mate, John, was there with a merry-go-round. He also had a knock-em-down.

'Give me a hand working this,' he said, 'you'll get a few bob out of it.'

I thought, that's good, and started working it. I got hold of the balls and had the money belt on. I was yelling out, 'Come and knock 'em down. Who'll have a go? One set down to win.' I was yelling out like that all day. There was a dance that night and I was so hoarse from shouting all day that I hardly had enough voice to ask a girl for a dance.

I had a good pair of dancing pumps I always wore to the dances. They were light, with thin soles. I was at a dance in the Rylstone Hall one time, and I got dancing with this girl for a good bit of the night. I asked if I could take her home and she said yes. I had no way of getting her home cos me little car had broken down and I was waiting to get it fixed. So we went on the bus to Kandos and I walked her down to where she lived. I was there till about one or two o'clock in the morning. There was no bus or train back that late, so I had to walk. It was about five miles from Rylstone to Kandos and I walked on the gravel road with these dancing pumps on and completely wore them out.

*My youngest sister, **Pat**, in me little 1929 Triumph Tourer.*

*Me, back left, **Pat**, **Peter**, **Maureen**, **Larry**, **Billy**, and Mum in the passenger seat, all crammed into me little car.*

Chapter Twenty-Two

Lucky Escapes

On me way home from shearing out Bourke one time, I called into Sydney and stayed with me Aunty Min for a week. She was one of Mum's sisters, and Billy Mac's mother. I drove Billy back with me to Rylstone for a holiday. We got to Rylstone in the morning. Mum said Dad was shearing out at Rawdon. 'That'll do,' I said, 'we'll go out and see him.'

So away Billy and I went, out to Rawdon. We went into the shearing shed and were talking to them on the board.

Dad said, 'Hey, Jack, get a handpiece and hook into 'em. We can cut out today if ya shear for three runs. We'll have ta come back tomorra for half a day otherwise.'

All I had on was a pair of shorts, no boots or anything. They give me a handpiece and I started shearing, barefoot.

Billy Mac come up to me, 'Uncle Stan said he's half a sheep in front of ya.'

I said, 'Jesus! He can't shear more than me.' So I hooked into them and away I went, going like mad.

After a while, Billy comes back up to me and says, 'Uncle Stan says he's a sheep in front of ya now. Ya can't catch him.'

I was going like mad, sweating me guts out. I found out I was shearing two to his one. They'd worked it out that the only way they were going to cut out that afternoon was if I was to shear flat out. So Dad was telling Billy, to tell me that he was a sheep in front of me, to make me hurry up—the lying old bastard! And I stuck the machine in me toe, too, *and* never got paid. Dad got that money. He was a cunning old bugger.

When we lived on Misery, Rawdon was a bloody big property. From Bylong Road to Mills's gate was around twelve mile, which would have made Rawdon four or five mile wide by about twelve mile long. She was a fair sized station. They had six shearers and they'd be there for about three weeks to shear all the sheep. A lot of them were two-hundred-a-day men. The government cut some of it up for settlement blokes after the war, for the returned soldiers. One of me mates drew a block on it.

There was a stock and station agent in Rylstone and he had a property near Tooraweenah, up near the Warrumbungle Mountains. One day he asked me and another young fella, called Harvey, if we wanted to go and do some crutching up at Tooraweenah. This young fella was just learning how to shear at the time. He had a little Austin A40 ute that he wanted to go in. But I wanted to take me little car. I'd just had it fixed, and I wanted to give it a good run.

So away we went, me in me little Triumph and Harvey in his ute. We got up the other side of Gulgong, when I hit a pothole and put a hole in me radiator. I left me car in a bloke's yard near the road and we went on in Harvey's ute.

When we got to Tooraweenah, Harvey said, 'Let's have a beer before we go out to the station.' We went up to the pub and there was a bloke sitting on a keg out in the sun.

'Any chance of a beer, mate?' I asked him.

'Yeah, mate,' he said. 'Wait till I put one on.'

He got off the keg, rolled it inside, put it up on the bench and poured us a beer out of it. It was that hot it would scald a bloody pig. 'That's no good to me,' Harvey said. 'Let's go!' So we left and went out to the shed.

When we were finished that shed, Harvey said to me, 'How about we go a bit further out, to Moree? There could be shearing out there.'

Away we went, but when we got to Moree there was no shearing. Over to Bourke we went—no shearing. A bloke there told us there was some shearing work over the border in Queensland. That'll do us, I thought. So we went up to St George and hung around the pub there, asking if there was anyone who wanted any shearers. A bloke in the pub told us there was a man out on the Mitchell road, who was crutching and wanted some shearers. So out we went to see him. He had a six-stand shed and put us on.

It was only a few weeks after Christmas, and it was bloody hot. We'd dragged our bunks out into the open air, hoping to get a breeze. We'd been working there a little while and it was our last night. We only had a few more sheep to do the next day and we were finished. We were lying outside on our bunks and Harvey was fiddling around with a rifle he'd bought off some joker. All of a sudden this big, white cockatoo flew past the huts, heading straight for the homestead.

'Look at this,' said Harvey. And he let drive with this rifle.

Well, you'd have been flat out hitting it with a bloody shotgun any other time, but Harvey managed to hit it with the rifle and knocked it clean out of the sky. Turns out it was the boss's pet cockatoo who'd been out for a fly around and was on its way home. There was a bloody row about that, I'll tell ya. Just as well we were cutting out or he'd have shot Harvey if he'd found out he'd done it.

We cut out and went back into St George, where we got on the booze. Late in the evening, Harvey went out the back to go to the toilet. It was a tin shed and there was a wire fence along it, bordering the pub and the houses. Harvey was staggering around out the back and bashed into this fence where there were chooks and ducks kept on the other side. One particular duck was sitting on a clutch of eggs and she started quacking and yelling. Harvey reached over and grabbed this duck and started pulling out feathers, yelling, 'Shut up, ya bastard!' Then the back door flew open and the owner come out armed with a shotgun. He opened fire at Harvey and blew half the pub dunny away. I grabbed Harvey and we left St George in a hurry.

From St George we went back down to Bourke, where a bloke told us there was still no shearing but there was fruit picking down in Victoria. We went down through Louth and were on our way to Wilcannia.

'Gee, we'll have to be careful down here,' I said, 'it's been raining and it looks like we're in for more.'

We only got about forty or fifty miles out of Louth when a great black cloud come over and down it came. It had been raining before that and we got bogged in the black soil. It stuck to the wheels like glue to a blanket. It builds up in your guards so your wheels can't turn. The car stopped right in the middle of the road. We couldn't move it an inch. We tried digging it out but it was no use.

'We'll be here for a few days now till this clears up,' I said.

We had no food with us, but we had a gun. Anyhow, there was a line of trees not too far away so I figured there had to be a creek or river not far from them. So we grabbed our swags and headed off through the scrub. We could see a tin roof shining off in the distance. We thought it might be a homestead, but when we got closer we saw it was a shearing shed. There was no one around because the shearing had finished. That did us for something to camp in and there was a river nearby. It was the Darling River.

We went poking around in the huts looking for food but there wasn't any. Harvey looked out the back and saw two loaves of bread out on the rubbish pile. They were as hard as concrete so we left them and went down to the river. We poked around and found a hook and line and dug up a worm from the bank, and put a line in. We caught a little yellowbelly that we cooked up and ate.

The next day we were starting to get pretty hungry. So we went and got the stale loaves of bread. Harvey soaked them with water from the water tank that was nearby, while I stoked up a big fire in the stove that was in the kitchen for the shearers' cook to use. We stuck the loaves in the oven soaking wet and heated them up. They tasted bloody beautiful!

After a day or two, it had dried out enough to dig the mud out from under the wheels of the ute and we were on our way again. We got to Wilcannia and stocked up on food. Then we went down onto the banks of the Darling and camped there for a day or two. I thought we might get some fish there because I'd heard that the Aborigines had made a fish trap near where we were camped. I asked another fella whereabouts it was and he told me. So I poked around down in the river till I found it. They'd made it by packing rocks together in a circle. Somehow, the fish were able to swim in and not get out again. The bloke had said there was always fish in it, and there were two yellowbelly in it when I looked, so I grabbed them. But like a bloody galah, I got out on the wrong side of the river to where I was camped. I had to try and swim across holding onto the fish. I had no chance. I let one go, and it wasn't long before I had to let the other one go, too.

The next day we decided to head down to Mildura and see if we could get on fruit picking there. Harvey thought it was a good idea to catch some fish and take them with us to Mildura to sell. We got about a dozen in the fish trap, put them in a bag and set off. We were getting down towards White Cliffs and it was getting hotter and hotter. We were nearly to Mildura and there was a hell of a stink coming from the bag. We had to chuck the fish—they were far to stinking to sell, or to eat. When we got to Mildura, we were told that the fruit picking was all finished and every bugger was leaving, so we went back to Broken Hill looking for work.

'If you're not born in Broken Hill, you've got no chance of getting any work,' we were told. So we camped out on the flats near Broken Hill for a couple of days and poked around the town, then we packed up and headed for home. I swam in the public pool in Broken Hill. That was the first time I'd been to a public swimming pool. I'd swum in plenty of creeks and rivers but not a pool.

When we got back to Rylstone, I woke up that I'd left me car in some bloke's yard near Gulgong. So Harvey and I set off again to get me car. We forgot to take a towrope with us, so we cut a piece of fencing wire from someone's fence and hooked it onto the car. Harvey took off and away we went.

I've never had such a rough ride in all me life. I thought I'd never make it alive to Mudgee. I reckon from Gulgong to Mudgee me car only hit the ground twice. I parked me car in a yard in Mudgee and left it. I thought, she's buggered, and I didn't have the money to fix her. I ended up getting it home somehow and give it to me brother, Peter, later on.

When I got back to Rylstone, Bobby, one of me cousins, who used to train racehorses, come up to see me about a horse he was training.

'Come out to the track with me and ride this bloody thing, it pulls like mad. I can't hold it,' he said. Mardawn it was called.

He took another horse as well. He had two he wanted to work. Off we went to the racetrack. 'We won't work them together,' he said. So we tied the other horse up in a stall and he took Mardawn out onto the track.

'On second thoughts, I better ride Mardawn in case the owner comes. He said he was coming out this morning. He don't like you. He wouldn't let you ride her.'

'He won't worry,' I said.

'Yeah, he will. I'd better ride her. But she pulls like mad.'

He started off just past the winning post and rode it round the track. As he come around towards the winning post the second time, the horse was flying. He was yelling, 'I can't hold her! I can't hold her!'

'Let her run!' I yelled back. 'She'll knock up.'

But no bloody fear was he going for that. As soon as he got near the winning post, he jumped off her in full flight. Holy, bloody hell! He went sailing up the track, spinning on his head like a top. What a bloody mess he made of himself. I ran out to him and he was buggered. He was knocked out flat. Geez, I thought, he's killed hisself. Just then the owner come along.

'What's happened?'

'Mardawn just threw Bobby,' I said. 'Ya'll have to get him to town, he's bloody crook.'

The owner got his car and brought it up onto the track and we put Bobby in the back. 'What about me horse?' he said.

'Bugger ya horse. I'll get it. Get him to town.'

He set off with Bobby and I caught Mardawn. I was supposed to be watching the other horse, but when Bobby fell off I forgot about that and raced out to him. So while all this was happening, this other horse broke away from the stall and took off around the track, full bloody pelt. I managed to catch him, too, and I was riding one and leading the other out the gate of the track, when the owner of this other horse come along.

'Oh, you've already worked him. How'd he go?'

I just said, 'He went all right.' Nobody was on him but he got a good work out.

After I got the horses back to the stables, I went up to the hospital to see Bobby, but they wouldn't let me go in. They said he was too crook and was delirious. So I went down to the pub and had a few drinks—then I was delirious.

That night after tea, I called in at the pub again on the way up to see Bobby and had a few more drinks. Then I got on the old motorbike I had at the time, to go up to the hospital. To get to the hospital you had to go up Abbot's Hill. It was a really steep, short hill. As I was going up it, I went to change gears and tipped the bike over backwards on meself. Down I went—hide off me everywhere. I got back on and kept going. When I got to the hospital they wanted to know what had happened to me. They thought I was there to get fixed up but I told them I was only there to see Bobby. They still wouldn't let me see him. They thought he had a broken neck, but he ended up being all right after. Geez, he was tough. It would have killed anybody else. He was pretty bloody crook for a while there, though.

Lucky Escapes

So anyhow, I was still poking around Rylstone and Anzac Day come up. I had a set of two-up pennies, and I used to get behind the pub with all the diggers on ANZAC Day, playing two-up. I had a good ring going down behind the bottom pub this particular ANZAC Day, when the copper come along.

'Righto! That's enough. Get out of here with them, Turner.'

'Righto,' I said.

Half an hour later, I was at it again. Then I moved it up to the top pub when they opened. We were playing it up in the bar and in come the copper. 'I told ya to cut it out. Now get out of here with them,' he said.

'Righto,' I said, and went back down to the bottom pub again.

I started the game up out the back. I had a good ring going so I got into the bar then. 'Up and do 'em, spinner! Up and do 'em, spinner!' I was yelling. I bent down to pick the pennies up off the floor and a big boot come down on top of one of them.

'Shift ya bloody foot off that,' I said. I went to grab his trouser leg, looked up and it was this bloody copper. He grabbed me be the scruff of the neck and lifted me up.

'I've told ya twice already and I'm not gunna tell ya again,' he said. 'Get out of here or I'll lock ya up.' He dragged me to the door, give me a boot up the arse and sent me down the stairs. 'If I see ya in town again tonight, Turner, I'll lock ya up.'

That's good enough for me, I thought, so I went home.

The stock and station agent come up to me in town one day. 'Will ya take a mob of cattle out to Tong Bong for me, Jack?'

I didn't have any work on at the time, so I said, 'Righto, mate.'

I saddled up me horse and went down to the stockyards to get the cattle. Me mate from town, Johnny, come with me. He was the one that was with me when we tried to pinch the watermelons. Gee, he was a funny bugger. Anyhow, we drove these cattle out to Tong Bong and were cantering along on our way back.

'Geez, I'm thirsty,' Johnny said.

'So am I,' I said. 'I'm dry.'

We got back to town and were riding up the street. Bugger this, I thought, I'll go in and have a beer. I was on Rainbow and he was a bloody good horse. I rode him straight up the steps and into the bar of the Globe Hotel.

'Is there any chance of a beer?' I said.

There were only half a dozen people in the pub but they all took off. Rainbow was slipping and sliding all over the place.

'Get out of here, ya bloody lunatic,' yelled the publican, 'or I'll get the copper.'

Chapter Twenty-Three

The Empty Rum Bottle

When I got back from Tong Bong, a bloke I knew asked if I wanted a pen out at White Rock. He said they had one shearer out there but they needed another one. He was a wool classer. He said he was starting that day and could take me out with him. So I grabbed me swag and some beer and a bottle of rum, and away we went.

The other shearer had started in the morning but he hadn't done many sheep. We stayed in a hut with three bunks in it. I put me swag in the hut, me bottle of rum on the table and the beer under the bed. Then I got changed into me shearing gear and did two runs. When I'd finished, I come back to the hut, got cleaned up and went and had tea. I went back to the hut and had a nip of rum and give this other shearer a snort. Then the wool classer come along and asked if I'd like to go into town with him and be the gate opener. There were half a dozen gates to open on the way to the town. So away I went.

He sorted out his business in town while I stayed at the pub. When he'd finished, he come and got me and we stayed there and had a couple of beers till closing time. Then we went home. He was staying at the homestead, so he dropped me off at the shearers' hut. In I went and lit the lamp and here's this bloody shearer sprawled out sideways across his bed, blind drunk, and me rum bottle empty. Next day, he was so sick he couldn't shear. He was buggered.

I run into the same joker about thirty years later, when me brothers, Tony and Billy, and I took Dad's ashes back to Rylstone. We tipped them out on the flat on Misery on Anzac Day, 1980. Then we drove down through Glen Alice to the places where Dad and I used to shear and go rabbiting, looking at the huts we used to camp in. We went up to one place where Dad and I did a lot of rabbiting and went looking for the old bloke who used to own it.

'No, he's moved,' the joker living there told me. 'He retired and moved to Sydney.'

'I used to camp in that old hut up there,' I told him. 'Can I take me brothers up and have a look?'

'Yeah, go up and have a look,' he said. 'There's an old bloke up there but he won't hurt ya.'

'Who's that?'

'Old Spencer.'

'Geez,' I said, 'I know him. I shore with him out at White Rock. I'll go up and see him.' Up we went, and he was sitting on the verandah. 'G'day!' I said.

'G'day.'

'You pinched a bottle of rum off me,' I said.

'No bloody fear I didn't. The only bottle of rum I ever pinched was off Jack Turner.'

'That's me!'

'Bloody hell,' he said, 'You was black when I knew ya.'

It would have been easily thirty odd years since I'd seen him. I used to have jet-black hair and a good suntan when I knew him. Me brother Tony said to me when we were leaving, 'Christ! He still remembered.'

It was two brothers that owned the property at White Rock back when I was shearing there. One was married to a big snob of a woman, and the other one was a real knock-about, old codger. Sugarbag we called him. He used to go to town on his horse with a sugar bag over his shoulder, and that's what he put all his groceries in. His brother would ride into town all dressed up with leggings and riding boots, and saddlebags on his saddle, but old Sugarbag didn't give a bugger. He was one of the boys. He lived in the shearers' hut. He cooked on an open fire in there. His bunk was up the kitchen end and the shearers' bunks were up the other end. He always had four or five big sides of bacon hanging up in his end, with the fire going all the year round and smoke everywhere. It was the most beautiful bacon I've ever tasted.

He said to me, 'Jack, you supply the rum and we'll have a snort each night, and I'll supply the bacon and eggs and we'll have a bloody good feed. It'll be better than that stuff ya get up at the homestead.'

'That'll do me, old mate,' I said. And by geez, we used to have some good feeds.

I helped cart the gravel that that homestead was built on while I was working for one of the carriers in Rylstone. He never had a tip-truck at the time. You had to shovel it on and shovel it off. Tip-trucks come later. Old Norm, the pig farmer, whose kids Dad and I looked after a few years before, he was the one that built that homestead.

It wasn't long after I finished shearing at White Rock that I was in the pub in Rylstone, and a joker come in and sit down beside me. Brian he was called.

We were yarning for a while and he said to me, 'Do ya know anywhere I can get a dozer driver, mate?'

I said, 'Yeah.'

'Where?'

'Me.'

'Can ya drive a dozer?'

'Yeah.'

'I got a job for ya,' he said. 'I'm gunna start clearing property at a place out over the Pinnacle Swamp Road. White Rock.'

'Oh, yeah,' I said, 'I know the place. I just finished shearing there.'

'Oh well, ya know it, that'll do.'

'I'll go home and get me swag and we can go.' So I went home and got me swag, packed a bit of gear and away we went.

Brian said, 'I'm camping in the huts there at White Rock.'

'We better take plenty of rum and grog,' I said. 'The old fella in the hut there likes a nip.'

Anyhow, away we went, and I started work out there. I didn't know much about dozer driving. I'd never even been on a dozer before. We were pulling the scrub down with a big wire rope and I got tangled up in it.

'You don't know much about bloody dozing,' he said to me.

'No,' I said, 'but I'll learn.' So he kept me on.

We were there for a couple or three weeks. We cleared the property and put a dam in for them.

Old Sugarbag and his brother that owned the property had another two brothers, and they each had a property down at Glen Alice. They'd both been prisoners of war. They also had two sisters that were nurses in the war.

The Empty Rum Bottle

They never come home. They were both serving on a hospital ship that got blown up by the Japs.

We went down to Glen Alice and cleared a big lump of ground for one of these fellas, and put a dam in for the other. We were working for them for about three or four months all up. We used to go to town of a weekend and get on the booze. One day, we were going back to Glen Alice after getting on the booze, and we had a heap of grog with us.

Brian said, 'Pull up here at this stock reserve.'

On the way down to Glen Alice, just out of Rylstone past the cemetery, was a TSR—Travelling Stock Reserve. There was a lot of scrub in it. We pulled up there and lit a big fire.

He said, 'We'll have a few drinks and camp here tonight, and go down to work in the mornin'.'

We had a bloody big fire going cos it was cold weather, and we got on the booze. I always had a comb in me hip pocket. I was always combing me hair when I was younger. Anyhow, I woke up in the morning and went to get the comb out of me pocket and one end of it was all shrivelled up. The heat from the fire had melted all the teeth and never burnt me trousers. I'm buggered if I know how it happened.

I come back to Rylstone when I'd finished dozer driving and was knocking around doing nothing much, when I met up with this bloke we called Sticky. He had the surname Glew so we called him Sticky, Sticky Glew. He was in the Buffalo Lodge, too. We were at a meeting in Rylstone one night. Now and then, they'd get people to sing a song or do a trick or whatever, to entertain us. Sticky and I were there this night and there was a bloke there doing tricks. Jeff he was called and he was a magician, so he reckoned.

He was doing different odd tricks and then he says, 'I want someone with a tie on to come up.' So Sticky went up. This Jeff said, 'I'm going to do a trick with you and your tie. I'm going to cut your tie in half but it'll be all right. It'll still be the same.'

Sticky said, 'That's all right.'

So he got a hold of Sticky, said a few words and cut his tie off about an inch from where the knot was. Then he said to Sticky, 'There's ya tie.' It was cut clean off in two pieces. Not much of a bloody trick.

Sticky and his brother were real keen fishermen, so we decided we'd go fishing. Away we went, out to Bourke, the three of us and Sticky's brother-in-law. A bloke in the pub there told us the best place to go fishing was down around Louth. That was about sixty mile out of Bourke. We drove out to Louth and had a few drinks in the pub and then went down to the river and pitched a camp. We set lines up there for a couple of days but never got anything. We were walking along the river this day, about half a mile from our camp, when we come across a professional fisherman. He'd been fishing for cod to sell and he had a bloody heap of them all laid out on the ground. We asked him how much he wanted for them. I think we paid about ten bob for these dozen or more fish. We packed them up in our old icebox and headed back to Rylstone with them.

Mum said she didn't want any and we had a job getting rid of them to anyone else. Sticky come up with the idea of getting the football club to let us use their name to raffle the rest of the fish. We'd give them five pound, and we might end up paying for our trip. The others thought it was a good idea, so I went to see the football club and asked them about it and told them we'd give them five pound. They said that would do them.

We give them five pound and got some raffle tickets. Away we went to the two pubs in Rylstone and raffled two fish. We sold fifty or sixty tickets at a time, for a bob each. Then we went to Kandos and sold them in the two pubs out there. We ended up with about ten pound more each than the trip cost us, and we still had two fish left when we got home. Me and Sticky ended up eating them. We had one fish each.

Chapter Twenty-Four

Condo

I think it would have been around 1951 by this time. I was poking around Rylstone but there was nothing much happening, so I went down to The Globe Hotel, drinking. I used to knock around with the brother of the girl who was a barmaid there. He and I used to drink together. He packed up and went to Sydney and I lost track of him. Anyhow, this barmaid said she'd just had a letter from her brother, Frank, and he was out at Condobolin. He was a mechanic out there.

I thought, that sounds all right to me. So I went home and packed me swag and said to Mum, 'I'm off out to Condo, shearing.'

I caught the train to Sydney and from there out to Condobolin. Frank's sister had told me he'd be at the Commercial Hotel. I carried me swag down to the Commercial Hotel and walked into the bar. I had a beer and asked the barmaid if she knew Frank. She said yeah and that he'd be in at about one o'clock. I stayed and had a couple of beers and then in walked Frank.

'What the bloody hell are you doin' here?' he said.

Frank was a good mate of the publican and he introduced me. The publican asked me what I was doing out there. I told him I was looking for shearing and asked him where I could stay.

'We got no spare rooms,' he said, 'but you can sleep on a bed on the verandah.'

Frank had a small room upstairs, so he said I could put me swag in his room. I slept on the verandah. I was there for two or three days. Then the shearing contractor come in looking for a shearer.

'That'll suit me,' I said.

'Where are ya camped?' he said.

'Here.'

'When can ya start?'

'Whenever ya ready.'

So that Sunday evening, I packed up and left with the shearing contractor. We went a good way out, about a hundred mile out from Condobolin. That shed went for about three weeks. I stayed there till the cut out come. Then I went back to the Commercial Hotel and got the same little bed out on the verandah. I was there for a week before another shed come up. It lasted a couple of weeks and then back I come again.

Frank had got a bigger room by then, with two beds in it. So I shared that room with him. By that time I'd got to know the publican and his family well. Frank and I used to drink with them at night and have our meals with them.

The publican had a daughter who was about four years younger than me. Her name was Brenda. She was a good-looking sort and I started knocking around with her. I was treated like one of the family then. It was six o'clock closing in those days. We used to clean up the bar after closing and have a beer and listen to the races.

She was a nurse and worked up at the hospital. When she was on day shift, she'd come in of a night and I'd sit for hours just talking and drinking and brushing her hair. She had long, dark hair. I used to brush her hair for hours on end. Then another shed would come up and I'd go out shearing again for a week or two. There were some good sheds out that way.

Then the shearing cut out for a while and I got a job with a bloke driving a truck, carting wheat and hay. This bloke had the first forty-foot semi-trailer to come to Australia. One time, we had a load of hay to take from Jemalong to Dandaloo. Six hundred bales of lucerne hay we put on the truck. A big load. We tied it all down with ropes. As we were going across a narrow grid, up the other side of Nyngan, there was a big plough disc on top of the strainer post. The bloke that was driving misjudged the gap and got a bit too close to the post, and the disc cut nearly all the ropes down one side. We looked back after we'd crossed the grid and saw bales of hay falling off everywhere. We had to load it all back up again. It took us bloody hours.

This bloke owned two trucks. He had the forty-footer and a thirty-six footer, I think it was. We carted a load of wheat on the forty-footer from the paddock into Bogan Gate. Six hundred and thirteen bags we loaded by hand that day. There was a hundred and eighty pound in a bag, if I remember right. That's nearly eighty-two kilos. Fifty-four ton went across the weighbridge at Bogan Gate.

After that, we did five trips to Adelaide carting pigs. I was his off-sider and spare driver. When we had a load of pigs to take down, we'd leave Sunday evening with them. First though, we'd get the pigs into the yard. There was about five or six boars in a load. We'd cut their tusks off with bolt cutters so they couldn't hurt one another. Then we'd let them fight all night so they'd be worn out and wouldn't wreck the float going to Adelaide.

While he was cutting the tusks off, I'd try and catch the next boar and tie him up ready. We used to put a rope around his jaw and pull it up tight. I threw a rope around this boar and he went swish with his nose. I thought, well, you missed me, mate. Then after we'd cut his tusks off, I bent down to untie the rope, looked down and there was blood everywhere. Gee, I thought, we've made a mess of him, but it wasn't him bleeding, it was me! He'd hit me hand and ripped between me two fingers with his tusks. I had to get it stitched up.

After we'd finished carting pigs, I come across a bloke who wanted a crutcher. That'll do me, I thought. One of the sheds we went to was Big Burrawong. It was cut up by this time, but it had been one of the biggest sheds around—101 stands on a double-sided board. But they cut the station into four sections. We were at the Burrawong shed.

I stayed in Condo for a while. One day I got a letter from Mum with another letter inside it. It was from Duncan. It would have been twelve months or more since I'd last seen Duncan in Sydney. There was a five pound note in it and a letter which read, *It took me a long time to get it, mate, but here's your fiver. Thanks very much.* He was a bloody good lad.

I was in the Commercial Hotel one day and a joker come in and he wanted a shearer out towards Lake Cargelligo for a couple of weeks.

'Righto. I'll go, mate,' I said.

He said, 'I'll take ya out.'

He had a Ford Mainline ute. It was a fairly new model. He picked me up on the Sunday afternoon. I was out there a couple of weeks or more, then the cut out come and we finished about dinnertime.

'When do ya want to go back to town, Jack?' he said.

'I want to go this evening, old mate.'

'Righto, I'd better take ya in now, cos I want to get back and do some work with these sheep and stuff.'

He threw me swag in the back of this ute and away we went. And, holy bloody hell, it could go! We were about a hundred mile out from Condo. It was a good road and he would have been doing a hundred mile an hour when we run into a flock of galahs. Well, they went everywhere. Half a dozen of them got wedged between the grill and the radiator of the ute. We only went another few mile when we had to pull over. The bloody noise they were making, you couldn't hear the revs of the car. When we pulled up we saw that they were all wedged arse first into the grill. Soon as we stopped, we poked a couple of them out with a stick and they all flew off. They weren't hurt but what a bloody racket they made.

While I was waiting for the next shed to come along, I got a job with the council. We poured a concrete causeway across a road just outside Condo. Two of us with shovels mixed the concrete. Forty shovelfuls of gravel on a flat surface and two bags of cement, we mixed it up with a shovel. That was one mix. We kept doing them all day till we finished the causeway.

After that I went to work for a station owner called Johnno. He had a big property about eighty odd mile out of Condo. He wanted a shearer that would do his own shearing and rouseabouting, and sharpen his own cutters—do his own experting. Experting means sharpening combs and cutters, and repairing your machinery. He just wanted the one bloke because he had to do his own mustering and cooking, while his missus was in Sydney. He wanted someone to poke along steady. He used to buy and sell sheep all the time—and he was a bugger for talking to himself.

He'd be standing on the board waiting for me to finish a sheep, and he'd be talking away to himself, 'Yes, I'll sell this many, and I'll buy that many, and I'll go to so and so and get some.' He used to talk like that to himself all the time.

There was an old joker who lived there with him. He used to do a bit of work around the place and help in the kitchen at times, but he was a bugger to get on the booze and go walkabout. He'd get on the grog and go away for a week or more into the scrub. You wouldn't see him for a while. Then when he got off the booze, he'd come back and stay for a month or so, then he'd go bush again.

When I first got there, Johnno told me that this old bloke had gone walkabout. I'd been working there for about a week and Johnno had been doing the cooking.

One morning, while we were having breakfast, Johnno said, 'This old codger must be comin' off the grog, he's been in and pinched a feed in the night. I'll trick him in a night or two.'

The house was quite big and it had a verandah all the way around it that was fly-screened. There were four doors on the verandah, one on each side of the house. All the rooms in the house had a door that led out onto the verandah. I was camped out on the verandah. So that night, he locked all the doors and only left one of the side doors open, so the old bloke could get in.

In the morning, we got up and Johnno said, 'He's been in again and got some tucker. I'll have some bloody fun with him tonight.'

That night, we had tea and after that, he told me to come and give him a hand. He got some old kerosene tins and an old billy and put them inside one another, and put some stones in them. Then he put them up on some shelves that were along the wall a bit higher than the table. He hooked a length of thin wire onto them and attached it to the door, so when this joker opened the door, it would pull all the tins down and make a racket. We went to bed and waited. About midnight we heard a clatter and a bang, then a yell, then we heard the fences outside rattling as he took off over them. He never bothered coming in to get a feed. It frightened buggery out of him. After a few days he come back, and he was all right then.

I was there for three or four weeks. On about the third week, Johnno's wife come back from Sydney and she brought a girlfriend with her to stay for a while. Now Johnno loved to play tricks on people. No one was safe. In the house, they only had kerosene lamps. One night, he went and put some pillows in this lady's bed and covered them up, and put his hat near them to make it look like there was a man lying in her bed. Later on, she took a candle and lit the lamp in her room, turned around and saw the figure in her bed. She let out a scream and Johnno's wife come in to see what was wrong.

'There's a man in my bed,' she said.

'No, that's just Johnno playing tricks. Don't worry about him,' said Johnno's missus.

A couple of nights later, Johnno come out onto the verandah where I was. 'You watch this tonight. Geez, I'll have some fun with this woman,' he said to me.

So he went and got into her bed, put his hat over his head and waited for her to come in. In she comes to go to bed. She lit the lamp and spotted the lump and the hat on her bed. Hah, hah, Johnno, she thought, you're not going to catch me again. I'm a wake-up to your tricks. And she started to get undressed.

Johnno thought to himself, I'd better get out of here, so he jumped up out of the bed. Well, the poor woman got the fright of her life. She took off outside screaming her bloody head off.

When I finished out at Johnno's place I come back to Condo. The publican where I was staying had a Peugeot car. One day he said he was going out shooting.

'Righto,' I said, 'I'll go with ya.'

Away we went, Frank and I, and the publican and his missus. Way out of town we went onto a quiet road. We saw a doe roo sitting up by the road. This bloke was going to have a shot at her.

'Wait till I get out,' I told him. 'Because she's got a joey in her pouch and if you hit her, she'll drop the little one, or he'll jump out and I'll grab him.'

So he let drive and shot the kangaroo straight through the head. She hit the ground and the little joey, he didn't know what he was doing. I raced up and grabbed him. He was biting and kicking and scratching and making a hell of a fuss. We took him back to the pub and the publican's missus nursed him and made a bag up for him to sit in. She reared him on milk. He was a great little fella. He used to hop around the bar of a night and play with us. We used to have great fun with him. He'd come in the bar with us in the evening and we'd look after him. When he got a bit bigger, we used to give him a little bit of beer in an ashtray and he'd drink it up. Then one night, we give him a bit too much and he was as silly as a wheel. He was trying to hop but he couldn't keep his feet, and he went slipping and sliding all over the bar room floor.

Then I got a job shearing at a station about thirty mile out of Condo, it was a four- or five-stand shed. The contractor there had one of the first Holden utilities that come out. We were going into town this particular Friday afternoon, him and me in the front and two rouseabouts sitting in the back of the ute. We were slowly driving along this dirt track through a paddock to get to the road, when he run into a mob of kangaroos. There were hundreds of them hopping everywhere. Suddenly a big old red roo hopped in the back of the ute with these two rouseabouts. Well, bloody hell! I've never seen such a shemozzle. The rouseabouts were yelling and trying to jump out, and so was the roo.

When I used to come into town of a weekend from shearing, the publican let me work behind the bar with them. Frank and I used to drink something terrible. We'd be drinking away, then we'd start drinking what we called 'depth charges'. That was a beer with rum in it. Gee, it used to put some fire into us.

We used to play darts of an evening after the pub closed. At that time, me brother, Tony, was an apprentice jockey in Sydney. We used to get the good oil off him. The pub was right opposite the Police Station. The old Crown Sergeant, he got to know about Tony being a jockey and us getting the good oil, and he wanted it, too. He used to let us keep drinking of a night after closing time, and he'd come over and have a drink with us. Tony used to ring at a certain time every Friday night with the good oil. This particular Friday night, I'd had too much to drink, and I was asleep on the settee in the office when Tony rang, and the Crown Sergeant picked it up.

'Is Jack there?' Tony asked.

'Yeah, but he's asleep. He's full,' the sergeant said. 'I'll take the message but if ya don't tip us a winner I'll lock him up.'

There was another bloke in Condobolin who had come from Rylstone. He left Rylstone before the war. He used to train coursing dogs. He always had a good coursing dog. He'd let me know about these dogs and I'd let him know about the horses. One day, we got word that the twenty-one squad—that was the undercover police—were coming up to raid the SP bookies.

I said to this fella, 'Don't have a bet here because the twenty-one squad's coming, so ya'll want to be careful.'

He went up to the billiard room, where there was another SP bookie, to back this horse that Tony had told us to back. He just got in there and the race was getting ready to start. He was walking up to the window to have a bet when the police come in and raided the joint. They grabbed him and all the rest of the blokes that were in there. He had to listen to the horse win and he didn't have a penny on it. And it paid about twenty to one.

I was working behind the bar for the publican one night and there was an old fella who used to come in. He used to do a bit of bag sewing and other casual work around the town. He always drank rum, straight. 'I'll have an over-proof, straight,' he used to say.

The publican had got in some Club 30 rum. It was thirty-three and a third over-proof. This old codger come in this day, and he had a couple of cockys with him.

'We'll have a drink,' he said. 'I'll shout. Two beers, and I'll have a rum please, Jack.'

'What sort of rum do ya want?' I said.

'Over-proof. I only drink over-proof.'

'Do ya want some water with it?' I said, and put the water bottle down beside his drink, and put the beers down.

'No. I don't drink that stuff,' he said. 'I'm a man, I only drink a man's drink.'

So I picked the bottle of water up and took it away, but I didn't tell him that I'd given him this bloody Club 30 over-proof.

'Here's luck,' he said. He took a big swig of the rum and went running up and down the bar looking for the water bottle. He couldn't speak—it took his bloody breath.

I'd been in Condo about twelve months or more, when Norm, the pig farmer whose wife had nearly died, come over to Condo to build a garage. He was a scaffolder and a builder by trade. They were building a garage on the opposite corner to the Commercial Hotel. He used to come and drink with Frank and me. Slippery we called him.

One day, I said that if we could get a plug of gelly—that's gelignite, we could get some fish the easy way.

'I can get ya the gelly,' Slippery said.

'I know where there's a waterhole,' I said. 'We'll go and blow it.'

'Righto,' he said, 'we'll go out Sunday.'

On Sunday, away we went—a couple of mile out of town it was—to a big waterhole on the Lachlan River. We had a seven-pound treacle tin, which we put about eight or nine sticks of gelly in and a fuse about a foot long. We lit it, then dropped it over the bank into the water hole and ran for cover. There was a big gum tree on the bank of the river, near where we dropped it in. We hid behind some other trees a fair distance away. There was an almighty explosion and the big gum tree shot straight out of the ground and landed on the other side of the river. What a bloody mess! We didn't get a lot of fish because it blew them all to buggery.

When we got back to town, the publican said, 'I thought the bloody Japs were here.' Didn't it make a row?

It was while Slippery was working out there at Condo that his eldest son was killed. Billy—he was one of the three kids that Dad and I had looked after years before. He was a passenger in a car coming from Lue to Rylstone.

The car hit a tree and the branches went straight through him. Dad was working as yardsman at the Rylstone Hospital at the time. He did whatever work he could get when he wasn't shearing or rabbiting. He told me he had to cut off the branches that were sticking out of Billy so they could get him in the coffin. What a bloody tragedy! He was only about eighteen.

At the next shed I got near Condobolin there was a young rouseabout that had a motorbike, and a couple of shearers from Crookwell that liked shooting. There were plenty of roos on this property that we used to shoot. I always had a .22 rifle with me and they had rifles. One weekend we decided to go shooting. There was pretty thick scrub and a clearing on either side.

I said to this young rouseabout, 'You and I will go through the scrub on the motorbike and we'll hunt the roos out into the open for the other blokes to shoot.'

We worked it all out and they said it would be all right, so away we went through the scrub on this motorbike. This kid was going like buggery on his bike and I had me rifle over his shoulder, just shooting at anything to make a noise and drive the roos out. The next thing, he and I were sailing backwards and the bike was going forwards. We'd run into a wire fence. The two wires were just above the handlebars of the bike and they knocked us clean off. How I didn't shoot him, I'll never know.

When I come back from that shed, I got word to say that me sister, Marie, was getting married, and I had to go home for the wedding. I thought it was a bloody long way to go by train, so I told Frank that I wanted a little car to drive home. He looked around and got me a little Morris 840 Tourer, 1947 model. It was a nice little car. I thought, right, I can go home now. I took Brenda, the publican's daughter, with me. I wrote and told Mum I was bringing her home for the wedding. We drove across from Condobolin to Rylstone. There was no special treatment given to anyone at home and she just had to bunk in with a couple of me sisters.

After the wedding, we drove back to Condo. There was no shearing at the time and I was short of money, so I was looking around for work. A bloke said that the council was looking for a burr cutter, to cut galvanised burr on the stock route from Condobolin out to Ivanhoe. A pound a day it was paying. That'll do me, I thought. I'll live in me car as I go and just cut burrs. I had a couple of water bags and a drum of water with me. I'd chop burrs in the week, then come to town on the weekends. I ate and slept in me car. I just cut burrs all day. I did more than me eight hours. At daylight I'd be up and at 'em, and cut till it was dark, then I'd go to bed. Cutting galvanised burr on the stock route, talking to meself. It was a bloody long way from town, too.

After that, I got a job with a builder who was building a picture theatre in Condo. I carried the concrete up the steps to pour the projector room floor. I carried two four-gallon buckets of concrete at a time, up the steps, all day till it was done. I got one pound a day for that.

When that job finished, I had nothing to do and was running short of money again. All the other shearing was finished, so a couple of the shearers got a job burning off on a station about fifty mile out of Condobolin. I found out the blacksmith in Condobolin wanted charcoal. He was paying four bob a wheat bag for it. So I went up to the baker's shop and got a dozen flour bags. They were the same size as a wheat bag. They held 160lbs of flour. Then I went out to these fellas where they were burning off and sifted the charcoal and bagged it. I got eight or ten bags. That's all that would fit on me little car. I had it tied on the bonnet and everywhere. When I was driving past the cop shop on the way to the blacksmith, a copper pulled me over.

'Well, Jack,' he said, 'there's one thing we can't book ya for and that's vagrancy.'

I was as black as buggery but it got me a few bob.

Frank and I had been living at the pub for a couple of years. I went away shearing for a few weeks and when I come back the publican had sold up and moved away. Brenda had gone with them. I never saw her again.

Frank and I shifted out of the pub after that. We didn't like the new publican. And he was charging us more than the other fella. Down near where Frank worked there was an old, one-roomed shop. It was next to the garage where he worked, so we rented that for about ten bob a week.

There was no furniture in it, so we got a double bed frame and set it on four kerosene tins. Someone give us a mattress and we put our swags on it. We used to camp together on that. We used the toilet and shower behind the garage where Frank worked to shower and shave and do our washing. We got a couple of tea chests, one we turned upside down and used as a table and the other we used for dirty washing. Instead of washing every couple of days or even weeks, we'd just go and buy a new shirt and throw the dirty one in the tea chest. One day, we decided to do some washing. We had a tea chest full of shirts and singlets. It took us all bloody day. We'd eat at the cafés or the pub for our meals.

I'd go away shearing, leave me gear there, and come in on the weekend if I wasn't too far away. When we were living in the pub, the milkman used to come in with the milk. We had a bottle of rum in our room and he'd pour us out a rum and milk when he was doing his rounds, about three or four o'clock in the morning. He'd give us a morning starter when he was delivering milk to the pub. This milkman, Jack he was called, would always have a drink with us, too, at three or four in the morning

When we shifted down to the shop, he said he'd come down there and give us a drink. He used to come in, sing out, 'Come on, you bastards, get up. Rum time.' And he'd pour us out half a glass of rum and half of milk. That was a nice way to start the day.

Then another fella that we knew come to town and he couldn't find anywhere to stay, so we said he could stay with us. Then there were three of us in the one bed. The next morning, Jack come in and sang out, and three heads struck up out of the bed.

'Bloody hell!' he said. And he poured out three drinks of rum and milk, and one for himself.

Anyhow, the next day we met another bloke and he had nowhere to stay, so we told him he could come down and stay with us. There were four of us in this double bed then.

Jack come the next morning yelling, 'Righto, get up,' and four heads stuck up. 'How many more are ya going to put in that bloody bed?' he said.

This shop we lived in had a big yard out the back. I had me car there one day and I said to Frank, 'Give us ya grease gun? I'll grease me car.'

I lay down under the car out in the yard to grease it, and I went to sleep. Frank couldn't wake me up. He and his mate that was there turned the hose on me and I was still sound asleep. Then they got me, tied me hands and feet to the front bumper bar and drove the car backwards around the yard, and I was still sound asleep. I don't know what time it was when I woke up but me feet and hands were tied to the bumper bar of me bloody car.

Me sitting next to the Morris 840 I bought to go home to Rylstone for Marie's wedding.

Wop *and me dressed up for Marie's wedding. Rylstone Hotel in background.*

*Me on the left of **Marie**, and **Peter** on the right. Mum behind Peter.*

*Me on the left with **Larry** in front, **Peter** on the right with **Billy** in front, dressed up for Marie's wedding.*

Chapter Twenty-Five

Smashed Up at Cooper's Sheep Dip

It was the end of 1953 when I left Condobolin. I was shearing out at a four stand shed near there, when I met up with a Scotsman called Tommy. We used to go to town together and yarn and drink. I'd decided to go down the Riverina looking for a bit of shearing.

'That'll do,' he said. 'Do ya want a mate? Cos I'll go with ya.'

'Fair enough,' I said.

I had me little Morris car. The two of us threw our swags in it and away we went. We just slept in the car. We stopped at Canberra and looked around there for a while. Then we got a shed out at Bungendore—a two-stand shed. The cocky was an Irishman.

There were two girls there. One of them was the station owner's wife's sister, and the other one was her mate. They'd both come up from Sydney to help do the cooking and look after the kids while the shearing was on, to give the cocky's wife a hand.

Tommy and me got onto these two sheilas and we were out every bloody night. We used to go into Canberra and all over the place with these girls. After a week or two, the boss got savage cos we were a bit sluggish shearing and we'd be late getting up. We met up with them one night after tea and one of the girls told us they weren't allowed to go out with us any more during the week. So we had to stay home till the weekend, then we'd go off with them.

This shed only lasted four weeks or so, then we got another shed but that only lasted a couple of weeks. The girls had gone back to Sydney by then but we'd got their addresses.

So after we'd finished another shed, Tommy said, 'Let's go to Sydney and see our sheilas.' So away we went to Sydney.

I went back to Mrs Mac's boarding house where I'd stayed before and she had enough vacancies for us. We stayed there for a while and got in touch with these two girls and were taking them out. I didn't want to go back shearing for a while, so I went out to the sheep dip factory where I'd worked before, and Tommy and I got jobs there.

I sold me car before the registration run out because the spring hanger that holds the back spring on had broken away from the chassis. I'd fixed it by shoving half a house brick into the chassis and tying the spring hanger onto the brick but it wouldn't have passed an inspection, so I got rid of it.

We were working at Cooper's Sheep Dip, and were getting on good there. We used to cart the sheep dip around in big trays on pallets. There was a hydraulic trolley that went under the pallets to jack them up and wheel them about. One day, I was waiting to push a trolley full of sheep dip into the kiln. I was sitting down on me haunches leaning over the trolley handle, with the T-piece between me knees. There was a ton of sheep dip on each trolley.

The trolley had a lever that you pressed when you wanted to release it, to lower the pallet. It should just ratchet down slowly but there must have been something wrong with the jack this day.

A bloke come along and said, 'Leave it there. We'll go have smoko.'

He pressed the lever to lower the trolley and the full weight of the sheep dip come down full pelt. The trolley handle flew straight up and hit me fair under the chin. It lifted me up in the air and I landed on me head on the concrete and split me head open. I was knocked out cold. I woke up in Ryde Hospital with the doctor stitching me up. What a bloody mess I was. I was silly as a wheel, delirious. They put me in a room with just a bed in it.

A bit later, some bloke come in and I said, 'How'd I get here? Where's me clothes?'

Anyhow, he found a bag with me gear in it and I put me clothes on. There was no bugger about except for the cleaner bloke that found me clothes, so I got out of there and got a taxi back to the boarding house.

'What's happened to you, Jack?' Mrs Mac asked.

'I had an accident,' I told her.

Tommy come home that night and said, 'I've been ringing up the hospital all day and they told me they didn't know where you were.'

'Yeah,' I said. 'I walked out of the bloody place.'

I had me head all bandaged up and could only whisper. I could hardly open me mouth. Me jaw was broken and me teeth were all smashed. Tommy rang up me sheila—Pat her name was. He told her what happened. Over she come that night and had a look at me. Then away she went and come back with a milkshake to feed me. After that she come over every evening and fed me soup through a straw till I could eat again.

When I got a bit better, a bloke told me to go to the compo office to get compo for it. So in I went to the compo office and they give me a form to fill out.

'I can't fill that out,' I said. 'I can't read or write.'

Nobody would fill it out for me or help me. Then a bloke come along and started asking me a whole lot of questions—what happened here, and what's this, what's that? I thought, bugger ya, and left. I never got any compo. I went back to the boarding house.

I was walking to the bank a couple of days later, and as I got to the door, a bloke come out and bumped into me. It was me mate, John, the showman. He was back working on the shows and had called into Sydney to get some knock-em-down balls and stuff. He'd just called into the bank at Burwood because that's where he had his money.

'Geez, mate,' he said. 'What's up with you? You're a bloody mess.'

'I got smashed up at Cooper's Sheep Dip,' I said. 'And I don't know what to do.'

'Come with us,' he said. 'We're goin' to Nelson Bay for a carnival and I've got room. It'll do ya the world of good. I'll look after ya up there. Get ya swag.'

I went back to Mrs Mac's and grabbed me swag. I left word for Tommy, rung up Pat and told her I was leaving to go on the shows with me mate, and away I went.

I met John down on Parramatta Road. He had a caravan and a Studebaker truck, a wife and two little boys. So into the truck I got with them. His wife, Greta, nursed one of the kids and I nursed the other, and away we went to Nelson Bay.

We had a great time there and I started to get better. It was the first time they'd been to a carnival there. John had just heard that it was a good ground for one. There was a heap of showmen there. John had a horse-a-plane and knock-em-downs. After we set up the joint, he wanted a loud speaker tied up in a tree.

'Give us a rope,' I said. 'I'll fix the bludger.'

I climbed up this big, palm tree. Fifty foot I went up and pulled the loud speaker up and tied it in the tree. The sound carried right out over the bay. We played records and sang out over it, calling people to play the knock-em-downs.

John said to me, 'I'll go ya halves in a knock-em-downs. You work it and we'll make enough money to split.'

I got a little tent to camp in and I used to eat in the caravan with them. We must have been there for a couple of months on that show, then the Lithgow show started.

'Come on,' John said. 'We'll go there. We'll get enough money there for you, too.' So we went to Lithgow.

The next show was Rylstone. I did the show at Rylstone with him, too. I was a lot better by then. I got the dentist there to make me a new set of top teeth. Me jaw had just started to come good.

After there, we went to Mudgee and then Gulgong and Dunedoo. Then the shearing started up again. 'I'll go back shearing now,' I told him. 'I'll be able to get a shed around Rylstone.'

'Righto,' he said. 'I'll see ya later.'

Back in Rylstone, I met the bookkeeper for Bob, the shearing contractor I used to shear for. 'Jack, I got two four-stand sheds at Coolah,' he said. 'Do ya want a pen and do ya know where I can get some others?'

'Yeah,' I said.

'And I've got the contract for Umbiella,' he said.

'Geez, I'll go.'

'Can ya get the men? Ya got about three months.'

'Yeah, I'll get 'em,' I said. So I lined the jokers up, and got a cook too, and told them when we were starting.

While I was waiting for the shearing to start at Coolah, I got a job with the council for a few weeks driving a '47 Ford tipper. The old engineer for the council was called Black but I used to call him Stump-jump. I was always at him for work and asking him to give me a go. One day, he told me to go down to Woodlawn and get five yards of gravel out of the river and take it out to a causeway that they were building at Kandos.

'Righto, boss,' I said.

I drove down to the river, got the planks out of the back of the truck, stuck them under the wheels, backed the truck down to the river and loaded five yards of gravel onto the truck with a shovel. Then I drove the five mile out to Kandos and unloaded it. I drove back to Rylstone and into the council yard in just under an hour and a half.

I walked up to Stump-jump. 'What do ya want me to do now, boss?'

'I told ya what to do,' he said.

'I've done it.'

'Don't tell bloody lies to me, son,' he said.

'He's done it all right,' said the yardsman.

'Go to buggery!' he said. 'Ask the yardsman for work, I've had enough of ya.'

Another day, I was working with the truck out near Cudgegong when it broke down. There was a truck driver there who was going to Kandos for a load of cement. The ganger told him to tow me back to Rylstone, to the depot, so they could fix the truck there. He hooked the rope onto me truck and away we went. It was a gravel road and he was fairly travelling, too. He didn't give a bugger about me. He was going like bloody mad. About half way back to Rylstone, one of his wheels flicked up a rock and smashed me windscreen. Here I was with glass spraying in on me—wind, dust and stones going everywhere. But he didn't stop—he just kept on driving till we got to the depot. It's a wonder I was still in one piece.

A week later, I run into a bloke in Rylstone. 'Do ya want a shed, Jack?' he said, 'A one-stand shed down in Bylong. There's over two thousand down there to shear. Do ya want it?'

'Bloody oath,' I said, 'I'll have it.' I had no car to get down there, and I'd sold me motorbike, but one of me brothers had a mate with an old motorbike he wanted to sell.

'How much do ya want for the motorbike?' I asked him.

'Eighty quid,' he said.

'Here ya are, I'll take it.'

So I rode the motorbike down to Bylong to the shed. When I'd finished shearing and I was on me way home, I had a buster off the bike and buggered me right wrist up, me shearing hand. It swelled up and I couldn't move it. This'll be bloody nice, I thought. I'm supposed to be going to Coolah and Umbiella, and I want to ring Umbiella. Be bloody nice if I get there and I can't shear.

I run into two blokes who were going to shear further down in Bylong and I was telling them about it. 'Can I come and shear with ya?' I said.

'No, Jack. It's only a little shed. They don't want any fast men down there,' they said. 'They got no rouseabout, ya gotta do it all yaself.'

'I'll shear for nothin',' I said. 'You can be the rouseabouts and I'll do the shearing. I don't want nothin', just me tucker, but I gotta work this bloody hand back into line before I go to Coolah.'

'Geez,' they said, 'that sounds all right to us.'

So back I went and shore there for three weeks, and me hand started coming good the last couple of days I was there. I was lucky I got that right.

So anyhow, I went back to Rylstone and it was just coming time to go out to Coolah. Sticky Glew was coming out to Coolah with me and he had a little Morris two-ton truck. We put all the shearers, the cook and a couple of rouseabouts in the back of this truck and headed off for Coolah, with him and me in the front. We had a heap of grog with us as well. As we were going along one of the back roads, one of these bloody ratbags in the back of the truck stood up to have a pee and just as he did, Sticky hit a pothole. He was thrown clean out of the truck onto his head. Everyone was banging on the roof of the truck yelling at us to stop.

'Man overboard, man overboard!' they were shouting.

We raced back and this bloke was laying flat on his back on the ground, out cold. They were all standing there wondering what to do with him, when I come up with a bottle of rum and a pannikin. I poured a heap of rum into the pannikin, lifted his head up off the ground and poured the rum down his neck. Well, he give a splutter and a heave and shot up, shaking himself. Geez, he come alive in a bloody hurry. He didn't know *where* he was.

'Ya silly bastard, you'll kill him,' the cook said.

But I give him another snort of rum and he come to properly. He had hide off him everywhere but no broken bones. And he was silly to start with, which the rum didn't help to make any better. After we got to the shed, everybody realised he was a ratbag. He was a bit slow, poor little bastard.

Everyone wanted to job him. One day, one of the shearers had him lined up and was just going to let him have it, when I walked past.

'Don't hit him,' I said, 'hit me instead.'

'Ya can't be shepherdin' him, Jack,' he said.

'You have a poke at me instead of him,' I said. 'The first bastard that hits him, I'll flatten.' I looked after him. He thought it was great to have someone looking after him.

After we finished Coolah, we went on to another shed and by geez, did he get into some trouble. The boss was going to sack him. He used to do everything arse-over-head. He didn't get anything right.

'No, leave the poor bastard,' I said. 'He's all right, don't worry about him. Get someone else to do the work but he's stayin' with us.'

Anyhow, we finished shearing there and come back to Rylstone. We had a few days there before we set off for Umbiella. We were in the pub one day and everyone was talking about who was going to ring Umbiella. It was a good shed. Good fast little sheep there.

'Here's fifty quid,' I said to the publican. 'Get whatever price ya can and put it on me, because I *will* ring Umbiella.'

'Geez, Jack. Ya fair dinkum?' he said.

'Yeah.'

'Well,' he said, 'I'll be in that with ya.'

We got down to the shed and we had plenty of grog in us. The contractor told us to do a couple of runs after dinner to feel ourselves out.

'Okay,' I said. 'That'll do us fine and dandy.'

After dinner, we went up to the shed and I flew into them straight away. I got round the lot of them. I got four sheep in front on the first run and eight on the second run. And I thought, I'm that far in front now that none of you bludgers are ever going to catch me. I rung Umbiella all right.

A few days before we cut out, we got thirsty and run out of grog. Glen Davis was only about twenty mile away. So down to Glen Davis we went one night after work. Into the pub we went, which at that time had the longest bar of any pub in New South Wales. There weren't many people there though. It was a ghost town more or less because the mines had closed down. No bugger had any money but I had plenty. This little rouseabout I'd been looking after at Coolah was there. He'd come to Umbiella, too. Fallin'Off we called him, after he fell off the truck.

'You get a pencil and paper,' I said to him, 'and everyone that borrows money off me, you write it down and how much he gets.'

Well, you'd have thought he was the best secretary in Australia. He looked after me all right. The next day he had a bloody list a foot long, who got money and how much they got. They all squared up on payday.

I noticed when we were in the pub at Glen Davis that the bar was covered with bags of beer. It was stacked as high as the bloody ceiling. They used to keep the beer bottles in bags like cement bags back then. A dozen bottles in a bag. The publican told me they had plenty of tobacco, too.

I said to the barman, 'Can I buy a bag of beer, mate?'

'Ya can buy the bloody lot if ya want it, mate. It's all for sale,' he said.

I never had a car at the time. I'd got a lift out to Umbiella with Harvey in his ute. Harvey was the one that shot the cockatoo in St George. He was shearing at Umbiella with us.

I said, 'What about when we cut out, we come down here and we'll fill ya bloody ute up with beer and we'll sell it back in Rylstone.'

'That's a good idea,' Harvey said.

So after the cut out, we went back to the pub and bought about twenty-five bags of beer and put it in his ute.

'There's a ball on next week,' I said. 'We'll tell everyone we've got plenty of beer for sale.' It was six o'clock closing back then so you couldn't buy beer at the pub after six. And beer was still pretty scarce in Rylstone at the time.

'How much of this tobacco can I buy?' I said to the barman.

'As much as ya want,' he said.

'Give us two pound of it.' It was hard to get tobacco in Rylstone. Things were still hard to get years after the war finished. We paid about three and six a packet, and we sold it for five bob a packet.

Back home we went and took it up to Mum's place. I had beer and tobacco stacked everywhere at home—all over the verandah and under me bed. A few days before the ball, we got around telling everyone we had beer and tobacco for sale. That way we had nearly all of it sold before Dad come home. We sold the beer for twice what we paid.

When Dad got home he said, 'What's all this beer doin' here?'

I said, 'I was going to sell it at the dance.'

'Get that bloody stuff out of here,' he said. 'I'm not havin' the coppers comin' up here and pinchin' us for black marketing.'

We only had a few bags left, so we put it in the back of Harvey's ute and sold it from there the night of the ball. Gee, we made some money out of it.

I went back down to Umbiella after that, splitting posts with Uncle Bob. We cut down this tree and it took us half a day. We got a hundred and twenty posts out of the one tree. It was a beautiful big tree.

When we'd just about finished, a cousin-in-law of mine come looking for me. He had a couple of trucks and used to cart cement from Kandos to Sydney, and he needed another driver. So Uncle Bob said he could finish up the splitting and I went with me cousin-in-law. Two diesel Morris Commercials he had. They used to carry about seven ton each at a time. We used to go through Lithgow and up over the scenic range to get to Sydney. It was a pretty steep hill.

This Sunday, I was going down with a load and cracked an injector pipe. The truck was missing like bloody mad. I started to go up the scenic range. I got a quarter of the way up and the truck couldn't take any more—she couldn't take the weight. So I took a ton off the load. There were twenty-four bags in a ton. I carried a bag at a time for about half a mile up this scenic range, till the slope was shallow enough for the truck to take it again. I drove the truck up and loaded all the bags back on, then drove to Sydney.

This cousin-in-law had a fruit shop in Kandos, as well. He had arrangements with somebody at the Sydney fruit and veggie markets to buy what he wanted for his fruit shop and bring it round to the government stores, where I used to cart the cement to. I just had to pick it up from there when I unloaded the cement. I was late getting back with his fruit and veggies this Sunday, cos it had taken a lot longer to get to Sydney, and he sacked me for being late.

I went back to Rylstone and got a shed then, down around Portland. I rode out to it on me motorbike. There was a young fella at that shed called Jimmy. He had a Holden ute. We shore there together, then we come back to Rylstone and did another little four-stand shed near there—out along the Cudgegong Road.

There was a lady wool classer at this place. She always wore a little white hat. She used to leave it on a bale of wool while she went over to the homestead for dinner. We used to eat in the shearers' huts. You'd have an hour off for dinner. We'd only take half an hour, then we'd be back at the shed washing our combs and cutters and loading our machines for the next run. When we come back to the shed this day, we got her hat and sewed it to the bale of wool. When she come back, we were watching her trying to pull this bloody hat off the wool bale. After we finished that shed, we done another shed down near Ilford.

This mate, Jimmy, said, 'How about we go to Crookwell? We'll go out there in me ute.'

'Okay,' I said, 'but I'll take me motorbike home first.'

While I was at home, Mum told Peter and me that Dad was coming home in a week or two and we had to scarify the front paddock and have it ready for him to sow. Dad owned the block opposite us in Dawson Street. It had an old house on it. I s'pose it would have been about an acre of land. He used to grow all our veggies in it. Peter was working at Charbon in the cement works at the time. He used to come home late every night. So we had to wait till the weekend to do it. Saturday come and we forgot all about the paddock. Sunday come and I thought, we better go and scarify that paddock for Dad.

'We can't do it yet,' Peter said. 'The boys have got the horse.' Our younger brothers had taken the horse to go out and get firewood.

'Don't worry about that,' I said, 'we'll use me motorbike.'

'What?' said Peter.

'We'll use the bike,' I said, 'it'll be all right.'

'Oh well,' said Peter, 'it won't take as long.'

I brought the bike around to the paddock and he got out the scarifier. We hooked a chain from it onto the motorbike. I started up the bike and took off. Geez, I had a job to stay on the bike and Peter had an even harder job trying to hang onto the scarifier. We only touched the bloody ground every twenty yards. Across the paddock we went. Inside of an hour, every second person in Rylstone was at the paddock fence having a look at the two lunatics trying to scarify a paddock with a motorbike. It took us nearly all day. By gee we had some fun with it. We were both as black as buggery by the time we'd finished.

When Dad come home he said, 'What the hell happened to the paddock out there? Half the bloody dirt's on the road.'

'They scarified it with a motorbike,' Mum said. 'What a bloody shemozzle.'

'If I'd have been here, I'd have shot the pair of 'em,' Dad said.

Peter reckoned the old bloke from across the road was talking about it for ten years. He thought it was the funniest thing he'd ever seen.

Me and Peter looked the dead spit of one another even though he was nearly nine years younger than me. One day, I was home from shearing and I put Peter's coat on to go down the street. I was standing outside the boot maker's shop, when this girl come up, put her arm around me and said, 'Did you mean what you said last night?'

I turned around and said, 'Who are you?'

'My God,' she said, 'ain't you Peter?'

When Peter was old enough to drink, we'd go down to the pub on a Friday night. One Friday night, a telephone worker had killed a big brown snake coming back from Bylong, and he had it in a bag. He was in the pub when we went in, and he told us he had this snake in a bag and wondered if we wanted to have some fun with it.

'Geez, give it here,' I said. 'We'll have some fun with it, all right.'

There was a parlour in The Globe Hotel. It was where the men would take their women, or the women would go to have a drink. Peter and I used to call it the sows' pen.

I went outside and got the snake out of the bag, washed the blood off its head under the tap and brought it back into the pub around me neck. When I walked in blokes were yelling and diving over everything to get away from me.

'Bring it round here,' said Peter, 'and we'll go into the sows' pen.' As we were about to go into the parlour, Peter said, 'You get hold of one end in ya mouth and I'll get hold of the other end in my mouth, and we'll pretend to be fightin' over it.'

So I got hold of it in me mouth behind its head and Peter got hold of it down near the tail and, as we walked into the room, we started pulling at this snake, yelling and running towards the women that were sitting in there. Well, they upset tables, screaming and running everywhere. We frightened buggery out of them.

The publican come out yelling, 'That'll be those bloody Turners. Turner, you get that thing out of here.' They didn't know it was dead to start off with.

That reminds me of another funny story. One time, Dad wanted to teach me three youngest brothers to ride bullocks. He'd bought an old house on a couple of blocks of ground, a few streets up from where we lived.

He said to me, 'I think we'll build a round yard up there.'

So anyhow, we built this yard. A bloody good round yard it was, too. The rails were about six foot high and the yard itself was about thirty or forty foot across the middle. A good, big yard for breaking in horses or riding a buck-jumper in.

There used to be a cattle and sheep sale about every fortnight in Rylstone. Dad said, 'I'll get the auctioneer to keep his eye out for a sturdy sort of a steer and we'll put him in the round yard, and we can teach the kids to bullock ride on him.'

After we'd built the yard, the stock and station agent come to Dad and said, 'I've got ya a good lump of a steer, Stan. He's down in the saleyard. You'll have to get him out today.'

When Peter come home from work that evening, Dad said, 'Come on, we gotta go down to the saleyard. The auctioneer's got a steer for us.'

We took a lasso rope and down we went to the saleyard, which was on the other side of the railway station. I went to get in the yard with this steer. I got through the fence and, geez, he come straight at me. He was as wild as buggery.

'Jesus!' Dad said. 'One rope's no good to him. We'll have ta get three.'

I went home and got a couple more lasso ropes. While I was away, Peter lassoed him and tied him up to the post. Then we put the three ropes on him.

Dad said, 'I'll go first and lead him. You two hang onto a rope each, one either side of him, and stop him from runnin' over me, and steer him.'

I said, 'Righto.'

We opened the gate and he took off. Dad went out the gate with this steer after him. By geez! Me and Peter had our riding boots on and we had our heels dug in the ground digging a furrow two inches deep. Holy Christ! Didn't he go. We had a job to keep him off Dad. Up the lane we went, about two or three hundred yards, before we come to the Glen Alice road. That was the main road. Then we had to turn right to go into Rylstone. About two hundred yards along from there was the railway line. We had to cross the railway tracks.

Either side of the road, where it crossed the railway line, there was what they called a viaduct. It was a cattle grid to stop any stock from getting off the road and going up the train line. As we were going along, Dad let the lead rope go a bit loose cos he seemed to be travelling all right, this steer. We got to the railway tracks but instead of going straight across the tracks, he turned right—and ya wouldn't believe it—he put his two front feet straight down between the rails of this cattle grid. Down he went. Well, what a bloody shemozzle! He bellowed and kicked. He couldn't get out.

Dad's sister lived on the corner just near the railway line and you could hear her screaming. 'Stan, ya silly bugger. Stan, ya lunatic, what are ya doin'? The train will be comin' soon.'

It was about half past five in the evening and the Mudgee train going to Sydney come through about half past six. Geez, what a panic. After a while, we got one end of the lasso rope under the guts of the steer and we lifted him up. We got him out of there and away we went again, up past the hospital. We were going down the hill towards our place and we come to Johnny's house. He was the one I was with when we tried to pinch the watermelons. His place had a fair sized yard.

Dad sang out, 'Can we put this fella in here for the night?'

Johnny said, 'Yeah.' So we stuck him in there.

Dad said, 'Don't go near him. He's bloody wild.'

We had to leave the ropes on him cos we'd need them again the next day.

Next morning we got up and Dad said to Peter, 'Ya can't go to work today. We gotta get that steer and put him in the yard.'

Up we went to get him, and he met us at the fence and come at us again. I jumped the fence and he come at me. Peter grabbed the rope while he was chasing me. He got one rope and Dad got the other rope. We got him out of the yard and he come at us again.

Dad said, 'This fella's too bloody wild. We can't put him in that round yard—he'll kill all the kids. He's too wild to ride, this bludger. We'll have ta take him out to the common and let him go.'

Well, bloody hell! We had about another mile, I suppose, from there out to the common. Down through the streets we went with this steer chasing Dad and us hanging onto him with the ropes. We were flat out keeping him off Dad. We got him out onto the common at last, tied him up to a tree and took two ropes off him.

Dad said, 'We'll go and get out of the way. Then you let him go and you can just jump up into the tree till he gets out of the way.'

I undone the rope and ducked behind the tree and he followed me round, horning at the tree. I got onto a limb and flew up this bloody tree. Well, he tore bark off the tree and stayed there for a good couple of hours. Then he got away a bit, so I got down and he come straight back at me again. Back up the tree I went. I had to sit there and wait till he got four or five hundred yards away, then I took off. By geez, he was wild!

Another time, me three young brothers, Tony—he was the eldest of the three—Larry and Billy, were riding somewhere on horses. Larry's horse started to bolt and he went sailing up the road past the other two.

Larry's yelling, 'I can't hold him.'

Me littlest brother, Billy said, 'Saw his mouth.'

And Tony said, 'Let him run.'

And Larry said a Hail Mary.

Larry used to chew like mad all the time. His mouth would be going like he was chewing. I come home from shearing one time and I bought two sets of Hop-along Cassidy cap guns and holsters. Larry and Billy would get these gun belts on and draw against one another. Dad used to think it was great fun. They had to wait till he said draw, then they'd draw. Larry was getting all on edge this time and chewing like buggery while he waited for Dad to say draw.

Dad said, 'If ya can't shoot him, ya can chew him to death.'

Gee, I used to get up to some capers with me little brothers. One time, I actually hung Billy. And if ya don't believe it, there's a photo to prove it. There was a big peach tree in our backyard, with a big limb sticking out. I got two lasso ropes and put one around under Billy's arms, under his shirt. The other one, I made a proper hangman's noose with and put it round his neck. Then I plaited the two ropes together so one wouldn't pull tighter than the other and threw it up over the limb. We tied Billy's hands behind his back and lifted him up off the ground, while one of me brothers tied the other end of the rope to the foot of a fence post. I lowered him down till the rope took all his weight but he was still off the ground, and raced and got me camera. So there's a picture of 'The Hanging of Billy'.

So anyhow, after we'd scarified the paddock with me motorbike, I left it at home and away Jimmy and I went in his ute to Crookwell. We did a couple of sheds there. Then we went on to Queanbeyan and shore there in a couple of sheds.

While we were there, Jimmy said, 'I wouldn't mind goin' to New Zealand, shearin'.'

'Gee, mate,' I said, 'I've been thinkin' about that, too.'

'We'll go to Sydney and book our boat tickets to New Zealand,' he said.

'That'll do. That sounds fair enough to me.'

We went to Sydney the next weekend and booked a ticket on the Oronsay. Thirty-one quid to go over to New Zealand. We had to get a tax clearance or something before they'd issue our tickets. We hadn't even done our tax—never got around to it. So the bloke at the ticket office said that if we could get someone to guarantee that we'd come back before the end of the next financial year and sign a form saying so, then we could go.

So I went round to a cousin of mine and said, 'Sign this form to say we'll be back in time to pay our tax next year, so we can get a tax clearance to go to New Zealand.'

'All right,' he said and signed it. Then we went down and got our tickets.

We went back to finish the shed off—it was a fairly big shed. Every shed voted in a union rep out of the shearers there. I did it once but they nearly drove me mad complaining about this and that. I wouldn't take it on again. The rep would write out tickets with the number of each stand on it, put them in a tin and each shearer would draw one out. That's how you picked which stand you shore at. Nobody wanted number one stand. That's what we called the exhibition stand because any visitor that come in would see that shearer first.

The rep would also write out a wet and dry ticket for each stand, which you'd leave on the ledge where your combs and cutters went. If it rained and they thought the sheep were wet, each shearer would shear two sheep, then the rep and an off-sider would come along with a tin each. One tin was to vote them wet and the other to vote them dry. Each shearer would put his ticket in, whether he wanted to vote them wet or dry. The rep would count the vote and if there were more wet votes than dry, the owner would have to turn the sheep out and we'd wait for them to dry before we'd shear any more.

On Thursday the rep of the shed, who lived in Sydney, asked us when we were going to New Zealand. We told him next week.

'Well,' he said, 'how about we have a long weekend and I'll go to Sydney with ya?'

'What do ya mean?' we said.

'We'll vote the bloody sheep wet on Friday morning, and we'll have Friday, Saturday and Sunday in Sydney, and I'll come back Sunday night.'

There was about three more days of shearing left after this Friday but we'd told the cocky we could only stay till the Friday.

Next morning, we got up and started shearing, then we heard this bloke calling, 'All shearers this way,' he said. 'They're wet. Let's take a vote.'

There were five shearers in this shed: Jimmy and me, and two others, plus this rep. One of these other shearers said, 'What the bloody hell's wrong? It hasn't rained.'

'They're wet,' the rep said. 'Take a vote.'

So me and Jimmy and the rep voted them wet, and the other two voted them dry. It wasn't a contract shed, it was a privately owned place. The cocky said, 'Well, it's no good bringing them back in after dinner to get ya to shear them.'

'Not a bloody chance,' the rep said, 'We won't be here.' It hadn't rained for a month and we voted the sheep wet.

*This is the photo I took when I hung **Billy**. He doesn't look very dead.*

*Me and **Tony** sitting on a bed on the verandah at Dawson Street.*

Chapter Twenty-Six

New Zealand

We went down to Sydney and spent the weekend there. I had two new pairs of trousers made while we were in Sydney. Big, bell-bottomed flares, with wide legs and a band around the top. I picked them up the day before we sailed.

I was twenty-eight when I went to New Zealand. Uncle Bob shore in New Zealand when he was young. It took him six weeks to get there in a sailing ship. It took us three days. Didn't Jimmy and I have some fun on the boat! We were drunk most of the time.

We had our first couple of nights booked at a pub in Auckland. The first night there, I unpacked me gear and hung me two new pairs of trousers in the wardrobe. Then we went out tearing around the town, drinking. We found out that there was no shearing left on the North Island so we'd have to go down to the South Island. We looked into hiring a car to drive down to Wellington, to catch the ferry across to the South Island, but we decided to go by bus instead. I packed me swag the next day and forgot about the trousers in the wardrobe and left them there. I'd never even worn them.

Anyhow, we caught the bus down to Wellington. As we were going along, I looked out the window and there in a paddock was a skewbald horse sitting up on its back legs like a dog.

I said to Jimmy, 'Look at this fella.' And I didn't have me camera.

We got down to Wellington and onto a boat that took us across to Littleton and then on to Christchurch. As soon as we got to Christchurch I bought meself a camera, but I never again saw a horse sitting like that.

Once we were in Christchurch, we hired a car. After a hundred mile we had to pay so much extra. I'd had to sign the papers to say I was the driver. We had our handpieces in our swags. In with mine, I had a pair of multigrips that I used to take me handpiece apart for cleaning. When we got out of town about a mile or two, I pulled over onto the side of a causeway and had a look under the dash. They'd put a sealed tape on the speedo so you couldn't undo it and disconnect it. They were a wake-up to that trick, but they weren't a wake-up to undoing it at the back. So I got under the car and unscrewed the speedo cable from the gearbox and plugged the hole with a stick. We drove this car all around the South Island for a couple of weeks looking for shearing and never had to pay for one mile over the hundred.

We got right down to Invercargill, then out to a little town called Winton. We pulled up at a pub there and asked around.

A joker at the pub said, 'There's a stock and station agent that looks after the shearers. He's out of town, about a mile and a half up that road there. Ya can see his house on top of the hill. Go and see him.' So out we went to his place.

'G'day, mate,' I said to him. 'We're looking for shearin'.'

'Who are you?' he said.

'We're two Australians. We've just come over and we can't get any shearin'.'

'Can ya shear?'

'Bloody oath, we can shear,' I said. 'If I can't shear two hundred a day in anything ya got, I'll go home.'

'Bloody hell!' he said. And went in and dialled up the phone. 'Hey Jim, I got two Australian shearers here, they'll shear a bloody million. Do ya want 'em?'

And this Jim bloke said, 'Yeah!'

It was a four-stand shed, the other side of Winton. I told him I'd be late starting because I had to take the car back to Christchurch and then catch the train down. Me mate, Jimmy, stayed there while I drove the car back. Then I caught the train back to Winton.

I got off the train and there was a joker there to meet me.

'You Jack Turner?'

'Yes, mate, that's me.'

'Come with me out to the shed,' he said.

So I hopped in his truck and he drove me out to the shed. They'd already started when I got there. I was half a day late. I got up there after dinner and Jimmy said to me, 'Geez! We're in bloody trouble here, mate.'

'Why?' I said.

'These sheep are as big as horses. I don't know how we're gunna shear them with this little gear.'

So I had a go at them and, bloody hell, there was a learner there shearing more sheep than what I was.

The contractor come along and said, 'By geez, you fellas will wanna sharpen up. Ya not doin' too good.'

I said, 'Where do ya get that bigger gear from? We'll have to modify these machines. We can't shear these bloody monsters with these little combs.'

'I'll send into town to get some chicken feet and combs and cutters for ya machines,' the contractor said. 'Poke on today, but you'll have to have the big gear tomorrow.'

'Righto,' I said.

So we poked on, but, by geez, those sheep were wide. They were bloody two foot across the back—big buggers.

Next day, we put the merry widow comb—that's the wide New Zealand comb—with the wider cutter on our handpieces. The chicken foot was the piece that held the cutter on. We had to change that, too, to suit the merry widow comb. It had two sets of prongs on it for the wide New Zealand cutter and comb. We put them on and that made a big difference. Away we went. Then we could shear a few.

The last shed we were at before we went to New Zealand, we'd made ourselves half a dozen pair of bag boots from the wool cap packs. That's a piece of hessian about two foot square that went in the top of the bale of wool to stop the wool falling out till the flaps got fastened. You could make a pair of bag boots out of the one cap, with just a packing needle and some binding twine. They were great for shearing in, wouldn't slip and would roll up nice to go in your swag.

Jimmy and I pulled our bag boots out this day and one of the New Zealand shearers said, 'They look good, where'd ya get them?'

Jimmy said, 'Anthony Hordern's in Sydney.' Anthony Hordern's was a big store in Sydney.

The New Zealand shearer said, 'What do ya call them?'

'Shearing boots,' Jimmy said.

This poor bugger wrote away to Anthony Hordern's to get a set of these bag boots and they sent him a big pair of leather shearing boots. You couldn't buy bag boots, you had to make them.

We finished that shed. Then we got a two-stand shed that was live-in. When we'd finished the first shed in New Zealand, we got paid three pound ten a hundred.

At this little two-stand shed the bloke asked, 'How much do ya want?'

'I don't know,' I said, 'What's the goin' price?'

'It's only thirty bob, the going price. But last year I had a good year and got good money for me wool. Will you shear for three pound?'

'Bloody oath, we will,' I said.

It was seven pound for a hundred in Australia, but three pound in New Zealand was good money. That'll do us, I thought. That was three pound per hundred sheep. If the cocky had had a bad year, you'd have to shear for the going rate, but if he'd had a good year, he'd give you a few bob more.

We finished shearing at that two-stand shed then went down to Invercargill, and on to Gore, and down to the Bluff. One place we stayed at in Whitecliffs was a Maori's joint. Mautau he was called, this bloke. He used to carry a hundred pound note around in his wallet. 'This is to bury me,' he used to say. He carried his funeral payment in his pocket. We stayed at his place for a week, holidaying, and then we got another shed.

After that shed cut out, we met up with a stock and station agent in one of the pubs. Charlie something-or-other he was called and he knew a lot of cockys who wanted shearers. He kept us going for the rest of the year.

It was coming on to Christmas by then and he got us a two-stand shed near Winton. The bloke next door to this shed had no place for shearing, and he wanted his sheep shorn at the shed we were at. So we said we'd shear them. He had a '52 Chev car and a crippled wife. He was a bloody drunkard, this bloke. Gee, he could drink, and he knew *everyone*. We spent Christmas there with him. He had a party every day and night.

Next shed we went to, they asked what time I'd knock off on Saturday.

'I knock off dinnertime Friday. I don't work Saturday or Sunday,' I said.

They used to shear Saturday and Sunday in New Zealand, but you couldn't shear before ten o'clock on a Sunday. Bugger that, I thought. Dinnertime Friday, I was finished. I wanted to get to the pub. We used to go to race meetings and dances. The bloke with the crippled wife used to lend us his car. Whenever we were shearing around Winton, we'd end up back at his place of a weekend. We used to get around in this bloody big Chev. We had a rip-roaring time.

After Christmas, we shore at a few more sheds and then the shearing finished and the crutching started. Crutching started about six months after the shearing, so it was time to go back where we'd first started shearing and start the crutching. It was the New Year by then.

We went to one shed and the joker there said, 'Do ya want us to pull them out and I'll pay ya less, or do ya want the full price and you pull them out yaself?'

'There's no bugger that can pull them out fast enough for me, mate,' I said. 'That's not on. I'll crutch eight hundred a day.'

'Bloody hell,' he said.

There was a sheet of tin I tripped over while I was talking to him. 'What the bloody hell is this doin' here?' I asked him.

'Mate, I'll tell ya something. There's a hole down there. One of you hungry, bloody Australians put it there.'

'How come?'

'He wanted us to pull the sheep out for him, and he was that bloody tired he couldn't bend down, so he cut a hole in the floor and stood down there and we'd pull the sheep out over the hole and he'd crutch 'em.'

'Be buggered,' I said.

'That's true, mate.'

Another shed we went to didn't have quarters for the shearers, so we boarded in town. They were all dry pubs down round Invercargill and places. It was a dry area. But the stock and station agents used to supply all the beer. You could buy it through them. The pubs had hardly any in a lot of places.

We were staying at this pub and the cocky was paying our board. He lent us a car to drive out to the shed. It was only a two-stand shed. But it was a good-sized shed and we were there for three weeks. The day of the cut out come and the cocky said we'd have a party for the cut out. 'That'll do us,' we told him.

We'd seen the mailman come past earlier in the day and drop off a couple of bags that looked like cement bags, down near the mailbox. That would have been about ten o'clock in the morning, and it was pretty warm weather. They were there all day. The last sheep we shore was about half an hour after the last run started at three thirty. We put it down the pen and the cocky said he'd go and get the beer. Down he went to the mailbox and brought back these two bags. It was two bags of New Zealand beer, and it was bloody near boiling, and he expected us to drink it.

'That'd poison a cat, mate,' I said, 'Ya couldn't drink that.' It was bad enough drinking it cold.

We went back to the little town of Otautau after that. We used to stay there a fair bit and shear in the sheds around there. We used to terrify the jokers there. We'd be up all night drinking.

One bloke said, 'I'll be glad when you two Aussies go home. You're bloody terrors.'

The contractor from around Otautau that we were shearing for was a Dalgetty agent. They've closed down now. They used to be a big stock and station agency in Australia.

He asked us, 'When are ya going home?'

'We gotta go home this year,' I said.

'Come back next year. I'll guarantee I'll get ya two hundred thousand to shear. There'll be plenty of work if ya come back.'

'That's good, mate,' I said. 'We'll be back next year.' But I never got back there.

Soon after, we sailed home on the Wonganella. Not long after we got to sea, we run into a storm. Gee, it got rough. An Australian trainer had bought some New Zealand racehorses and was bringing them back to Australia. They were tethered in their stalls in the bottom of the boat. It got that rough that quickly, the strappers couldn't get down to the stalls in time to untie them all and the most expensive horse got thrown off his feet and broke his neck. It was that rough the captain said if we didn't get out of it by midnight we'd have to turn around and go back. It was so rough, you'd go to reach for your glass and it wouldn't be there. It was down the other end of the table. I'd have sooner been riding a buckjumper and trying to have a drink, than trying to drink on that boat.

When I left Australia, I had to sell me motorbike to get the fare over. I left Australia with a hundred pounds. It cost us twenty-nine pounds on the Wonganella to come home and when we got back to Australia, I landed with a hundred pound Australian money. And I'd been shearing for a year. I had a good time and I met some good people. It was great fun over there.

We landed in Sydney in June 1956 and caught the train back home. Jimmy got off at Wallerawang to go over to Portland and I kept on the train to Rylstone. I got off the train, swung me swag over me shoulder and walked home. I walked in the door and Mum said, 'Gee, am I glad to see you. Dad's bloody crook. He's got heart trouble.'

I walked in to see him. He was lying in bed. 'Holy bloody hell,' I said. 'What's up, mate?'

'Ah, Johnny,' he said, 'I wanna see Queensland before I die.'

'Holy Jesus,' I said. 'I'd better look around and get a shed so I can get some money to take ya to Queensland.'

Chapter Twenty-Seven

A Mob of Galahs

I got a shed—a four-stand shed it was—down round Wallerawang way. There were four of us at this shed. I still had me merry widow gear on me handpiece.

I said to these blokes, 'They're all good looking sheep at this shed. I'm not gunna change this handpiece. Tell him not to count them out. I'll shear the good ones, and I'll shear more than you blokes, and we'll just split the cheque four ways. We'll get a quid out of this quick, with this bloody big, wide comb.'

'Geez, that sounds all right,' they said.

So we started. Bloody hell! They shore two while I was still on me first. The wide comb was getting stuck in the dense wool. I could *not* push it. I had to take it off and put me little gear back on. It was impossible to push that wide comb through the wool. How they do it today with these big, wide combs, I don't know. It must be different sheep. I got me own gear back on and got into them. Finished that shed and then done another one.

Then I got another big shed, an eight-stander, out Orange way. I finished there, made a few quid and went back home.

Me brother, Tony, the apprentice jockey, had just finished riding in Sydney and come home.

'Dad's crook,' I told him. 'And we've gotta take him to Queensland.'

'I've got some money in the bank, in the AJC,' he said. That was the Australian Jockey Club. 'We'll go down and get it, and we'll get a truck and take him to Queensland.'

'That sounds all right,' I said. Away we went down to Sydney and he got this money out of the AJC.

We had a cousin in Sydney that knew a fair bit about machinery and everything, so we went and seen him about a truck. He had a look in the paper and found us a good, cheap truck, a '52 International. It had a crane frame on the back, because it had been used as a crane, but the crane had been taken off. We bought it, and home to Rylstone we come in it.

There was a bloke in Rylstone that had pulled a tip-truck body off a truck and put a semi on it. He told us we could have the tip body for ten pound. I bought it and fixed it onto our truck. Another fella had an old army canopy tarp and frame. I got that for about five pound and put that on and made the back all waterproof. We took Dad and Mum's mattress out and laid it in the back, and packed all our camping gear in it. Then the five of us kids still living at home, me, Tony, Pat, Larry and Billy, plus Mum and Dad, headed for Queensland.

Me oldest sister, Marie, had married an Air Force bloke, and he was based at the Amberley Air Force base in Queensland. They lived in a house in Ipswich. Dad said, 'We'll go up there and see Marie, and once I've seen Queensland I'm set.'

So away we went in this truck. Mum and me in the front, and Dad and Pat, and the three youngest brothers, Tony, Larry and Billy, in the back. Before we left, I thought, I'll have to be able to keep in touch with Dad in the back. If something falls off or they need to stop, I won't be able to hear them call out with the tarp down. So I got a lump of garden hose, stuck it through the driver's window and ran it along the outside of the truck under a rope, and then fed it into the back of the truck and hooked it up there.

I used to blow in it and they'd pick it up and ask what I wanted. Then I'd talk into it and they'd put it up to their ear, and they'd talk and I'd put it up to my ear. We had our own two-way. Dad would say if he wanted to pull up, or if something had gone wrong, or they wanted to stop and look at something. It was our telephone and was good fun.

We camped at the foot of the Moonbi Ranges the first night. We got up to Queensland by the next night and went out to Marie's place and stayed there. Mum and Dad camped in the truck in the yard and us kids slept under the stars. There was a bloke next door to Marie who was mad on horses and punting. He found out that Tony Turner, the jockey from Sydney, was up.

'Geez,' he said, 'I've got a friend at Deagon who's got racehorses. Come out to Deagon and I'll introduce ya to me friend up there. We'll go on the train.'

So away they went on the train, this bloke, Tony, and me youngest brother, Billy, who was also a jockey in Rylstone. He took them to Deagon and they met up with a couple of trainers there. They talked with them and had a couple of rides.

Anyhow, they come back to Ipswich that night and Tony said to Dad, 'We're stayin' here.'

'What?' Dad said.

'We're goin' up to the stables at Deagon, they're gunna give us a job there. One fella's gunna finish apprenticing me and another fella's gunna apprentice Billy.'

'All right,' Dad said. 'We'd better go up and see 'em.' Dad was coming good by then.

We drove out to Deagon and met the trainers. Billy and Tony took their swags and they stayed there. Dad said, 'All right, Johnny, let's go back home and sell out and come to Queensland to live.'

'Bloody hell!' I said. 'Righto, that'll do me.' So we set off back to Rylstone.

On the way up, when we camped the first night at the Moonbies, Dad left his plumb axe there. We'd decided to take a different road home and go along the coast, but after we set off Dad remembered his axe.

'I want to go back down to the Moonbies where we camped and pick up me axe,' he said.

'It mightn't be there,' I said.

'It'll be there.'

So we turned off course and went back down to the Moonbies. It was there all right.

We got back to Rylstone and Dad said, 'We'd better start work and get some money and organise things to sell out.'

He'd come good by then and could work again. The doctor told him he'd had a heart attack but that never worried Dad. Once he was feeling all right, he went straight back to work. And he shore till he was well into his seventies. Not bad for someone with a bad heart.

Billy Mills come up home a couple of days after we got back. He and his wife, Beth, were growing spuds on Nullo Mountain and they needed diggers. We took the canopy off and all the gear out of the back, and drove the truck up, Dad and Larry and I. It was raining and we got bogged on the way up, and it was night as well. I had to walk for a couple of miles to Billy's house. He got his tractor and come and towed us up to a big shed near his house. We camped in there. It was raining, cold and foggy. There was a big drum in the shed, so we filled it up with wood and got a fire going.

Next day, Billy took us out to the paddock where the spuds were and we picked them up and bagged them all day. We got five bob a bag. Billy ploughed them out and we picked them up and bagged them. We put them in a four-gallon kerosene tin, then four of those was a bag of spuds. A kero tin was a quarter weight of spuds.

That night, geez, it was cold. We cooked our dinner over the fire in the drum and then got into our swags. They were on the ground. We'd put a heap of bushes down, then a bag wagga, then our blanket and another wagga on top of it. We kept the fire going all night. We got up the next morning and the fog was that thick you could hardly see.

Anyhow, we got to work. There was me in one row, Larry in the next and Dad next to him, going along picking up spuds. The fog was that thick that I couldn't see Dad and he couldn't see me, and we were only about three or four feet away from each other. It only took us about a week and we were finished.

'Let's get back out of this and down off this bloody mountain,' Dad said. Strike me pink, it was cold.

There was a shearing contractor in Rylstone who used to have a shed up near Warren. It was a six-stand shed. About a week after we got back from potato bagging, he told us he wanted a shearer and a rouseabout, and asked if I wanted a pen.

'Yeah,' I said. 'I'll go.'

'What about taking ya truck and taking the rest of the shearers and the rouseabouts up with ya,' he said.

So I put the canopy back on the truck. Larry and me mate, Sticky, come out with me. We were in the front, and three others in the back. We got about half way there, when one of the rouseabouts in the back was singing out.

'I want to get in the front. I'm sick back here, I can't stand it,' he said.

We pulled up and Sticky got out. 'I'll fix ya,' he said. 'That's no trouble.'

So he got a lump of wire out of a cocky's fence, tied it onto the back of the truck and let it drag on the ground. 'There ya are,' he said. 'That'll stop ya feelin' sick, mate. It does me wife. I gotta put it on the car every time for her. That wire draggin' on the ground takes the static out of the car or some bloody rubbish. Anyhow, it works.'

We got back in and set off. He never complained again.

We got more than halfway to Warren and pulled up at this café for dinner, and Sticky said to him, 'Are ya all right, mate?'

'Yeah, mate, good,' he said.

We had dinner and were all getting back into the truck to set off again, when Sticky said to me, 'Watch this.'

He went over and unhooked the wire. We got into the truck, set off and not a word out of the rouseabout the whole way up.

Larry, me brother, was the picker-up for us at Warren. He was only young—about fourteen, and he was that bloody little that he couldn't reach the wool table to throw the fleece on. We had to put a box at the end of the table for him to stand on so he could throw the fleece up properly.

While we were at Warren, the creeks were in flood. Sticky and I found a sheet of corrugated iron one day, about ten or twelve foot long. We bent it in half, punched holes in the ends and tied the ends together so it looked like a canoe. We packed it with clay both ends. Any holes, we filled in with clay. We put a couple of boards in the bottom of it to stop it folding in on us. Larry, Sticky and I took it down to the creek, got in it and went spinning for cod.

Sticky had a fishing line—he loved to fish. So he's sitting in the back fishing, holding this line out, and I'm rowing, and Larry was up the front. We were in this flooded creek. Suddenly, the canoe started to leak. The water was coming in up Larry's end. He got a fright and come running down our end. All the water ran to our end then, and down we all went—sunk the bloody boat. I looked around and there's Larry up in a tree. I don't think the bastard even got wet he got out of there so fast.

He's in this tree singing out, 'Jackie, Jackie, Mr Glew can't swim.'

We all had big rubber boots and boiler suits on. I looked around and Sticky's head is bobbing up and down in the water. By geez, I had a battle to get over to him.

When I got up to him he says, 'Don't worry about me, mate, I'm just trying to get the canoe.'

We shore for another week. Then I went into Warren on the Saturday morning. I thought, if we're going to Queensland, I'd better buy meself a new gun before I go. At that time I didn't know where we were going to end up in Queensland. So I went in and bought a repeating .22 rifle and some other gear that we wanted, and went back to the shed.

On the Sunday, I said, 'We'd better go and try this gun out.'

We asked the owner if we could go shooting. He told us to shoot every roo we could see and all the galahs as well. Anyhow, Sticky, Larry and I were walking through this paddock and we come across this old hay shed. There were thousands of galahs flying out of this shed. The owner had it all fenced in but it had been let go. The wire around it was hanging down everywhere and the galahs had got in.

I said to Sticky, 'Are you thinkin' what I'm thinkin', mate?'

'I think so,' he said. 'We'll fix this up and we'll get a quid here.'

Galahs make good pets and we thought we could sell them. We climbed up on top of the hay and pulled all the wire back up and tied it in place. But we left one section open where the birds could still get in, and we hinged this bit of wire. Then we attached a real long bit of wire to the hinged piece, and fed it way out down the paddock under a tree, a good hundred yards away. We tried to pull the hinged bit shut a couple of times and it wouldn't work. So we went back to the hut and Sticky found a cotton reel in his swag.

He took the cotton off it and said, 'This'll do the trick.'

Back to the hay shed we went and put the cotton reel under the wire on the beam we had it running over, and tried it. It went like a clock.

We left the wire open all week. We found half a dozen of the cocky's steel posts around the property and a lump of net wire. Between the two rows of shearers' huts we hammered in the posts and put the wire around them and over the top and made a big cage. It would have been about fifteen foot long and about five foot wide. The next Sunday, we went up to have a look at the hay shed and there were thousands of galahs in there. We pulled this wire up and locked them in.

I had an old pair of boiler maker's gloves in me truck that I used for shearing burry sheep. I put them on to get these galahs. We had to get the galahs down to the hut. So we got a wool pack, filled it up with galahs, took them down to the hut, emptied them into the cage, then went back and got another load. We kept going till we had a few hundred.

Well, the racket they put on was unbelievable. What a bloody row they made.

The other shearers were bellowing at us, 'What are ya gunna do with them? They'll send us mad with that racket.'

Of course, we had to feed them all, too. The cocky we were working for had some big wheat silos on the other side of the homestead. So we went over there one night and got a bag of wheat, and fed the birds the wheat and watered them. This went on for a couple of weeks while the shed was going.

Not long before we cut out, one of the young blokes was out shooting this day, and he shot a doe kangaroo and she had a joey in her pouch. So he caught the joey and brought it back with him. He had him tied up in the yard and was playing with him and feeding him, giving him a drop of milk. Then another rouseabout was out in the bush and caught a little sucking pig and brought him home. He made up a little yard for it, put netting around it, put him in and fed him with scraps from the cookhouse. Anyhow, the cut out come and we were all ready to go home.

'I got no way of taking this kangaroo home,' said the young bloke. 'Do ya want him, Jack?'

'Give him here,' I said. Then the other bloke said he couldn't take the pig. 'Give him here,' I said, 'I'll take him, too.'

So we covered the canopy on me truck with netting and put the galahs in the back of the truck. Holy hell! What a bloody row they kicked up. We loaded up our stuff, then we had to put the pig in, then we had to put the kangaroo in as well. Larry and Sticky Glew and I got in the front. I told the others they had to find their own way home cos I couldn't fit them in. We got our cheques and set off back to Rylstone from Warren. On the way we went through Gulgong.

'We'll go and have a beer here,' Sticky said.

So we pulled up and headed into the pub. The streets are real narrow in Gulgong and we'd parked the truck in the middle of the street. We were in the pub having a beer when a copper walked in. He lifted his hat and said, 'Who owns that green Inter out there?'

'I do,' I said.

'Get it out of town quick or I'll lock ya up,' he said. 'The bloody racket coming from that, ya can't have that in town.'

'Geez, let's go,' I said to the others. Away we went back to Rylstone.

Dad had an old house up the street from where we lived. It was on a couple of acres of ground he'd bought. At one time, Uncle Bob had kept fowls in it. The verandah was done up for a fowl house. So that's where we put these birds.

Sticky said, 'I know a joker who'll buy these.'

'Righto,' I said. So we had the roo, the pig and a few hundred galahs all locked in this old house.

Dad come home. 'What a bloody racket,' he said. 'What are you gunna do with them?'

'Sell 'em,' I said.

Sticky went down the street and come back saying there was a bloke that would give us five bob each for the galahs.

'Let him have 'em,' I said. He come up and took the lot.

The poor little kangaroo, he died, so the dogs had him for a feed. Then we were left with the pig. I decided to sell the pig and went down to the pub asking around. Another bloke that I'd shore for a few months earlier was in town and someone had told him that I had a pig for sale.

He come up to see me and said, 'How much do ya want for him?'

'Sixpence a pound, live weight,' I said.

'That sounds all right,' he said. 'Where'll we go to weigh him?'

'Down at the Post Office,' I said.

The Post Office had a set of scales outside that you put a penny in to weigh yourself. We took the pig down there. The Post Office was next door to the Police Station. It was about ten o'clock at night. Well, this pig was screaming and squealing and carrying on, while we were trying to weigh it. What a bloody racket it was making. Finally, we got it weighed and he give me the money, and away he went with this pig still squealing. It's a bloody wonder the copper didn't come out and pinch me for disturbing the peace.

I did a couple more sheds around Rylstone, then I got a shed down around Ilford. I think it was a three-stand shed. Larry come with me as the picker-up and rouseabout.

At this shed, we only had a few left in the pen this day. The musterers were late bringing the mob in and there was only a half a dozen or so sheep left. So we were mucking around, me and the other fellas.

One bloke said, 'I'm gunna shear this bloody sheep left handed.'

The other fella said, 'Well, I'm gunna shear mine back to front.'

And I thought, I'll shear the bastard upside down. So I got hold of the sheep and, instead of sitting him on his bum and shearing him, I stood him on his bloody head and shore his back legs first, then round his belly. What a shemozzle!

'You're a ratbag, Turner,' they said.

It took a bit of juggling to get the wool off him and not cut him about.

It was cold bloody weather at the time, at this shed. Geez, it was cold. One morning the bell went for breakfast. Larry got up and looked out the window.

'The bell's gone, Jackie. Come on, get up,' he said. 'Look out the window, there's snow.' And there was about six or eight inches of snow on the ground.

'Get back into bed,' I said, 'I'm not shearin' in this. It's too bloody cold.'

'But the bell's gone,' he said.

'Bugger the bell,' I said, 'I'm stayin' here.'

All the others went and had their breakfast and then come back to the hut.

Anyhow, the bloke that was running the shed come down. 'Come on,' he said, 'the breakfast bell's gone.'

'Bugger the breakfast bell,' I said, 'I'm not shearin' in this. Ya'll kill the bloody sheep, and us, too.'

'Come on, Turner, get out of bed,' he said.

'Like bloody hell,' I said. 'I'm not gunna work in this. Bugger the shearin'. And if ya have any sense you'll get back into bed yaselves.'

So everyone went back to bed till after dinnertime when the snow had cleared up a bit. By geez, it was cold.

I didn't know it at the time, but that was the last shed I ever shore in.

*Left to right- **Larry**, me, **Pat**, **Tony**, and **Billy** in front, in Marie's back yard in Ipswich, Queensland, 1956.*

***Larry** getting a haircut at Hatton Station, Warren. This is the shed we were at when we got the galahs. And one of the last few sheds I shore in.*

Mum, **Tony,** **Larry** *and* **Billy** *in the truck, ready to drive to Queensland the first time.*

Me and Dad in Marie's back yard in Ipswich, Queensland, 1956.

Chapter Twenty-Eight

Look Out, Queensland

We come back to Rylstone and started getting ready to move up to Queensland. We needed a caravan to take with us so we had somewhere to live while we were looking around for a place. We didn't know how long it would be till we had a house. Larry, Uncle Bob and I went to Sydney in the truck to get a caravan. We stayed in one of Uncle Bob's houses while we were there. One big room had four beds in it, so we all slept there. That night, Uncle Bob hooked a fishing line onto the bottom of the blankets on Larry's bed. In the middle of the night he kept pulling the blankets down off Larry. The first time it happened it give Larry a hell of a fright. He couldn't work out what was going on cos everyone was still in their beds.

We saw a van in *The Sydney Morning Herald* the next day and went and got it, then set off for home that night. On the way home, the skylight on the van worked loose and blew off in the wind. The caravan never had a safety chain either, so I made one up out of a bit of rope. Coming down a hill outside of Lithgow, the van jumped off the tow ball and it was only the rope that saved it. When I got it home, I had to build a new hatch for the top of it and I put a proper safety chain on it, and a new coupling on the tow ball.

I don't think we had any animals left at home by that time, cos there was no bugger home to look after them. Tony and Billy had stayed in Queensland. Maureen had joined the Air Force and was living in Darwin, and Marie and Wop were married. Peter got married while I was in New Zealand. Bryan was still on Charlton, he never come home again, and Dad, Larry, and I were away shearing and working most of the time. There was only Mum and me youngest sister, Pat, at home. So we never had to worry about getting rid of any animals.

We left Rylstone on October 7th, 1956. It was Mum's birthday. I was nearly 30. We loaded the pots and pans and cooking gear, and anything else we needed, into the truck and the caravan. The beds off the verandah that us boys used to sleep in, we shoved three or four of them in the back of the truck under the canopy. We left all the other furniture, even our big, twelve-foot table. We couldn't take that. One of me cousins in Rylstone was an auctioneer, so Mum made arrangements with him to sell the house and the furniture after we'd gone. I think she only got a hundred quid for the whole lot, house and all.

I think Dad had sold Misery years before, so we didn't have to worry about selling that. He hung onto the house and block of ground opposite Dawson Street, cos Peter and his wife were living in it. Land wasn't worth much in those days.

Dad was only in Queensland a couple of years, then he come back to Rylstone, shearing. He'd stay with Peter, or Wop sometimes. He'd go for a few months and come back for a while, and go off again. He come down to Rylstone to look after Uncle Cliff, and Uncle Arthur, when they were dying. He used to just pack up and go.

'Ya can't dig up an old tree and plant it somewhere else, Jack,' Uncle Bob told me. Dad kept coming back. He was shearing around Rylstone long after he'd turned seventy.

I wasn't drinking at the time we left. I'd decided to give the grog away for a while cos I didn't know what was in front of me. I hadn't had a beer for a month or so. I wasn't going down to the pub at the time so I didn't have a send-off. I just packed up and left. Uncle Arthur was living at the Globe Hotel in town then. When we were ready to leave, the publican brought him up to say good-bye. I had a billycan and lantern sitting beside the truck ready to load. As the publican was backing out of the yard, he backed straight over the bloody both of them. I had to buy a new billy and lantern before we left.

Once we got going on the road, we called into Mudgee to see Aunty Cis, Mum's sister. She was in hospital, but she wasn't real sick cos she recovered and lived till she was ninety-eight. From there we went onto Coolah. One of Dad's sisters had two sons up there. So we went up and seen them. We set off from there for Moree. I still had the lump of hose going from the back of the truck into the cabin for our two-way.

Just before we got into Moree, I heard a 'cooee' down the two-way.

'What's up?' I said.

'There's somethin' wrong with the caravan,' Dad said.

So I pulled up on the side of the road, got out and had a look. There were bolts that held the caravan frame onto the chassis. The nuts had come off the two front ones and she was lifting up and down. I had to sneak into Moree, nice and steady, and buy a big lump of rope. I used that to tie the van down onto the chassis on either side. We stayed in a parking area in Moree and then got to Queensland the next day.

When we got close to the border, I sung out down the two-way to let Dad, Larry and Pat know we were about to leave New South Wales. As we crossed the border, I thought to meself, look out Queensland, the Turners are coming.

We settled in Brighton. I built Mum and Dad a house there before I went to work in the tin mine up at Irvinebank. That's where I met me wife, Betty. She was a little Pommy nurse working in Mareeba Hospital. We settled in Brighton, too. Bought a nice new little house only a few streets from Mum and Dad's place. It had electricity, running water and an inside toilet so I thought it was pretty flash. We raised our three kids there. I always thought I'd go back to the bush, always wanted to, but that never happened. We're still in that same house in Brighton.

The house I built for Mum and Dad is still standing so I must have done a good enough job. It's changed a lot over the years, like places do. Tony's wife, Hazel, lives there now. They moved in after Dad died and Mum went to live in a nursing home. Tony's not with us anymore. He's with Mum and Dad and Peter but the rest of us are still here. And we all get together in that house whenever anyone comes to visit. There's been a Turner in that house since I first started building it in 1956. It's a hell of a lot bigger and better than our old house on the farm, that's for sure.

The little house on Misery is still there, though. Me daughter, Jacqui, and I went down to Rylstone a few years ago and I guided her out to Misery and showed her our old house. It's falling down now. I don't think there'll be anything left of it soon. It's a bloody shame really—it was a great little place. It was only an old slab hut and it wasn't real big, but it housed all of us and we were happy there, despite the name. Some of the best memories of my life were lived out in that old hut on Misery. I had the best childhood any kid could ever have and I'd go back tomorrow if I could. But I can't ever go back, I s'pose. Besides, I'm happy with my life and where I am now, even if it is a long way from Misery.

Glossary

Board	The floor along the wall of a shearing shed where the sheep are shorn.
Burgoo	What Jack's family called porridge.
Catching pen	Small pens inside the shearing shed, next to the board, used to keep sheep before shearing.
Chute	The opening next to each shearer's stand where the shorn sheep exit into the count-out pens. Each shearer had his own count-out pen so a tally could be made of how many sheep he shore in each run.
Cocky	The farmer or property owner.
Cocky's joy	Australian slang for golden syrup.
Crutching	Removal of the wool from around the sheep's tail and between the rear legs.
Cut out	The completion of shearing in a shed for that season.
Dodger	Slang term for bread.
Gun	The top shearer in a gang, or shed. A shearer who could shear 200 or more sheep a day.
Handpiece	Machine shears that a shearer uses to shear the sheep.
Lance Skewthorpe	Famous Australian rough-rider (1870-1958).

Lug	Slang term for ear.
Machine	Shearer's handpiece.
Overhead gear	Equipment above the board, used to power the handpiece. In Jack's time they were usually run by a diesel or petrol powered motor. The earlier versions were steam powered. Now most are electric.
Pen	Short for the catching pen. 'A pen' is also a figure of speech shearers use when asking for, or talking about, a shearing contract. For example, 'Can you get me a pen on Charlton?' or 'Do you want a pen?'
Penner-up	The shed hand responsible for keeping the shearers' catching pens filled with sheep.
Picker-up	The shed hand who picked up the fleece and threw it up onto the wool table.
Pinched	To be arrested by the police.
Presser	The shed hand who compresses the wool into a bale using a wool press.
Ringer	The fastest shearer in the shed.
Ring the shed	To be the shearer to shear the most sheep in a shed.
Rocky Ned	Famous Australian buck-jumping horse known as the four-legged fury.
Rouseabout	Shed hand who picks up fleeces and does other odd jobs.
Run	A two hour shearing period. There were four runs in a typical shearing day.

Setting hoe	A setting hoe was made especially for trapping. It had a wooden handle about 18 inches long, a hammer head on one side of the head end, and a blade like a mattock, about 2 inches wide, on the other side of the head. The hammer part was used for banging in the pegs of the trap and the blade part used for digging out a hole to lay the trap in.
Shed	Short for shearing shed.
Spanish-winch	To Spanish-winch something, a piece of wire or rope is tied to a post or tree then onto the vehicle that needs to be moved or towed. A sturdy stick is hammered into the ground halfway along the wire or rope and another strong stick used to slip under the wire or rope and is then wound around the centre stick shortening the wire or rope and moving/towing the vehicle along. When the vehicle reaches the centre stick the procedure is repeated until the vehicle is clear of the bog.
Stand	The place on the shearing board occupied by each shearer.
Stockholm Tar	A sticky, dark substance made from pine tar and used as an antiseptic.
Stringhalt	The involuntary and exaggerated flexion of one or both hind legs as a horse walks.
Surcingle	A strap made of leather that fastens around a horse's girth.

Tar boy	A young shed hand or rouseabout whose job it was to put Stockholm Tar on any cut the shearer made on a sheep.
Wireless	Old-fashioned radio.
Wool classer	A person who grades the fleece according to its quality.

About the Authors

Jack Turner

Jack Turner has entertained many friends, family, and acquaintances over his long life with the tales of his younger years. He is a quick-witted larrikin who loves to laugh and make others laugh.

Jack was born in Rylstone, New South Wales in 1926, and raised on a farm called Misery. He moved to Queensland in 1956 and lives in Brisbane with his wife of 54 years, his three children, five grandchildren and one great-grandchild.

A former shearer with no education and a rough and ready upbringing, Jack's 'that'll do me' attitude has stayed with him throughout his long life and seen him through many a scrape. Hard-working, and with the ingenuity born from being raised in the bush, Jack has built and fixed everything from houses to toys.

He has had too many jobs to mention, met too many people to remember, and had too many adventures to record. He has lived an ordinary life full of extraordinary stories.

For further insight into Jack's life and character please visit his blog: www.blackjackturner.weebly.com

Jacqui Halpin

Jacqui Halpin is the second born of Jack's three children. As a child she was enthralled by the stories of her father's early life. His knack for telling a yarn inspired her own love of storytelling.

Jacqui is a children's author whose stories have won prizes in writing competitions and been published in anthologies. She is currently writing a series of junior fiction novels inspired by her father's adventures growing up.

As an experienced writer she was the obvious choice to record Jack's life but she still feels honoured that he trusted her with his precious memories. Jacqui has recorded and edited A LONG WAY FROM MISERY over many years, but does not regret one minute she has spent working with her dad on 'the book'.

For more information about Jacqui and her writing please visit her website: www.jacquihalpin.com or follow her on Facebook www.facebook.com/jacquihalpinwriter

www.ingramcontent.com/pod-product-compliance
Lightning Source LLC
Chambersburg PA
CBHW021120300426
44113CB00006B/219